W9-DDX-058

THE PRESIDENTS

OF THE UNITED STATES

MAXIM E. ARMBRUSTER

The
Presidents
of the
United States,

and Their Administrations
from Washington to Ford.

Sixth Revised Edition

Horizon Press   New York

Acknowledgment is made to the following for their courtesy in making available the illustrations: p. 6, Zygmunt A. Stopinski; p. 7, 12–18, 20–34, 36, 37, The Library of Congress; p. 8, The New York Historical Society; p. 9, The Century Club of New York; p. 10, Ash Lawn Plantation; p. 11, The Corcoran Gallery of Art; p. 19, Mrs. John B. Lavelle; p. 35, The Honorable Herbert Hoover; p. 38, The New York Times; p. 39, Allegheny County (Pa.) Democratic Committee; p. 40, 42. The White House; p. 41, Republican National Committee.

To

the memory of my son

Bryan T. Haralson

ACKNOWLEDGMENTS

I have given credit in the footnotes of the text to the various publishing houses who have given me permission to quote from their respective publications. I thank also Mr. David K. E. Bruce of the American Embassy in London, for permission to use the fascinating description of Thomas Jefferson in his book *Revolution to Reconstruction*. Especial thanks go to the late Emil L. Schmidt for his invaluable criticism and suggestions during the writing of the manuscript, and to Mr. James H. Bailey, Richmond, Va., for his kind suggestions.

For taking out time to reply to my inquiries, I thank also Mr. Leon A. Arkus, Carnegie Institute Department of Fine Arts, Pittsburgh; The Chicago Historical Society; Mr. Charles Francis Adams, Waltham, Mass.; Mr. George Paul Bellon, McKees Rocks, Pa.; Mr. Guy L. Bushby, Los Angeles Department of Recreation and Parks; Mr. James Callaghan, Youngs Memorial Cemetery, Oyster Bay, L. I.; Rev. J. Rolland Crompton, Binghamton, N. Y.; Federal Deposit Insurance Corporation, Washington; The First Parish Church, Quincy, Mass.; Mr. John T. Flynn, Bayside, L. I.; Mr. Ralph D. Freer, Pittsburgh; Miss Bess Furman, Washington; Dr. Wilbur H. Glover, Buffalo Historical Society; Mr. E. Russell Hall, Auburn, N. Y.; The Hayes Memorial Library, Fremont, Ohio; Mr. William Henry Harrison, Sheridan, Wyo.; Historical Society of Pennsylvania, Philadelphia; Henry E. Huntington Library and Art Gallery, San Marino, Calif.; Illinois Division of Parks and Memorials, Springfield, Ill.; Mr. William Kaye Lamb, Public Archives of Canada, Ottawa, Canada; Miss Anna Lantz, Carnegie Library, Pittsburgh; the Library of Congress; Mr. Stefan Lorant, Lenox, Mass.; National Park Service, Washington; *New York Journal-American;* Ohio Historical Society, Columbus; Republican National Committee, Washington; San Francisco Public Library; Mr. Judd Sheppard, Pittsburgh; the late Senator Robert A. Taft of Ohio; Thomas Jefferson Memorial Foundation, Monticello, Va.; U. S. Department of Defense, Washington; U. S. Department of the Treasury, Washington; *U. S. News & World Report,* Washington; Virginia Historical Society, Richmond; Dr. Carl Hermann Voss, Saratoga Springs, N. Y.; George L. Cashman, Springfield, Ill.; Mr. Hugh Sidey, *Life;* Col. Frank E. Mason, Leesburg, Va.

I should state also that, without the excellent collection at Carnegie Library in Pittsburgh, Pa., this book could never have been written.

CONTENTS

George Washington, 1732–1799

Birthplace: Westmoreland County, Virginia

Presidential Term: 1789–97

Vice-President: John Adams

John Adams, 1735–1826

Birthplace: Quincy, Massachusetts

Presidential Term: 1797–1801

Vice-President: Thomas Jefferson

Thomas Jefferson, 1743–1826

Birthplace: Shadwell, Virginia

Presidential Term: 1801–09

Vice-Presidents: Aaron Burr, George Clinton

James Madison, 1751–1836

Birthplace: King George County, Virginia

Presidential Term: 1809–17

Vice-Presidents: George Clinton, Elbridge Gerry

James Monroe, 1758–1831

Birthplace: Monroe Hall, Virginia

Presidential Term: 1817–25

Vice-President: Daniel D. Tompkins

John Quincy Adams, 1767–1848

Birthplace: Quincy, Massachusetts

Presidential Term: 1825–29

Vice-President: John C. Calhoun

Andrew Jackson, 1767–1845

Birthplace: Lancaster County, South Carolina

Presidential Term: 1829–37

Vice-Presidents: John C. Calhoun, Martin Van Buren

Martin Van Buren, 1782–1862

Birthplace: Kinderhook, New York

Presidential Term: 1837–41

Vice-President: Richard M. Johnson

William Henry Harrison, 1773–1841

Birthplace: Charles City County, Virginia

Presidential Term: 1841

Vice-President: John Tyler

John Tyler, 1790–1862

Birthplace: Charles City County, Virginia

Presidential Term: 1841–45

Vice-President: None

James K. Polk, 1795–1849

Birthplace: Mecklenburg County, North Carolina

Presidential Term: 1845–49

Vice-President: George M. Dallas

Zachary Taylor, 1784–1850

Birthplace: Orange County, Virginia

Presidential Term: 1849–50

Vice-President: Millard Fillmore

Millard Fillmore, 1800–1874

Birthplace: Summer Hill, New York

Presidential Term: 1850–53

Vice-President: None

Franklin Pierce, 1804–1869

Birthplace: Hillsborough, New Hampshire

Presidential Term: 1853–57

Vice-President: William R. King

James Buchanan, 1791–1868

Birthplace: Cove Gap, Pennsylvania

Presidential Term: 1857–61

Vice-President: John C. Breckenridge

Abraham Lincoln, 1809–1865

Birthplace: Larue County, Kentucky

Presidential Term: 1861–65

Vice-Presidents: Hannibal Hamlin, Andrew Johnson

Andrew Johnson, 1808–1875

Birthplace: Raleigh, North Carolina

Presidential Term: 1865–69

Vice-President: None

Ulysses S. Grant, 1822–1885

Birthplace: Point Pleasant, Ohio

Presidential Term: 1869–77

Vice-Presidents: Schuyler Colfax, Henry Wilson

Rutherford B. Hayes, 1822–1893

Birthplace: Delaware, Ohio

Presidential Term: 1877–81

Vice-President: William A. Wheeler

James A. Garfield, 1831–1881

Birthplace: Moreland Hills, Ohio

Presidential Term: 1881

Vice-President: Chester A. Arthur

Chester A. Arthur, 1830–1886

Birthplace: Fairfield, Vermont

Presidential Term: 1881–85

Vice-President: None

Grover Cleveland, 1837–1908

Birthplace: Caldwell, New Jersey

Presidential Terms: 1885–89; 1893–97

Vice-Presidents: Thomas A. Hendricks, Adlai E. Stevenson, I

Benjamin Harrison, 1833–1901

Birthplace: North Bend, Ohio

Presidential Term: 1889–93

Vice-President: Levi P. Morton

William McKinley, 1843–1901

Birthplace: Niles, Ohio

Presidential Term: 1897–1901

Vice-Presidents: Garret A. Hobart, Theodore Roosevelt

Theodore Roosevelt, 1858–1919

Birthplace: New York City

Presidential Term: 1901–09

Vice-President: Charles W. Fairbanks

William Howard Taft, 1857–1930

Birthplace: Cincinnati, Ohio

Presidential Term: 1909–13

Vice-President: James S. Sherman

Woodrow Wilson, 1856–1924

Birthplace: Staunton, Virginia

Presidential Term: 1913–21

Vice-President: Thomas R. Marshall

Warren G. Harding, 1865–1923

Birthplace: Blooming Grove, Ohio

Presidential Term: 1921–23

Vice-President: Calvin Coolidge

Calvin Coolidge, 1872–1933

Birthplace: Plymouth, Vermont

Presidential Term: 1923–29

Vice-President: Charles G. Dawes

Herbert Hoover, 1874–1964

Birthplace: West Branch, Iowa

Presidential Term: 1929–33

Vice-President: Charles Curtis

Franklin D. Roosevelt, 1882–1945

Birthplace: Hyde Park, New York

Presidential Term: 1933–45

Vice-Presidents: John N. Garner, Henry A. Wallace,

Harry S. Truman

Harry S. Truman, 1884–1972

Birthplace: Lamar, Missouri

Presidential Term: 1945–53

Vice-President: Alben W. Barkley

Dwight D. Eisenhower, 1890-1969

Birthplace: Denison, Texas

Presidential Term: 1953-61

Vice-President: Richard Nixon

John F. Kennedy, 1917–1963

Birthplace: Brookline, Massachusetts

Presidential Term: 1961–63

Vice-President: Lyndon B. Johnson

Lyndon B. Johnson, 1908–1973

Birthplace: Gillespie County, Texas

Presidential Term: 1963–69

Vice-President: Hubert H. Humphrey

Richard Nixon, 1913- 1994

Birthplace: Yorba Linda, California

Presidential Term: 1969–1974

Vice-Presidents: Spiro T. Agnew, Gerald R. Ford

Gerald R. Ford

Birthplace: Omaha, Nebraska

Presidential Term: 1974–

Vice-President: Nelson A. Rockefeller

THE PRESIDENTS

OF THE UNITED STATES

1

★

GEORGE WASHINGTON

☆ ★

		Electoral
VOTE OF 1789:	George Washington	69
	John Adams	34
	John Jay	9
	Scattered	26
		138 [1]
VOTE OF 1792:	George Washington, Federalist [2]	132
	John Adams, Federalist	77
	George Clinton, Anti-Federalist	50
	Scattered	5
		264 [1]

☆ ☆

WITHOUT GEORGE WASHINGTON IT IS PROBABLE THAT THERE WOULD never have been a United States of America. One can speculate on all kinds of ways in which the status of the thirteen colonies would have been changed—for changed they would have been in any case—but it is hardly likely that the end product would have been the republic the world today knows. It is more probable that the United States should have become the most enterprising of the dominions of Britain.

High on the interior walls of the public library in San Francisco can be seen this inscription:

CHARACTER IS THE GOVERNING ELEMENT IN LIFE AND IS ABOVE GENIUS.

This dictum, of anonymous origin, proclaiming in a wonderful economy of words a profundity of universal application, explains

[1] Only one-half this number of electors took part in balloting.
[2] Although we think of Washington as being elected by the whole people, and above party, he was definitely a Federalist by the time party line-ups had been defined.

George Washington. Because he exhibited character of such magnitude, the colonies won their independence. Because of his character the poor colonials were kept together in some semblance of an army. Because of his character, delegates were willing to assemble "in order to form a more perfect union" and present to the world what is today the oldest written constitution extant. Because of his character factional strife was deferred in the new government, and political parties, early in American history dividing into the two main cleavages representing "democracy" and "oligarchy," postponed their smoldering rivalries.

Character in a man, especially as it enters into the fate of a nation, is an indefinable thing. Integrity is but a small element of it; intelligence is only its messenger. It is not genius, for as the proverb maker has indicated, it is above genius. It is not knowledge alone either, or courage alone, or religion, or love of nature, or mysticism, or a belief in mankind. It is a composite of all these.

George Washington, like so many others of the world's great men, has been called cold and heartless. Alexander Hamilton, who certainly should have known him, said his heart was a stone. Yet, how can one have character, which means hewing to the line of principle, without dismaying those who conceive of character in the narrow terms of folksiness, philanthropy, and personal favoritism?

It has often been seriously submitted that great people should never marry, since among the world's great idyllic marriages have not been many. But is it not true that these men were really married to their destiny, were in harmony, so to speak, with their guiding star, which alone engrossed their total soul and to which alone they were willing from childhood to commit themselves completely?

Both Washington and Lincoln, the man with whom he is most often compared, were personally ambitious on a mighty scale. Yet both also would not strive with Fate in order to realize their dreams: there was too much dignity in them for that. Rather, they were able to recognize opportunity, as Fate, in her own good time, *presented* them with opportunity. This is an aspect of greatness: not to force issues for self-advancement; to be ambitious, yet not to sacrifice a shred of personal dignity to bring events for the self to pass. Few public men have ever been able to accomplish this miracle, because few men with such an understanding of psychological forces are ever attracted to public life at all.

Little is known of George Washington's boyhood, but the indications are that it was a serious boyhood. His father, Augustine Washington, begat four children in his first marriage and six in his second, with Mary Ball; George was the eldest of these six children.

In the Northern Neck, that peninsula between the Potomac and Rappahannock Rivers, where Washington was born February 22, 1732,[3] lived many of the well-to-do families of Virginia. Augustine himself owned about six plantations and had an interest in a foundry besides. But principally associated with Washington's life were three plantations: the one on Pope's Creek, where George was born, near the ancestral home on Bridges Creek, and called only in later years Wakefield; the one called Ferry or River Farm, across the river from Fredericksburg, where the widowed Mary Ball Washington spent a large part of her life; and the one on Little Hunting Creek, originally called Epsewasson, later called Mount Vernon.

Young George Washington's seriousness had quite a number of causes. The loss of his father when the boy was only eleven was of course a serious matter. He was never on very affectionate terms with his mother—also a serious matter in a boy's, or a man's, life. The seriousness of the teen-aged Washington is certainly apparent in his copying into an exercise-book the "Rules of Civility and Decent Behavior in Company and Conversation"—110 of them in all—perhaps from his half-brother Lawrence's library.

He had the perfect older brother in Lawrence, the new master of Mount Vernon, and to his home he eventually went to live. There he met the prominent people of the colony and gradually became interested in the profession of arms. Although he had little formal schooling, the things he learned from Lawrence and the stories he heard from Lawrence's guests made up this lack and fired his ambition to be someone of importance. He was a materialist in every sense of the word, but only on the most honorable of

[3] In the family Bible it reads February 11, 1731/32, the reason being that England and her colonies were still on the old Julian calendar which was eleven days behind the Gregorian, later adopted, and which recognized March 25th as New Year's Day instead of January 1st.

terms: rather different from most materialists of that time and of today.

Repeatedly, in his early years, Washington referred to winning honor and renown, so that, although he "received the call" to his various undertakings for the colonial government in a literal sense, he was nevertheless always ready when the call came. It is unmistakable that from his early years Washington had a "sense of destiny" about himself.

Some men of destiny find their greatest adventures in the realm of the metaphysical and in striving with the infinite. Washington was not of this type. He strove with the familiar finite: he knew his adventures lay in the realm of matter. He chose a military life for that reason. And because he loved physical adventure, he was a natural choice for the expedition which first brought him to public notice—delivering the message from Virginia's Governor Dinwiddie to the French commander at Fort Le Boeuf near Lake Erie, demanding that the French evacuate the Ohio Valley. This was in 1753; he was Major Washington then. This was how the French and Indian War, which opened the Seven Years' War, started; it was to be concluded ten years later with the expulsion of France from the mainland of the New World. Fought on four continents, the Seven Years' War was, in effect, a World War of that period.

The portrait painter Gilbert Stuart has said of Washington that "all his features were indicative of the strongest and most ungovernable passions," adding, however, that the passions were always under complete control. A nature such as this could not avoid being impulsive in youth. Certainly in the Jumonville affair in southwestern Pennsylvania we see this impulsiveness revealed. The French claimed that their commander, Jumonville, and his handful of men were out under a flag of truce when Washington opened fire, killing Jumonville and nine men. Some weeks later, when Washington was compelled to surrender his Fort Necessity,[4] he had to sign capitulation papers acknowledging himself as an assassin. We must not forget that while these incidents were taking place, war had not yet been declared between England and France.

Washington's attack on Jumonville has generally been consid-

[4] Outline of foundations of this stockade ascertained only in 1953.

ered rash. He was to become considerably less impulsive in the years after that attack and to demonstrate a quality which is another hallmark of greatness—growth. Some occupants of the White House even in later times never were able to demonstrate that quality.

The one event before the Revolution with which Washington's name is most notably associated is Braddock's Defeat, or the Battle of the Monongahela. It is interesting first of all, of course, because General Braddock insisted on following his own counsel instead of Colonel Washington's about the best way to fight in the American forests. The lonely grave of Braddock in the Pennsylvania hills is more eloquent than any account of the outcome which nearly every schoolboy knows by heart.

But the Braddock affair is noteworthy also for its revelation of the perennial dignity of Washington's character, to say nothing of his bravery. Washington had resigned his commission and was living at Mount Vernon when Braddock arrived for the purpose of subjugating certain French forts, the first to be Fort Duquesne at the forks of the Ohio. Washington was anxious to take part in these expeditions, but he wanted participation only on his own terms for he felt they were the only honorable terms.

The colonials had been informed that all troops serving by commission signed by the King—British troops—should have rank above those serving by commission of the provincial governors—American troops. This was the event which caused Washington to resign, and he was not going to volunteer for the King's service now, ardently though his spirit yearned to do so. But Fate, that inscrutable architect, solved the problem for Washington—and for America. General Braddock invited him to join his official family as an aide-de-camp where the problems of precedence would never arise. Washington accepted. Rejecting Washington's recommendations on fighting the Indians, Braddock was defeated and killed, and Washington's star rose. After Jumonville and Fort Necessity, Washington sorely needed this restoration of prestige. From now on he would be a man seemingly passive to fame, yet achieving it; not anxious for any honor and not showing the suffering of frustration when he did not receive it.

The causes, prosecution, and success of the American Revolution have been recited often and well, its every aspect subjected by scholars to such minute research and exposition that the event has been placed perfectly in the tableau of Western history where its whole array and effect can be clearly seen. It is of no consequence now to deplore what the foolish George III did or what the radical Sam Adams did.

America has arrived at its present place in history as the consequence of an infinite and complex variety of circumstances, of action and reaction. Conjecture as to other causes, other results, although interesting, is fruitless. We do know that perhaps the most significant hour in the nation's destiny was struck at the close of World War II, but no man can know how long America's political ascendancy will last, what shape the future of this unique people will take.

However, the lessons to be learned from the study of the character of those men who have performed shaping deeds in the life of a people are always instructive. Man is an inexhaustible mine of fact. As all men are related by a common humanity, whatever is said or learned about any man, however great, is said or learned about all of us. As it is true of all men, it is true of Washington that a study of his nature reveals things we never knew were there, innumerable facets we never suspected. But the study of greatness is even more deeply complicated. There is, for example, a kind of duality in those we call great which baffles most men; and insight into this duality is difficult of explanation because to apprehend it requires some measure of the quality of greatness itself.

If to be a great general one must be a tactician, Washington was not in that sense a great general. He had had experience only in provincial contests and Indian fighting. He has been referred to as "the planter and frontier colonel." His genius, as we have said, was in keeping an army together, in the face of every defeat and every conceivable limitation, by the force of his character alone. U. S. Grant performed greater military feats; but he had not this quality of inspiring loyalty towards himself when cold, starvation, epidemics, poverty, homesickness, desertions, battle defeats, treason, a jealous Congress, and seemingly Heaven itself all conspired to spread hopelessness among the people and envelop his troops in debilitating despair. In a sense, then, the great victory of

Washington was the victory over despair. The military victories were subordinate to this.

Bunker Hill (Breed's Hill) was fought on a June day in 1775; George Washington had accepted the command of the Continental armies only the day before. He humbly acknowledged his inadequacy for the post and took command July 3rd in Cambridge, Massachusetts. For sixteen years—since he had helped General Forbes in the capture of Fort Duquesne—he had been living quietly at his Mount Vernon plantation overseeing his extensive holdings and shipping his tobacco. Very little of the remainder of his too short life would now be passed among his beloved acres.

When Washington took command, Paul Revere had already made his famous ride; Lexington and Concord had been fought; Ethan Allen had already taken Fort Ticonderoga and Crown Point; and American troops had invaded Canadian soil. Thus it was that the first year of the war—1775—passed into history.

In the following March, the long siege of Boston for which Washington had made great preparations compelled the British to evacuate that port. They never returned. New England was in the hands of the colonials; but a series of defeats was now to follow Washington. The most serious of these was his loss of the Battle of Long Island. He eventually lost Manhattan Island also; in fact New York was in the hands of the enemy for the duration of the war. Washington lost again at White Plains; he had to surrender Fort Washington and Fort Lee and retreat into Pennsylvania.

However, on Christmas night, 1776, Washington made his famous, now almost legendary crossing of the ice-jammed Delaware and surprised the Hessians who were celebrating the holidays in their German style, capturing 1,000 of them together with the town of Trenton, and suffering only five American casualties. Some days later he took Princeton in another surprise attack, as a result of which the British withdrew from New Jersey altogether. The year 1776 came to a close.

There was not another victory for the Americans until August of the following year, when 2,000 Green Mountain Boys under John Stark won the Battle of Bennington. This weakened the British under General Burgoyne and had much to do with his surrender at Sarotoga in the following October. But between these two victories Washington lost two battles—Brandywine and

Germantown. Almost immediately on the heels of these serious defeats the American General Horatio Gates won his trouncing victory at Saratoga, where Burgoyne had to give up one-fourth of the King's forces fighting in America. Saratoga is believed to have been the event that was needed to bring success to Benjamin Franklin's efforts in France for a military alliance with that nation.

Propaganda was afoot at once to disparage Washington and present Gates as the real hero of the Revolution. But Washington met this problem as he met all his other problems: he refused to become overwrought and even sent some of the adverse reports about himself direct to Congress for that body to dispose of as it saw fit. The conspiracy against Washington [5] fell flat and Gates and his sycophants were discredited.

The British moved into Philadelphia, Washington retreated to Valley Forge for the winter, and the year 1777 ended.

Valley Forge would be an epic in the life of any nation. The privations of that winter are known too well to require recounting. Washington was in anguish for his remaining troops. Three thousand of his army had deserted to the British. But the saddest part of all is that the people were indifferent to the cause of independence, often preferring to sell food to the British to selling it to their own soldiers and receiving in return the Continental currency in which they had no faith.

It is pure romantic manufacture that Washington during these dark days went into the forest to pray for God's help. Washington never made ostentations of this kind; in fact, his contemporaries say they never saw him kneel even in a church, to say nothing of the snow-encrusted floor of the Pennsylvania forest. Even his pastor condemned him, while he was President, before his own congregation, for not partaking of communion and showing a disregard for other outward amenities of religion.

But Washington was religious, whether the religionists of his day recognized it or not. When he wrote Sally Fairfax, whom records now seem to reveal as the only woman he ever deeply loved, telling her how he regretted that her marriage prevented him from pressing a suit of his own, one sentence read: "But experience, alas! . . . evinces an opinion which I long have enter-

[5] Known in history as the Conway Cabal.

tained, that there is a Destiny which has the control of our actions, not to be resisted by the strongest efforts of Human Nature." Certainly this is tantamount to recognizing God, regardless of whether the recognition fits in with any denominational dogma respecting the Deity or not.

To show how even at Valley Forge Washington could see, beyond the present suffering, the glory of an America which was to be, we need only glance into a letter he wrote at this time to his stepson Jacky Custis: "Lands are permanent—rising in value—and will be very dear when our independency is established." There was never any doubt in his mind of the outcome.

No one knows exactly why the British General Howe,[6] quartered in Philadelphia, did not go after Washington's weak army at Valley Forge; however, Howe was recalled and his place given to Gen. Clinton. Of course, now France was in the war—not so much because she had particularly libertarian aspirations but because, as happened in Europe for centuries, she wished to humble her ancient enemy England. Clinton left Philadelphia for New York to anticipate the arrival of a French fleet which was to attack Newport. Washington pursued Clinton at once and compelled him to fight the Battle of Monmouth in July 1778. Because of the defection of Gen. Charles Lee, the Americans' second in command, the battle was a draw.[7]

Washington now headed for White Plains, and we do not hear of him in an engagement again until Yorktown, where the war ended. However, in the Ohio Valley things were happening under the leadership of Lieut. Col. George Rogers Clark who occupied Kaskaskia and Vincennes, laying the foundation for the Northwest Territory, that vast slave-free tract which was actually to decide the economic and social character of the future young nation. It was important also because one of the causes of the Revolution had been the proclamation by the mother country that further white settlement must stop at the Appalachians. Of course, all this was now of no effect and America was to expand westward as much as she pleased, the trek not ending for over a hundred

---

[6] It was Howe who sentenced Nathan Hale, the young American spy, to death.
[7] Lee, born in England and once an officer under Braddock, was court-martialed and later dismissed from the army.

and fifty years from the time of the incidents recorded in these pages.

However, the war was moving to the South, and with the fall of Savannah to the British, the year 1778 ended.

One of the outstanding traits in Washington's character, both while he was Commander-in-Chief and when he was President, is made manifest by his custom of conferring with others before making decisions. He treated his officers and his Cabinet as colleagues, and while this endeared him to his subordinates, it always raised the criticism by his enemies of overcautiousness. Because he had no great need to satisfy his ego he could easily accept a rejection of his plans when an alternative was shown to be the wiser policy. His confidence in himself was strong enough to prevent him from considering an abandonment of one of his ideas a reflection on his own ability. Here again is greatness. Although Washington cared more about results than any reflection upon his ability, his particular way of caring revealed his ability.

The French trusted Washington completely and gave him entire control of the forces they sent to America. The first, under d'Estaing, did not fare well, although Washington had planned to combine the force with American troops and liberate Newport. The plan failed because of hurricane-like storms. The fleet of d'Estaing then headed South, his thirty-five ships aiding the Americans in the attempt to recapture Savannah. When this also failed, d'Estaing sailed for home. Washington's inactivity was irritating him as the strange, uneventful year of 1779 ended.

The following year was as bad as the Valley Forge winter. The heaviest American defeat of the entire war took place at the fall of Charleston when the British General Clinton captured 5,400 men and four ships. After this there was a mutiny in Washington's camp at Morristown, New Jersey, when rations were cut for six weeks to one-eighth of normal quantities. Then there was Gates's loss of the Battle of Camden with 2,000 casualties. And on top of it all came the treason of Benedict Arnold. . . . It was the blackness before the light of victory.

Yet, in this discouraging time Washington made one of his moves of genius. He selected Nathanael Greene as Gates's successor in the South. Greene was an organizer, quick in decision, and soon had a real striking force assembled. His appointment came soon after a signal colonial victory at Kings Mountain in which the British commander was killed. On this aggressive note the year 1780 ended.

The French recognition of the independence of the American nation and the consequent French-American military alliance was as certain a portent of the outcome of the contest in the colonies as Vicksburg was to be in the Civil War. The second French force, that under de Rochambeau, arrived with 5,500 men in the year before the close of the war, but it was at first inactive. It was a highly disciplined and well-behaved army, and Washington was counting on it to help him free New York.

At this point messengers arrived with reports of the plight of the British General Cornwallis on the neck of land between the York and the James Rivers. Greene had been giving battle to him in the Carolinas all winter and we hear again familiar names like Cowpens—a colonial victory—and Guilford Courthouse. The hapless Cornwallis had become trapped in Virginia; luck plus the shrewdest calculation came to Washington's aid. While feigning elaborate preparations for an attack on New York, he and Rochambeau marched their armies to the Chesapeake. There the French fleet, which had arrived just in time from the war theater of the West Indies, evacuated them to the beleaguered peninsula which was to produce a denouement greater than Waterloo. The "sense of destiny" was around everybody. The troops felt it, the generals felt it, the French felt it, the yeomanry felt it. Lafayette was there, and Hamilton, and von Steuben; the ill Jacky Custis also. Together—16,000 of them, with the French fleet blocking escape by sea—they converged on Yorktown. Cornwallis was without alternative to capitulation save that of virtual destruction. He surrendered his 8,000-man army on the very day his compatriot Clinton debarked from New York to rescue him. The day was October 19th. . . . And the year 1781 passed into history.

George III wanted to continue the war, and Washington himself believed that additional hostilities would be necessary to secure final freedom. After all, the British still held New York, Charleston, and Savannah, and had 30,000 troops in the colonies. But the feeling among the British people was that the Americans would never be subdued, so the King gave up the effort. At length Rochambeau sailed for home with his troops; and two years after the battle at Yorktown peace was signed with England. Eight years of war and twenty years of wrangling with the mother country had enabled the thirteen states to "assume among the powers of the earth, the separate and equal station to which the Laws of Nature and of Nature's God entitle[d] them." Washington resigned his commission.

But the years at Mount Vernon were to be few. Strong men in the various independent states knew that the old Articles of Confederation, by which the provincial governments had been held together in war, were too weak for times of peace; that without a stronger vehicle for union they would again be prey to foreign depredation and, worse still, to local rivalries.

At the Constitutional Convention, called in Philadelphia in 1787 for the purpose of tightening up their union, the delegates asked George Washington to preside. He more than any other man would be free from sectional prejudice and he alone stood as the catalyst capable of bringing all dissident interests into harmony.

In three months the work was finished and the momentous convocation was concluded; and the novel idea of a President, to be named by an Electoral College of educated, mature, and selfless citizens, meant to everybody but one thing, namely, that George Washington should be that President.

Again he accepted public "honor," that thing he had thought so important in his youth. He no longer felt it to be so important. He felt only that, since he alone could unite the separate independent governments, he should bear the responsibility of the first Presidency in order to achieve that unity.

The Electoral College met and voted in February 1789, the only time it was ever to meet in the same year as the inauguration, and unanimously voted for Washington to head the new Federal government. By the time he had formally been notified by the messengers and arrived in New York, the first national capital, it was late April. On the 30th of that month he took the oath.

In the following year the capital was moved to Philadelphia pending the construction of the new "Federal City" on the banks of the Potomac. In 1792 the Electoral College voted to have Washington take a second term. Again he acceded, but afterwards declined the third term—a precedent followed by all succeeding Presidents except Franklin D. Roosevelt whose decision to break this unwritten law resulted eventually in the adoption of the Twenty-Second Amendment.

On December 14, 1799, George Washington died at Mount Vernon and was buried in the old tomb on the estate. His remains and Martha's now repose in a newer tomb built in 1831.

Washington was not a great humanitarian. If he had been, he never would have chosen a military career. Military life presupposes an acquiescence in the need for violence and its resultant bloodshed and privations. Since human affairs seem, however, to have shown a pattern of violence, resorted to from time to time in order to realize national aims, whether real or vague or factitious, military departments in the social structure of peoples would appear necessary. A nation is fortunate at such times if it can furnish a leader who possesses magnanimity as well as those qualities which direct the application of physical force. Washington possessed that magnanimity.

Being born to wealth, he naturally had the wealthy man's acquisitiveness. Before he was seventeen, he was the owner of a plantation of 550 acres. When he married the wealthy widow Custis, he added 15,000 acres to his holdings. Ferry Farm, where his mother lived, had been willed him outright at his father's death. Mount Vernon came to him at Lawrence's death, and he increased this property from 2,500 to 8,000 acres. After the war, he went into the Pennsylvania territory around Fort Necessity where he owned land and sought to make the squatters on his acres there remit a regular rent.

But Washington's love of his country was greater than his materialism. He took command of the Continental armies on the condition that he would serve without pay. ". . . I long ago despaired," he wrote, "of any other reward for my services than the satisfaction arising from a consciousness of doing my duty, and from the esteem of my friends."

Washington's relations with women were exemplary. There is no record of even a slight indiscretion anywhere. His marriage to Martha Dandridge Custis can be called successful. She had four children; only two were living when she married the man she always referred to as "the General." All her children were dead by the time the war was over. Martha lacked practical abilities and was not an efficient manager. Her spelling was so poor that her husband often had to write her letters for her.

Washington's mother lived to see her son reap his worldly honors. His relations with her were dutiful but not affectionate. She owned 400 acres and some slaves in her own right before she married Augustine Washington; her spelling was worse than Martha's. When George was fourteen and planned to go to sea, his mother objected; and although his brother Lawrence urged the sea as good experience, George in the end obeyed his mother. It was probably better that he did not go: he obtained some additional schooling, became a surveyor for Lord Fairfax's vast holdings, and became acquainted with the prominent people of the colony instead. But this meant also that Washington would be destined not to see the other parts of the world, the only time he ever left America being when he went with Lawrence to Barbados for reasons of the latter's health.

No analysis of Washington's character would be complete without a consideration of his natural paternal instinct. Not having children of his own, he had a natural fondness for the children of others. When Martha's last child, Jacky Custis, died, Washington adopted as his own the two youngest of the remaining four small children. One of them was his namesake, George Washington Parke Custis, who built Arlington house and became the father-in-law of Gen. Robert E. Lee. The famous Savage portrait of the Presidential family, now hanging in the National Gallery, shows the Washingtons with these two children.

The story of Washington and the young Marquis de Lafayette is as interesting and beautiful as any comparable story the Scriptures tell. Lafayette was fatherless, Washington was childless. The two needy souls met at a critical time and loved each other devotedly, so that when after Yorktown the younger man had to return to France and his family, it was with a sad heart. Washington later had the joy of lodging the marquis's son, George Washington Lafayette, under his own roof at Mount Vernon.

In appearance Washington was every inch the general and aristocrat. He had great reserve and dignity, even shyness, and was not voluble in conversation. Jefferson said that "his colloquial talents [were] not above mediocrity." He was six feet two inches in height and his appearance either on horseback or on foot evoked comment. Again Jefferson says: "His person, you know, was fine, his stature exactly what one would wish, his deportment easy, erect and noble." While in Barbados he had contracted smallpox and his features bore the scars of that scourge.

The English always have thought of Washington as one of their own. During the War of 1812, as a British naval force sailed down the Potomac after having set fire to the public buildings in the national capital, the British admiral ordered the bell of his flagship tolled as his fleet passed Mount Vernon and Washington's tomb. Sulgrave Manor, in Northamptonshire, whence Washington's ancestors came, is kept up beautifully and visited regularly. At Washington Old Hall, in County Durham, where William of Wessington lived in the twelfth century and founded the family, plans are envisaged for the restoration of the sorely dilapidated home still standing there.

The Farewell Address of George Washington to the American people, published in the late summer before he left office, is part of the literary heritage of the United States; although Alexander Hamilton is known to have written the greater part of it, its outline is believed to be Washington's, and its philosophy certainly is. With all its ornate language, its final theme of avoiding Europe's endless quarrels is most often stressed today. In the first half of the twentieth century, the American nation twice disregarded this solemn adjuration. It is not possible at present to state conclusively whether the United States was truly without alternative when she partook in the two most recent world wars. Certainly those wars appeared as entirely new threats to the generations who had to fight them. To the tired and disillusioned Washington they might have appeared as useless as they did to Herbert Hoover in the twentieth century.

If the times immediately ahead bear out the soundness of Washington's advice that, "Against the insidious wiles of foreign influence . . . the jealousy of a free people ought to be constantly awake"; and that "a passionate attachment of one nation for another . . . leads also to concessions to the favorite nation of privileges denied to others, which is apt doubly to injure the nation making the concessions, by unnecessarily parting with what we ought to have retained, and by exciting . . . a disposition to retaliate in the parties from whom equal privileges are withheld"—

then the Farewell Address will be not merely a literary but a great sociological heritage for the American people. But time must prove this.

One of the pastimes of the American people is comparing Washington with Lincoln. A few similarities these two had. Both were tall and spare. Both were in a way a product of the West. Both were lacking in a provincial outlook and were unmistakably federalists. Both possessed the great quality of magnanimity.

But it is in their contrasts that these two—the one the founder, the other the preserver, of the nation—are interesting. Washington was reserved and diffident; Lincoln was folksy and familiar. The one was orderly and an excellent administrator; the other was haphazard and a mediocre administrator. The one was strictly nonpolitical; the other knew the craft of politics and used it. The one was emotional and passionate; the other was phlegmatic and quiescent. The one was overly serious, sombre; the other possessed a sense of humor bordering even on the melancholy.

Often old nations are able to produce several sons whose devotion can magnify the national name; but it is unparalleled that in a new country two such giants should have arisen in less than a century and out of soils so widely disparate as those that brought forth these two.

George Washington had his detractors when he was living and he has them today. John Adams, his successor in the Presidency, could not understand why a man of such limited intellectual horizon should receive so much adulation. Jefferson said of Washington's mind, that it was "great and powerful without being of the very first order." Washington recognized that his mind was not a truly extraordinary one and was humble enough to defer to other minds. Is not such recognition of itself the hallmark of a great mind?

The hostility of Tom Paine is well known. In one of his letters to Washington he wrote: "As to you, sir, treacherous in private friendship, and a hypocrite in public life, the world will be puzzled to decide, whether you are an impostate or an impostor; whether you have abandoned good principles, or whether you ever had any . . ." A Philadelphia paper, the *Aurora*, edited by Franklin's grandson, was virulent in its castigation of the President, writing that "the American nation has been debauched by Washington."

Even today Washington is referred to as a martinet, a hater of the ordinary man, pomp-loving, snobbish, and irreligious. Students of political philosophy no doubt have their biggest complaint against him in his excessive reliance on the Hamiltonians. To those with strong democratic impulses it comes as a shock to read that Washington did not shake hands at his levees but merely stood apart in high military regalia with sword, and bowed formally to those who came forward.

But in all these things we must do what most find it so difficult to do: judge a man by the standards, the temper, and culture of the age in which he lived.

The enigma of Washington is in part the enigma that the man with limited opportunities sees in the man with special opportunities. Greatness is in reality half the gift of destiny, half the result of the soul's coming through its own crucible. Men generally see only the first half.

George Washington had his limitations; it is possible to say that he was too purely an empiricist. But he was a national hero because he loved his country as selflessly as it is possible to love one's country. He is a world hero because he was willing to discipline himself to develop to as high a point as was possible for him.

2

★★

JOHN ADAMS

☆ ☆

		Electoral
VOTE OF 1796:	John Adams, Federalist	71
	Thomas Jefferson, Republican	68
	Thomas Pinckney, Federalist	59
	Aaron Burr, Republican	30
	George Washington, Federalist	2
	Scattered	46
		276 [1]

VOTE OF 1800: *See* under Thomas Jefferson

☆ ☆

IT SEEMS IMPOSSIBLE TO LIVE A FORTHRIGHT LIFE WITHOUT MAKING enemies. The reason is simple. Social arrangements of whatever nature are based in part on some deceit. They do not admit of complete frankness. They do admit of opportunism, of the temptation to be all things to all men, and of choosing the way of least resistance.

A great person nevertheless might follow a forthright life with a minimum of friction. To be completely without enemies is of course out of the question; but to be "wise as serpents and harmless as doves" is a technique that can be perfected if we put our minds to it. The fact that honest John Adams was not a master of this technique explains most of his troubles with his contemporaries, but it does not cause us in our time to admire him one whit the less.

There is a similarity in the rugged quality of the services of such men as John Adams, Grover Cleveland, and William Howard Taft, that might provide material for the student of physiology and physiognomy; there is a similarity in the fleshy physical construction of these men also. A fleshy man rarely is thought of as a deceptive man and nearly always imagined a generous one.

[1] Only one-half this number of electors took part in the balloting.

John Adams was the first of his family line to achieve prominence. There were at least four reasons for this. He was the first
of his family to be able to obtain an education; from his mother's
people, the Boylstons, he inherited ability and a predisposition to
accomplishment; through his wife, the former Abigail Smith, he
was enabled to widen his connections considerably; and he was,
of course, a man possessed of a sincere patriotism and a high code
of honor so that positions of trust naturally came his way.

Like George Washington, Adams lived on ancestral lands which
came to him from the original migrator from England, the first
Henry Adams. It may be clarifying to observe that John Adams
was the third noteworthy person in direct descent from Henry to
bear the name John, his father also being called John, and Samuel
Adams's grandfather likewise. His mother was Susanna Boylston.
John was the eldest of three sons and was born on October 30,
1735 in a house that still stands, in Braintree, Massachusetts, in a
parish of the town later incorporated as the separate municipality
of Quincy. He was thus three years younger than Washington,
and seven years older than Jefferson who died on the same day
Adams did—July 4, 1826.

The facts of American history are not so strange as the miscon-
ceptions about them so many Americans have. Many people are
handicapped by knowledge acquired from the heroic tales which
are fixed in the folklore of any nation. Also, in grade school we
are imbued with certain ideas; in high school we are given a somewhat different version; and in college still other things are stressed.
By this process, it is hoped that things will be set in their proper
perspective.

What the average American thinks about the so-called "Boston
Massacre" of 1770 is an outstanding example of half-knowledge
with respect, not only to the teaching of history, but to compre-
hension of its simple facts. Probably no more than three per cent
of living Americans know what really happened at the Boston
Massacre; nor did most Americans living in 1770 know what happened. It is not that the facts are hidden: it is merely that people
generally do not take the trouble to avail themselves of accurate
descriptions and details.

The regrettable thing about misinformation is not only that the
misinformed do not seem to care much about what really hap-

pened; worse still, the press will sometimes go along with such an attitude. The press of 1770 was no more interested in printing an objective statement of what happened than was the press of a century later.

Even though he was called "the Atlas of American Independence," Adams was not by nature a revolutionist. But as a lawyer he hated the infamous Stamp Act which required the affixing of stamps to all legal papers as well as newspapers. And from a national point of view he hated the act also because the colonists had never given their consent to it. Adams never in his life opposed any public policy for purely personal reasons.

When the people of Boston precipitated the Boston Massacre, that is, when a mob of the townspeople attacked a patrol of British "lobsterbacks," needling, jeering, and pelting them so that they had to defend their lives with their muskets, the attack resulting in several deaths, it was John Adams who defended the British captain and his soldiers in the trials which followed. He won acquittal for seven of them. His words to the jury are timeless:

"Facts are stubborn things. And whatever may be our wishes, our inclinations, or the dictates of our passion, they cannot alter the state of facts and evidence."

By 1770 almost all "obnoxious" acts passed by Parliament had been repealed. Yet the mother country and her American colonies misunderstood each other more and more, and the First Continental Congress was called in 1774. Among those present as delegates were John Adams, George Washington, and Patrick Henry. At the Second Congress, called the following May, Adams was the one responsible for Washington's appointment as Commander-in-Chief of the united military forces. The following year, when complete independence from Britain was definitely decided upon, it was Adams who seconded the motion of Richard Henry Lee for a declaration of such independence. And when the Declaration was actually drawn up, it was Adams who worked the hardest for its adoption by Congress.

After July 4, 1776, Adams was to have practically no time for himself or his family until his retirement from the Presidency in 1801. In 1755 he had been graduated from Harvard; he was admitted to the bar in due time. Thereupon he had acquired a practice which he himself admitted was the best in the entire colony.

But as his interest in public affairs increased, his earnings correspondingly decreased, so that he had to practice great frugality. New Englanders did not live on borrowed money.

In 1778 Adams was sent to Europe to try to obtain a treaty of alliance with France, only to find that this had already been accomplished by the American commissioner there—Benjamin Franklin. However, Franklin's accounts were in confusion, his incompetent grandson being a hindrance rather than a help as secretary. Franklin's great popularity at the French court roused Adams's ever-present jealousy, and he sailed for home.

At once he plunged into the work of framing a new constitution for Massachusetts and indeed was its principal author. He had been home from Europe but three months when Congress again sent him to France; for it was felt the end of the war was nearing and that an able agent for the United States should be on hand to negotiate peace and commercial treaties.

The Adamses had never been noted for tact, and John Adams's bluntness was not an asset to the new American nation at this time when the utmost diplomacy was needed everywhere. Adams was more than ever disgusted with Franklin, who was not the serious man Adams was, nor nearly as hard a worker. In fact, Adams was guilty of insubordination on this trip and was actually reminded by the French government that he was not the authorized person with whom they meant to deal. At length, he went to Holland as American Minister, and here his indefatigable efforts achieved recognition for the young republic; also several much-needed loans.

Finally, with John Jay and Franklin, he arranged for the treaty of peace with Britain, and his statesmanship and continued hard work were again unequaled. He was appointed the first American Minister to the Court of St. James, a post which both his son and grandson were later to hold. In 1789 he was elected the first Vice-President of the United States.

It is unfortunate that Adams had a capacity for envy and jealousy, even vanity. With all his amazing talents and opportunities, he still did not feel secure. A touchy man, rather than a sensitive one, he could not avoid showing his jealousy of Washington whom he looked upon as merely a military hero and thus inferior to the scholar. Adams did not see that the scholar's calling is not necessarily the *ne plus ultra* of human callings. Intellectually, he was the superior of every one of his contemporaries, Jefferson probably excepted; and some modern scholars say he was the greatest political thinker America has ever produced. No other person of his times or probably since has known so much about the theory of government. His best known works on this subject are *Discourses on Davila* and *Defense of the Constitutions of America.* He believed that democracy had its demagogues as well as oligarchy; so neither the capitalist class nor the working class could receive him with open arms.

Like Washington, Adams was a Federalist because he was at heart a conservative. But the Federalist Party was being managed completely by Hamilton and his followers, and these men conceived of the Federalists principally as the vehicle for the creation and maintenance of a powerful moneyed interest. The disparity between Hamilton's ideas and his own scholarly, more humane concepts of public service was a hard enough obstacle for Adams to overcome; coupled with his irascibility and envy, it created a gap between himself and Hamilton which never closed. Washington also had his differences with the rash young Hamilton, even in their army days, but they never blinded him to the possible worth of Hamilton's talents for public service. But to Adams Hamilton was just that "bastard brat of a Scotch pedlar." Whereas in Washington we have a devoutly patriotic man who did not let the demands of his ego interfere with his usefulness to his country, in Adams we have as devoutly a patriotic man who was not shrewd enough to conceal the requirements of his ego. That was Adams's weakness, great though his services were, unimpeachably honest all his policies and statements.

In the election of 1792 Adams received a larger percentage of the votes for the Vice-Presidency than he had at the first election. But by the time 1796 came around, the Anti-Federalists had coalesced into a real party; and that group plus the hostility of Hamilton's bloc in the Federalist Party was to give Adams a hard run and make him the first one-term President. After his election the sensitive Adams was outraged and bitter, smarting under Hamilton's rebuke and the narrow margin by which he had won the contest. Jefferson, receiving the second largest number of votes, became the Vice-President, although he was of a different party. This latter anomaly never again took place in American politics.

Adams's monumental service to his country while President was his averting of war with France. In fact, Adams had once made it known that he wished his epitaph to proclaim that that was his outstanding accomplishment. An outstanding accomplishment it was: he almost alone kept his head during the provoking crisis between France and the United States.

In 1793 those old rivals, England and France, were again at war, and Washington as President had proclaimed America's complete neutrality. Nevertheless, Hamilton and other Federalists in the Government were sympathetic to England, while Jefferson and his Democratic-Republicans were sympathetic to France and her revolution which they considered a people's movement.

But, as was the case in the wars of the twentieth century, England, through her control of the seas, seized not only enemy shipping but American shipping bound, or presumed to be bound, for enemy ports; and, as was the case in modern times, she defined all manner of cargo as contraband besides weapons and ammunition. In addition to this, impressment of sailors on American ships into the service of George III, who was still reigning, heightened the bad feeling. Washington finally sent John Jay to England to settle the differences between the two countries and Jay brought back the famous but highly unpopular Jay's Treaty which Washington signed. Although some important concessions were made to the Americans, the treaty was silent about seizure of American ships. The foreign policy of the United States as we know it today was actually formulated in those days; the sympathies of the United States were to be always with Britain thereafter in that nation's contests with any other European power.

France, angry over Jay's Treaty, began reprisals against American commerce. By 1797 she had captured three hundred American vessels (England had captured a similar number). In the Presidential campaign of 1796 the French Minister to America committed the unheard-of indiscretion of asking the American people to vote the Federalists out of office. France was also not happy over her old alliance with America, formed in the dark days of the Revolution when the United States had agreed not to make a separate peace with England—a provision the young nation very conveniently circumvented. Lastly, the XYZ Papers were laid before Congress by President Adams in which the nation was informed that three French diplomatic agents, known only by the aforesaid letters, would agree to treat with America provided they were paid certain bribes and France were given a loan.

By now the nation was at fever pitch. Even Jefferson was alarmed by France's actions. Actually, although few Americans realize it, an undeclared war existed between France and the United States for two years, 1798–1800, in which France was soundly beaten, the Americans capturing eighty-five of her ships and losing only one of their own.

Adams prepared for war, while doing all in his power to prevent war. He nominated Washington as Commander-in-Chief again. Three frigates of America's new navy, authorized a few years previously, were launched in 1797, the *United States*, the *Constitution*, and the *Constellation*. In 1798 the Navy Department was organized as a separate unit from the War Department.

By 1800 Napoleon had come to power in France. He was anxious to patch things up with America so that he could develop the French West Indies unhampered. Adams seized the opportunity thus afforded, and in the Treaty of Morfontaine achieved the cherished peace while at the same time obtaining the release from the defensive alliance America had with France from Revolutionary days. The Hamiltonians now were furious. What they wanted was war with France; and the President, who had always piqued them because they could never control him, now alienated them for all time, thus forfeiting his chance for the coveted second term. But peace was realized, and Adams, alone, was the architect of it.

The Alien and Sedition Acts passed during the Adams Administration have been severely criticized by historians. For times of war these acts do not appear as harsh as they were publicized to have been, and one wonders why writers made such a hue and cry over them. The rising Republicans made capital out of them by insisting they were a monstrous invalidation of the First Amendment. In times of peace, it is true, they would have been; Adams himself did not try to enforce them, and less than a dozen persons had to stand trial for violations thereunder.

One feature of these laws was that dealing with naturalization, whereby the length of residence was raised from five to fourteen years before the conferring of American citizenship. As we of the twentieth century behold the impact of contemporary immigration on what social order America has, we wonder if the fourteen-year probation can actually be called severe.

In 1800 Adams might have been re-elected if Hamilton had been on his side; but that powerful and aristocratic young man, frustrated in his passion to have American armies led against the French nation, was determined to defeat the President. This he intended to do not by insuring the election of a Democratic-Republican but by throwing his influence to another Federalist who would be amenable to him. He did not succeed, for, by opposing Adams and splitting his party, he brought into office that group which was anathema to him, the Democratic-Republicans and their popular following.

On the morning of March 4, 1801, in order that he might not behold the installation of his successor, John Adams left the new capital city of Washington and the executive mansion which he had occupied for a few months as its first resident. But before he left he performed one last act which was to affect profoundly the weal of the American people to the present day: he sent to the Senate the name of John Marshall to be Chief Justice of the United States. It is Marshall, of course, who interpreted the Constitution to the young nation and gave that document the tone by which it is recognized today.

The Federalists did not trust popular movements; hence, to Washington and Adams, both Federalists, clung the suspicion of a love of monarchy. In fact, Adams had once expressed himself as believing that fewer evils attached to hereditary succession than to frequent popular elections, and even in his old age he does not seem to have entirely surrendered this belief. Such sentiments, combined with his vanity, elicited from his detractors the designation of "His Rotundity."

Nevertheless, when he became President, Adams discarded every semblance of monarchical trappings and even declined the four white horses that Washington had used while in office. What Adams wanted was, to use his own words, "the principle of a free government formed, upon long and serious reflection, after a diligent and impartial inquiry after truth." Adams sincerely made that diligent and impartial inquiry, but unfortunately the bulk of his countrymen did not, and do not even now; nor do the citizens of any other nation concern themselves with any such inquiry. For most people, inquiry after Truth is not a particularly thrilling adventure.

With the many disappointments and personal hostilities that his fervid nature brought to him, it was a blessing for Adams that he had the kind of wife he had in Abigail, who, despite her unusual intellectual equipment, bore the long separations from her husband with stoic resignation while, according to her letters, she suffered the pains of loneliness. "I cannot sometimes refrain from considering the honors with which he [Adams] is invested, as badges of my unhappiness," she wrote. The letters of Abigail Adams are famous; they give a graphic picture of her times. She was a member of the talented Quincy family who have had such a great influence on the life of Massachusetts. Her income cut down by her husband's long absences, she had to look after the farm and be a mother to three sons and two daughters, while maintaining her interest in public matters. She did not live to see her son become President—the son who wrote in his diary:

"Had she lived to the age of Patriarchs, every day of her life would have been filled with clouds of goodness and love. There is not a virtue that can abide in the female heart but it was an ornament of hers. She had been fifty-four years the delight of my father's heart, the sweetener of all his toils, the comforter of all his sorrows, the sharer and heightener of all his joys."

It is fitting that this brave woman, her tempestuous husband, her adoring son, and the latter's own wife should lie together in the First Parish Church of Quincy where their rough-hewn sarcophagi speak to us of domestic felicity, disinterested scholarship, unqualified patriotism, and monolithic character.

John Adams worked incomparably hard to keep the peace. It cost him his re-election; but today it is clear that he, and not the warmongers of Hamilton, chose the wiser road. Jefferson, whose characterizations of his contemporaries are so telling, said of him: "He is as disinterested as the being who made him." Belatedly, the American people are coming to concur in that judgment.

3

★★★

THOMAS JEFFERSON

☆ ☆

VOTE OF 1796: *See* under John Adams

		Electoral	House of Rep.
VOTE OF 1800:	Thomas Jefferson, Republican	73	10
	Aaron Burr, Republican	73	4
	John Adams, Federalist	65	14 [2]
	Charles C. Pinckney, Federalist	64	
	John Jay, Federalist	1	
		276 [1]	
VOTE OF 1804:	Thomas Jefferson, Republican	162	
	Charles C. Pinckney, Federalist	14	
		176	

☆ ☆

PLATO IN HIS *Republic* YEARNS FOR THE APPEARANCE OF THE "philosopher-king" as the only ruler who would be fit to govern in the ideal state. For many students of history Jefferson typifies this kind of ruler, eclipsing even Marcus Aurelius.

Of course, we have never had an "ideal" state; not so much because it is impossible to find worthy rulers as because people by nature could not grasp the significance of philosopher-king rule if it were given to them. We presume that Plato meant to include the quality of magnanimity in the philosopher-king principle; Jefferson had that quality. John Adams was certainly a philosopher-king, even if he did not always possess magnanimity.

When the mores of a people are vital enough to produce a titan, such as Jefferson was, and when such a titan actually finds his way to the nation's highest official seat, we can only marvel ʰthat

[1] Only one-half this number of electors took part in the balloting.
[2] Two states did not vote.

society—and especially so primitive a one as eighteenth-century Virginia—was able to train and nurture such a genius and bring him forward so that all might benefit from him.

Thomas Jefferson's great and lifelong passion was egalitarianism. How this complex man came to embrace such a social concept is not clear. He was born an aristocrat. Peter Jefferson, his father, was a well-to-do landowner of several thousand acres and held some small public offices, such as justice-of-the-peace and burgess. He died when Thomas, the third child and eldest son of many children, was fourteen years old. Thomas's mother was Jane Randolph; that family name also betokened influence in the colony of Virginia. Jefferson's birthplace, called Shadwell, was a plantation near Charlottesville. Also near Charlottesville was Monticello, that unique and famous home, thirty years in the building, where Jefferson died at eighty-three.

Jefferson's life defied many of the rules and standards by which men and events usually are gauged. Most men who have accomplished great things in their youth have failed to live to the traditional three score years and ten. But here we have a man who at thirty-three authored a document as great as Magna Carta, and who was active at an age which many statesmen fail to reach. He lived from April 13, 1743, to July 4, 1826.

At thirty-one, Jefferson wrote a paper as superb as the Declaration of Independence he was called upon to draw up at the Second Continental Congress. This was *A Summary View of the Rights of British America*, presented to the Williamsburg Convention of 1774. The *Summary View* is one of the greatest manifestoes ever written in the English language. In this disquisition Jefferson appeals to the precedents of old Saxon law and behavior to substantiate the complaints of the Americans against the Crown. He makes the astonishing analogy that, as Saxon ancestors had left their Northern European wilds to establish a new society for themselves on the island of Britain—and were unmolested by a mother country in their efforts to work out their destiny—so Americans were entitled to a parallel right under similar circumstances. The one migration, he pointed out, was like the other. There could be no valid answer to this demonstration.

To show that England had no right to dissolve any American legislature, he asked how a body like Parliament, which is elected by only 160,000 men, could control a nation of between three and four millions of people which the Parliament had never seen and would not be likely ever to see? He went on to ask how an American accused of killing a Britisher in the colonies could be fairly taken to England for trial, as the mother country required, where he would "be tried before judges predetermined to condemn."

And Jefferson complained, as he did again in the Declaration, that the Crown prevented the normal desire of Americans to prohibit further importation of slaves, thus outraging Americans in their own consciences. And then there was the matter of the English troops quartered in America for the purpose of surveillance, thus subjecting the civil to the military authority—and for the maintenance of a third of which Americans were being duly taxed. Then, in his noble summation, he exhorts:

"Open your breast, Sire, to liberal and expanded thought"— his humane appeal to the eventually disordered mind of George III. This "raw meat" the Williamsburg Convention could not bring itself to consider in the open, but privately it was mulled over, sniffed at, and by some delectably accepted. Published copies found their way to England. Jefferson was famous.

Jefferson's educational preparation for leadership was excellent. It was one of those marvelous coincidences, seen so often during America's early history and hardly at all today, when the opportunity and the right man met. After being graduated from the College of William and Mary, Jefferson entered the law chambers of George Wythe, one of the most scholarly lawyers in all the colonies.

To Wythe he owed much. And from Governor Fauquier's "Attic society" where the learned and the artistic of the day gathered, and where Jefferson himself took part in the musical performances, he learned more. He spent five years with Wythe before considering himself sufficiently prepared for admission to the bar. Even in so recent an era as that of Calvin Coolidge it was not necessary to study law more than a couple of years for admission, and Patrick Henry received his license after only a few months of reading. But Jefferson's passion to exhaust a subject before he could say he knew it was a matter of unshakable integrity.

Had Jefferson never written the Declaration, had he never taken it upon himself to buy Louisiana, he would still have achieved greatness through his role in converting the dominion of Virginia from a royal province into a democratic commonwealth. Upon his return from the famous 1776 session of Congress at Philadelphia, he was re-elected to the legislature and undertook in earnest his struggle for the rights of man, which had begun when he first went to the House of Burgesses in 1769. He was appointed to a committee to revise the laws and constitution of Virginia.

First of all, Jefferson succeeded in outlawing the ancient principle of entails by which a landowner decreed for all time how his property was to be disposed of. It took almost three years to present a completely revised legal code for Virginia; 126 separate bills were returned while it was being accomplished. Primogeniture was abolished which, with the abolition of entail, struck an almost fatal blow at the basic composition of the Virginia social order—an order, incidentally, without which the world might never have heard of Thomas Jefferson. In the new criminal code the death penalty was retained only for murder and treason.

But Jefferson's greatest accomplishments during this time were with respect to religion and education. That Jefferson himself considered his acts in these fields as taking precedence over all his other achievements is revealed in the epitaph he composed for himself. He asked to be known to posterity only as the author of the Declaration, of the Statute of Virginia for Religious Freedom, and as the father of the University of Virginia.

One of the things the Americans had never liked was paying for the maintenance of an established church in the colonies. The established church was, of course, the Anglican, or Episcopal, Church. In New England, Pennsylvania, and New York the state church was not strong; and after July 4, 1776, even the southerners who were the mainstay of the Anglican Church in America were dissenters, since they no longer recognized the King as the head of the church. But Jefferson wished to separate church and state completely and finally achieved adoption of his measure which stipulated that support for any religious body should be rendered only by the communicants themselves and that in all cases it should be voluntary and never compulsory. Even George Washington thought this too radical a step.

Jefferson's conception of a system of free education for all youth except slaves was remarkable for those times. Not only were grammar and high schools to be made available to boys and girls but also free college training to all those who were talented and definitely showed promise. However, this does not mean that Jefferson believed in mass education: he did not believe in that any more than his great political opponent Alexander Hamilton did. He believed in an aristocracy of the intellect: he believed in *selective* education, to be available freely to all who had a natural yearning toward such an intellectual aristocracy, regardless of personal wealth or previous background. And he believed also that a public library should be maintained by the state. But it was only in his later years that his state agreed to erect the free University of Virginia, the design of the buildings and layout of which he was himself the author and artist, and to which he hoped the great and liberal minds of Europe and America would come to teach.

During the years 1779–81 Jefferson was the wartime Governor of his state; he was not considered a successful one. By temperament he was distinctly unmilitary. The British occupied the capital, Richmond, and he himself only narrowly escaped capture at his own home of Monticello. He was severely criticized for his conduct of the gubernatorial office at this crucial time, and he was sensitive to the criticism of the public. The Revolutionary War never was a really popular uprising, although an untrained and patriotic yeomanry led by a fearless and devoted general won it. It was estimated that only one-third of the populace desired the rebellion, one-third were opposed to it, and one-third were indifferent. It is believed that of those who opposed it—the Tories —as many as 100,000 left the colonies never to return. And while there were in Virginia many planters whose heavy debts to their British agents were being handed down from father to son, and who longed for a pretext to be free of these generations-old obligations, still Virginians were at heart Englishmen who thought of England as home and, like the Washington family, sent their sons there to be educated. It was hard to be Governor of Virginia at a time like that, and to a hypersensitive being like Jefferson it was

just about impossible. He was therefore more than glad to retire
to Monticello.

It was just about this time, in 1782, that his wife died. Jefferson
was distraught. Martha Wayles Skelton was a childless, wealthy
young widow when Jefferson, a promising young lawyer, married
her. Jefferson's daughter wrote that her father was at the sickbed
night and day, that as the end came he fainted, and she had feared
for his life. His grief was so deep, she wrote, that she dreaded even
to think of it. But for such an extraordinarily intuitive and specu-
lative nature, reacting with the utmost sensitivity to experience,
it is to be expected that the loss of a loved one might have deeper,
more enduring consequences than for an average man.

In 1783 Jefferson was elected to the Congress of the Confederation and here his efforts were made manifest in two important acts.
He was responsible for the decimal system of coinage that was
adopted for the nation; and he recommended an ordinance for the
government of the nation's western lands which was the basis of
the famous Northwest Ordinance of 1787.

Inasmuch as we shall soon have to consider in these accounts
the great national crisis posed by the institution of slavery, of
which Jefferson said, "I thank God I shall not live to witness its
issue," it is interesting in analyzing Jefferson's character to see
just what this owner of 10,000 acres and 200 slaves did about
Negro bondage. When he was only in his early twenties, his very
first legislative effort in the House of Burgesses had to do with the
emancipation of the slaves; the proposal was rejected. In his
Summary View he lashed out at the King for refusing to allow
the American dream of emancipation to be realized. In the Declaration, the paragraph pertaining to the slave trade, where he spoke
of "the *Christian* king of Great Briton [*sic*] determined to keep
open a market where *men* should be bought and sold," was de-
leted by Congress in deference to those states who still dealt in
the African slave traffic. Back in the Virginia legislature again,
where he put through his society-rocking reforms, he returned
to his old proposal of prohibiting further importation of slaves,
and again his colleagues warned him of the certain failure of such
a bill.

In his book *Notes on Virginia*, first published in France, Jefferson's abhorrence of slavery is unmistakably revealed. And while his

original bill for the government of the Northwest Territory was not accepted by Congress, a substitute one, setting forth his position on slavery in that vast tract, was passed by Congress. This act determined for all time the economic status of the American nation; for, by unqualifiedly banning slavery from all territory north of the Ohio, these lands were rapidly opened to Northern and Eastern settlers and formed the great free states of Michigan, Illinois, Indiana, Ohio, etc., the admission of which created the ascendancy of the free states over the slaveholding ones.

Finally, when he was President, Jefferson signed the bill forbidding all further traffic in slavery after January 1, 1808. Thus, when he was nearly sixty-five, the dream of his youth came to pass. There is romance in this progression of events, and inspiration as well.

In 1784 Jefferson was sent to France to work with Adams and Franklin in developing some commercial treaties for the new nation, and the following year he succeeded Franklin as the American Minister there. His five years in Paris were additional education for the young widower who was never to marry again. He was to devote all his energies to the continuing fight for the rights of sovereign man, and to bringing up his two young daughters. Everything he beheld and experienced in Europe was to feed the voracious genie in him that was bent on improving the lot of man.

He beheld at close range the vicissitudes of the government of Louis XVI and his tragic queen Marie Antoinette. Lover of France that he was, he experienced both pleasure and trepidation at the coming revolution there. He conferred with Lafayette about the crisis and recommended a constitutional monarchy on the British model rather than an outright republic like that of the Americans for which he felt Frenchmen were not yet ready. He witnessed the fall of the Bastille in 1789 a few months before he sailed for home.

The esthetic side of Jefferson's nature was also nourished and enlarged in this cultural capital. Thomas Jefferson was not only an artist; he was even somewhat Bohemian. When, while he was President, he received the British minister in carpet slippers, it was primarily because of this streak in him rather than, as his foes declared, because he wished to affect an identification with the common man. It is only natural that the mercurial propensities of the kind of life he found in a Gallic people would appeal to him much more than the saturnine, mercantile English temperament. It is not hard to predict where Jefferson's feelings would lie when later in his own country the people were to split up into pro-French and pro-English sympathizers. Every aspect of his nature predisposed him to France; and now, with a genuine revolution coming on, in which the authoritarianism he so hated would be abolished, his love for France increased the more. It was only later, when Napoleon's power threatened the United States at New Orleans, that he became more realistic and wrote that America might have to "marry ourselves to the British fleet and nation."

Washington's appointment of Jefferson as America's first Secretary of State followed Jefferson's return from France. His fundamental beliefs regarding man and his relations to the state were never so accentuated as in the Cabinet where he clashed often with Hamilton. In his famous assertion, "Your people, Sir, your people is a great Beast," Hamilton succinctly stated his philosophy; in his sharp realism, he was in part correct. Jefferson's whole philosophy was the sovereignty and essential regnancy of man; he, in the idealism of his thought, was in part correct. But since the United States has become a nation closer to Hamilton's concept than to Jefferson's, it is in order to inquire into the reasons.

They are many, and belong rather in the study of economics and sociology than in biography and psychology. Even a superficial glance, however, shows that people in the main are materialistic rather than idealistic. Jefferson's native unselfishness in desiring to realize an ideal society for the young American nation misled him into taking inadequate account of the inability of people to appreciate his philosophy as readily as Hamilton's. If they could be led to some mercantilistic pasture where the harvest of materialism could quickly be gathered, they would hardly mind Hamilton's nomenclature, "great Beast."

Jefferson studied government and the rise and fall of peoples more profoundly than any other statesman of his time with the exception of John Adams. He thought the issues out, but Adams, although a less attractive personality, saw the picture more realistically, if not more clearly, than Jefferson.

Thomas Jefferson was the greatest artist-scholastic ever to appear at the helm of a nation. His gentle conception of life was a natural outgrowth of his loving nature. But the artist-scholar is in the minority in an aggressive world.

Jefferson resigned from President Washington's Administration in 1793 and devoted his efforts to building up the Democratic-Republican Party, which he called, simply, Republican. The excesses of the French Revolution had made the term "democratic" odious in the world and politicians did not wish to risk the liability of having that word as part of their official designation.

In 1796, when he received the second largest number of votes in the Electoral College, Jefferson became the Vice-President. It was obvious that with the expansion of the West, and the Adams-Hamilton feud, frontiersmen were coming into their own; and that Jefferson, the frontier planter and champion of the individual, would be the next President.

The defects of the Electoral College were exposed for the first time in the 1800 election and had to be corrected at once by a Constitutional amendment. Not having anticipated the growth of political parties, the framers of the Constitution could not foresee that, when the Presidential electors met to cast ballots for President, they would do so along party lines. Since each elector had to vote for two men (the one receiving the highest number of votes becoming the President, the one receiving the second-highest, the Vice-President), we now realize that a Federalist would vote for two Federalist men, a Republican for two Republican men; it was almost inevitable that two candidates would receive the same number of votes.

When, therefore, the two Republicans in the 1800 election—Jefferson and Burr—had an equal number of votes, the contest was sent, as the Constitution provides, into the House of Representatives. There, to the credit of Alexander Hamilton's true statesmanship, the election went to Jefferson, to whose whole philosophy of society he was so antagonistic. But Hamilton knew what could be expected of the egoistic Burr, and subsequent events proved him to be eminently correct.[3] In the 1804 election, when the elec-

---

[3] Burr later killed Hamilton in a duel. In 1807 Burr was tried for treason and acquitted; but his political life was done, tragedy stalked him, and he died forsaken.

tors cast separate ballots for President and Vice-President, Jefferson won easily over his Federalist opponent.

The outstanding accomplishment of Jefferson's first term was, of course, the purchase in 1803, on his own initiative, of the vast Louisiana Territory at four cents an acre, doubling the area of the American nation and producing thirteen new states. America had had commissioners in France with two million dollars to spend, dickering for the cession of New Orleans and West Florida. Jefferson was alarmed at the prospect of an imperial power on the other side of the Mississippi endangering American commerce. Napoleon, fearing there might be a united English-American force marching against Louisiana in the event he declared war on England, sought to head off such an alliance and made a bid for American friendship by selling all Louisiana outright.

Again opportunity and the right man met and Jefferson, ignoring his Constitutional scruples, grabbed at the bargain and told Congress about it afterwards. Thus even Jefferson saw that in the day-to-day performance of practical affairs, decisions often have to be adjusted to circumstances; and that at such a time it would do no good to argue about whether you were a "strict constructionist" or a "loose constructionist" in your view of the Constitution. It is contingencies such as these which fanatical theorists lose sight of in their zeal to foist nostrums on their societies.

But Jefferson's second term was not as peaceful as his first. Europe's perennial conflicts were impinging upon America's domestic tranquillity again, England and France were locked in struggle, and again all neutral shipping was being suppressed by the combatants. Again, because of her superior sea force of seven hundred warships, Britain's depredations were the worst, and this, together with a renewal of her old practice of impressment of American seamen, angered the Americans. The fact that a Francophile was in the White House also did not help the British cause.

The President, whose horror of violence precluded his ever taking the American nation to war, obtained the passage of an embargo act. This kept American ships off the seas altogether, and it was hoped in this way to coerce the combatants into respecting American rights. All it did was to tie up American shipping and threaten ruin to the merchants, seamen, farmers, and fishermen.

Jefferson knew the embargo had failed and had substituted the Non-Intercourse Act, forbidding trade only with England and France until such time as they decided to treat American shipping with respect. France purported to comply—purported only—and the result was that the embargo was directed just against England, hastening the useless War of 1812. Jefferson, like Washington, declined a third term, and retired for good to Monticello; his successor Madison had to deal with the inevitable war.

Jefferson's talents and temperament fitted him for the management of domestic affairs, and all the high achievements of his statesmanship reveal this aspect of his abilities. No other American President ever was so interested in the agriculture of his country. While traveling in Europe he always looked for some new staple that the American planter might adopt to rotate his crops. It was possibly his greatest disillusionment that the United States did not remain an agrarian economy, and that so many of his glorious plans for her had therefore to be discarded.

By his appointment of the able Swiss Gallatin as Secretary of the Treasury, he consistently reduced the national debt, even at the expense of the national defense; it was below sixty millions when he left office. West Point Military Academy was nevertheless established during his first term.

Of course, no biographical vignette can tell the whole story of Thomas Jefferson. His interests seem to have covered everything except metaphysics and such physical recreation as we today call sports; he was as talented as Leonardo da Vinci. The historian Beard calls him the most civilized man ever called to the Presidency. To discuss his *Notes on Virginia* alone would take countless pages. Some idea of the universality of his concerns is gained from Mr. David Bruce's delightful account of him:

> Jefferson loved birds, flowers and trees, and was more moved by the note of the mockingbird than by the grandest European art. He held the same opinion as did John Adams of the necessity for Americans of his generation to devote their attention to utilitarian objects in order that their descendants might cultivate artistic ones. His mind turned with ease from a discussion of Greek vowels to the invention of the swivel chair and the leather buggy top. He was the inventor of a plow which won him a prize from the French National Institute of Agriculture; the principle of its

moldboard is in common use today. His own inventions he never patented, wishing the people to have free use of them. Grieved by the dreadful mortality among laborers in the Southern wet rice fields, whose working life is supposed to have averaged only eight years, he strove to introduce the cultivation of Egyptian, Algerian and Italian rice, and attempted to import some, as well, from Cochin China. He sent over olive trees from France for experimental planting in South Carolina and Georgia . . . and he promoted as well the cultivation in the South, of figs, mulberry trees and sugar maples. . . .

During his long residence in France he was in frequent correspondence with American friends, and communicated to them his ideas on such varied subjects as innovations in wagonmaking, with designs for cabriolets, and balloon ascensions, properties of minerals, new mechanical processes, astronomical phenomena, literature and philology. . . . He proposed to compare the vocabulary of African Berbers with that of the Creek Indians, to see whether there could be any foundation for the suggestion that the Creeks were descendants of the Carthaginians. His mind roved from speculations on the practicability of a canal through the Isthmus of Panama to the arrangement of a private aviary and the best manner of packing china cups and saucers.[4]

Jefferson loved friends and glorified friendship. One story can illustrate this side of his character. When Dabney Carr and he were boys, they used to rest under an oak tree not far from where Monticello was built. The boys pledged to each other that they would be buried together under that oak. While Jefferson was away, Dabney Carr died and was buried in the local cemetery. When Jefferson returned, he had Dabney's remains disinterred and deposited under the tree where now Jefferson and his family rest, and the spot can be seen by all who visit that classic home on the hill. Any age would be refreshed by a story like this.

Jefferson had, of course, the finest library in the country. In 1800 the Government had authorized the creation of the Library of Congress, but during the War of 1812 it was burned by the British and Congress had to start all over again. Jefferson's library was then purchased by the Government as a new beginning for the Library of Congress. Jefferson often read works in their original

[4] David K. E. Bruce: *Revolution to Reconstruction*, pp. 99–100; Doubleday & Company.

tongues in order to get closer to their meaning. Imagine a President of the United States in the twentieth century writing to a correspondent as Jefferson wrote to Dr. Joseph Priestly:

> I enjoy Homer in his own language infinitely beyond Pope's translation of him . . . and it is an innocent enjoyment. I thank on my knees Him who directed my early education, for having put into my possession this rich source of delight: and I would not exchange it for anything which I could then have acquired, and have not acquired.

Jefferson's descendants today are legion but they are all through his two daughters, the only ones of his six children to reach maturity. Shortly before he entered upon his second term, he lost his youngest daughter also—his household had always been familiar with death. Thomas Jefferson Randolph came in time to be his favorite grandson.

In reviewing the life of a Washington or a Grant or a Roosevelt, one is conscious of a life of acts, of business having been done in the world of matter, and of one's having noted it all objectively. But in studying the life of Jefferson one feels as if one has himself had an emotional experience—whether good or ill—of having been imbued with a force, confronted by an onslaught of ideas; of having been subjected to influences not easily revocable; of having been unable to take a detached view of what was done or said. One experiences a similar sensation in exploring Woodrow Wilson's life: there is a certain neurosis around the whole matter the sense of which one cannot shake—relieved, in Jefferson's case, of course, by the evangel's genuine goodwill and benignity. In both Jefferson and Wilson we see this zealous absorption with an ideal to an extent that obscured for them the practical considerations to which their propositions were tangent. A main difference between the two men is that Jefferson did not hold personal grudges—one of the qualities that gave him his great charm, a charm that even his enemies acknowledged.[5]

On July 4, 1826, John Adams died in his ninety-first year. His last words were said to be, "Thomas Jefferson still lives." In their last years these two old political opponents, co-workers in the

---

[5] Although Alexander Hamilton was his most vigorous opponent, Jefferson kept a bust of him in the hall at Monticello.

greatest sociological undertaking of the Western world, now both widowed, had recovered their friendship and were enjoying a happy correspondence. Adams's philosophy had not essentially changed; a true realist's seldom does. But we suspect that in his inmost soul the ever-learning Jefferson had perceived that much of his own philosophy could never be applicable in the America which was emerging. That was for Arcadia, which neither he nor those to come after him would ever see. It was a transcendently beautiful conception, this felicitous land, which Beethoven might have envisioned when he composed his *Pastoral Symphony* or Corot have contemplated in one of his tranquil landscapes. And it was right that the ideal should have been striven after in America. It was right also that a near-god should have fathered this idyllic concept. But it could have functioned only in a land where the other dwellers were comparably noble.

As if even in death to transcend the past and perplex the future, Thomas Jefferson died the same day as his friend, a few hours before John Adams. It was the fiftieth anniversary of the promulgation of the charter of freedom of the American states with which they had both had so much to do.

The rumblings of "the irrepressible conflict," which was to make all men free and equal as the Declaration stated, could already be heard.

4

****

JAMES MADISON

☆ ☆

		Electoral
VOTE OF 1808:	James Madison, Republican	122
	Charles C. Pinckney, Federalist	47
	Scattered	6
		175
VOTE OF 1812:	James Madison, Republican	128
	DeWitt Clinton, Federalist	89
		217

☆ ☆

JAMES MADISON, THE DISCIPLE OF JEFFERSON, SUCCEEDED HIS MENTOR in the President's House.[1] It is significant that a political party today would hardly risk running a Presidential candidate like Madison: it would be that certain it could not win with him.

James Madison, son of James Madison and Nelly Conway, had about as drab a boyhood for use as campaign material as one can think of, although it never seemed drab to "Jemmy" Madison. Eldest of ten children, he was frail, slight, and introspective. He never took part in any of the usual boyhood activities, but preferred to keep to his studies and his solitary walks in the Virginia woods.

The America of the early days was fortunate that it had scholars and not mere "personality men" to get its ship of state launched and into the navigable waters of a national life. To the Father of the Constitution—James Madison—America is greatly indebted, even though he was not a great success as President because of his poor administrative ability.

[1] Official designation of the President's residence during this time. Although on occasion it had been referred to as the "White House," it was only after its burning by the British, when the still-standing walls were painted white to conceal the ravages of fire, that the latter name came into general use.

Port Conway in Virginia's King George County, where Madison was born March 16, 1751, is no more. It was a small settlement of Madison's mother's people, where Nelly simply went to have her baby. After the birth, the child was taken back to the ancestral estate, Montpellier, in Orange County, Madison's home for the whole of his long life, where he died and is buried. The estate was in the family for about a century before James was born; it is obvious the Madisons were members of the slave-holding aristocracy of Virginia who could afford fine education for their children and who were thus constantly furnishing men for government service.

Madison, of course, never wanted for any material thing. His education was obtained privately and at the College of New Jersey, later to become Princeton University. His name is principally associated with three things—the creation of the Federal constitution; the part authorship of the papers known as *The Federalist;* and the War of 1812. We should add a fourth, for it is highly important—a half century of collaboration with Thomas Jefferson.

Jefferson was in France when the Constitutional Convention met in Philadelphia in 1787 with George Washington presiding. It was probably best that he was in France. And it was best also that such radical leaders of the Revolution as Patrick Henry, Tom Paine, and Sam Adams, were not present either. These men were in truth revolutionists; they were of no service in erecting a new social order. But the fifty-five men who did comprise the Convention produced a work that has been a marvel of the civilized world. It was the first written constitution ever presented to any people.

The sessions of the Convention were held in secret, but Madison kept a daily record of the proceedings and debates which was published after his death as the *Journal of the Federal Convention.* It was at this great gathering that the quiet and unassuming James Madison revealed his deep understanding of the organization of political societies. It was here that his boyhood walks in the woods and his years of sequestered study came to fruit.

And Madison was not without political experience. As a youth of twenty-three he started out by becoming a member of his local Committee of Safety charged with the defense of the colony. In

1776 he was a member of the Virginia convention which carried that province directly into independent statehood. He became a member of his state's first Assembly where he advocated what was almost tantamount to the disestablishment of the Anglican Church. He was a member of the Governor's Council at the time Jefferson was Governor. He was a delegate to the Second Continental Congress. In the Congress of the Confederation he was considered its ablest member. In the years 1783–86 he was back in the Virginia legislature where he took up Jefferson's battle for the separation of church and state.

Madison and the other delegates understood that the real problem of the 1787 Convention was to erect a Federal structure which would supersede the confederation of thirteen sovereign states— the only national Government the United States had. They agreed that the Articles of Confederation, for the amending of which the Convention had been called, were moribund; that an altogether new start would have to be made. Madison realized further that the new Government, if it was to have its laws enforced, should, as he wrote to Jefferson, "instead of operating on the States . . . operate without their intervention on the individuals composing them. . . ." In other words, the national Government would be *directly* paternal toward the citizens of the nation, not indirectly through the jealous state governments.

The framers of the Constitution were men of property; most of them were lawyers. The impetus to all their deliberations, therefore, was the protection of private property. It is safe to say that the majority of them did not trust the people and did not believe in democracy *per se*. Hamilton wanted the President elected for life. Charles C. Pinckney said that to elect members to the House of Representatives by popular vote was nonsense. But the leaning away from monarchical influences so paramount with the majority of the delegates, the predisposition to a society functioning within the periphery of the "inalienable rights," especially the inalienable right of liberty, the willingness to embark upon a revolution in the political field to supplement the victory of the revolution won in the military field, became the complex of emotions that produced the legacy for Western civilization which caused Gladstone to declare that "the American Constitution is the most wonderful work ever struck off at a given time by the brain and purpose of man."

Jefferson from his distant place of influence bemoaned the absence in the new charter of a guarantee of personal rights. He was witnessing from his post the brewing of the French Revolution. Instinctively hating authority, he possibly had a premonition of those violences which were shortly to take place in unhappy, monarchical France. James Madison offered for consideration of the First Congress, in the form of the first ten amendments to the Constitution, a protection for the people of these personal rights—amendments since known as the Bill of Rights. In two years the three-fourths number of state ratifications for the amendments had been secured, and they became part of the basic law of the land.

Madison's work for the Constitution did not end with the adjournment of the 1787 Convention. With Hamilton and Jay, he wrote the masterful set of essays, called *The Federalist*, in support of the Convention's work. At heart Madison was a nationalist. In the two alignments which were arising over the matter of the new constitution—the Federalists and the Anti-Federalists—Madison definitely, by temperament, belonged to the former. It is strange that he ever became Jefferson's ardent lieutenant. In fact, it was because of his strong nationalistic views that he failed to be elected to the United States Senate. However, throughout the eight years of Washington's Administration he was a member of the House of Representatives and was considered its ablest member. For eight years he was Jefferson's Secretary of State and in 1809 fell heir to that sage's mantle—and woes.

The War of 1812, like every other war, had its ostensible cause and its actual cause. The ostensible reason was the British orders-in-council which again interfered with American ocean commerce during the titanic struggle then being fought between England and France. The actual, immediate reason for the war was the shrieking of the "War Hawks"—the same kind of shrieking that went up from the same kind of people over the same kinds of issues before the Mexican War and before the Spanish-American War. All societies periodically have their war hawks, the kind of people to whom the ennui of unexciting peace is simply unbearable. When economic and social conditions contain the tinder for war, it is often this element which sets it aflame.

The Founding Fathers with their scholarly understanding of government and society were disappearing. Thirty-six years had passed from the signing of the Declaration of Independence to the outbreak of the new war with England. A new generation had grown up and was feeling its strength. Like every new generation, it had to learn about life and history for itself: the cautionings of the Fathers meant little to them. Like people in every age, they said, "But *this* situation is *different.*" Younger men were being elected to the Congress, and among the "comers" were Henry Clay of Kentucky and John C. Calhoun of South Carolina. Young men like this were anxious to "do something," to carve a niche for themselves; and, again like people in government everywhere, they rationalized their clamorings as supreme patriotism.

It was such young men who were called War Hawks, because they wished to risk war and annex Canada and the Floridas. The Westerners in their expansion program had been having trouble periodically with the Indians, and the British were the Indians' traditional allies in these years. In fact, Tecumseh, the great chief of the Shawnees, who lost his life during the 1812 War, was a brigadier-general in the British army. This sort of thing did the British no good when Americans were chafing under their orders-in-council and American shipping was being subjected to one indignity after another.

The shouts of the West and the South for hostilities could no longer be resisted. One Congressman declared that the great Disposer of Human Events had intended that the St. Lawrence and the Mississippi should belong to the same nation. How often in the imperialist program of the United States would such pontifical chatter be heard in the halls of Congress—for the consumption of a public which not only paid such officials to serve its interests but would also be required to offer its youth in meaningless slaughter to fulfill the boastings of warmongers.

Before his first term was up, Madison asked Congress for a declaration of war against England, citing 6,057 instances in which the British had impressed American seamen in a three-year period.[2] The vote of approval was by no means unanimous, but it carried; in the Senate the vote was only 19 to 13.

[2] Nevins and Commager: *A Short History of the United States,* p. 165; Random House.

All the New England states were against the war, as their economy was so tied up with shipping that the curtailment of it meant only suffering for them. In addition, they were strongly English in sympathy and, further, were the last stronghold the Federalist Party had in the nation. So unsympathetic were New Englanders to the war that they called the Hartford Convention in 1814 to consider their grievances; there was even talk of secession. They would lend no money to the Government for the conduct of the war and even resisted orders to call out their militia for the national defense. After the war, this group was held in such contempt for its lack of patriotism that the Federalist Party died, never to come to life again.

The war, of course, was unsuccessful, although American children learn in a vague way that the United States won a second war from England. The American military and naval program, to which John Adams had given such splendid attention, was allowed to lapse by Jefferson and Gallatin in their zeal for economy. In fact, the United States owned not a single large warship at this time.

A few salient events in the conflict are worth remembering. The navy of George III—who was still on the throne, but who was by then entirely insane—blockaded America from New England to New Orleans. The British invaded Maryland, captured Washington, burned the Capitol, the President's House, and other public buildings. The President's House had only the charred outer walls remaining. Dolley Madison,[3] the First Lady, became a heroine by escaping with the Lansdowne portrait of Washington; the picture hangs in the White House today. Commander Oliver Hazard Perry won his famous victory on Lake Erie. Resistance at Fort McHenry prevented the capture of Baltimore and gave birth to *The Star-Spangled Banner*, which Francis Scott Key wrote while he was a prisoner on board a British ship outside the Fort.[4] Fort Dearborn (Chicago) was captured by the British. Detroit was lost and regained. The league of the British and the Indians was ended by Tecumseh's death at the Battle of Thames River. Andrew Jackson came into national prominence by his capture of New Orleans.

[3] Mrs. Madison signed her name Dolley, not "Dolly," according to Bess Furman: *White House Profile*, pp. 54-55; The Bobbs-Merrill Company.
[4] Voted by Congress the national anthem only in 1931.

If Morse's telegraph or the steamboat had been in commercial use, there might not have been a War of 1812 at all. The orders-in-council had been repealed by Britain only twenty-four hours before war was declared, but America had no way of knowing that. Also, a treaty of peace had been signed in Europe between Britain and the United States when Jackson fought his Battle of New Orleans—but he had no way of knowing that either.

The war settled nothing. Mr. Madison's government was glad to get out from under "Mr. Madison's War," as the Federalists called it. However, the war did serve to unite the American people and gave rise to a new nationalism. It was the beginning of the abandonment of the old idea of a federation of separately sovereign states: America was growing up into an imperialist power, to be a peer of other imperialist powers, as Hamilton had foreseen.

Her population was increasing. At the first census, in 1790, it was 3,900,000; in 1800 it was 5,300,000; in 1810 it was 7,239,000. New states were being added to the original thirteen. While Washington was still in office, Vermont, Kentucky, and Tennessee were admitted; Ohio was next in 1803; then during Madison's Administration Louisiana and Indiana were added. Internal improvements were coming fast. The national Government in 1811 financed the Cumberland Road, or Old National Route 40, which was distinctly a factor in opening up the West. Fulton had sailed his steam-driven *Clermont* up the Hudson in 1807, reaching Albany from New York in thirty-two hours. Canals were being dug. An American literature was beginning to flourish with the emergence of Irving, Bryant, and Cooper. The first protective tariff was enacted in 1816, and this, together with Chief Justice Marshall's broad construction of the Constitution, added to the internal growth of a mighty nation. Only one cloud was on the horizon—the black man's bondage.

In middle life Madison had married Dolley Payne Todd, a young widow many years his junior; their marriage was a happy one. They had no children but Dolley had a small son and Madison brought this boy up as his own. The boy grew up a kind of wastrel and caused his parents a good deal of anguish.

Dolley was official hostess for both Jefferson and her husband when these men were in their respective Presidencies. She was the first popular First Lady the nation ever had and was a familiar figure in Washington society even into Polk's Administration. Noted for her social qualities, tact, and concern for her husband's problems, she shone brilliantly at gatherings, her gowns, turbans, and bird-of-paradise feathers being always the topic of comment at such times. In later life, when she was in an impecunious position, the Government paid her $25,000 for some of her husband's papers. The other woman in Madison's life, his mother, lived with him at Montpellier until she was ninety-seven.

Obeying Jefferson's solemn, rather strange entreaty to him in a letter—"Take care of me when dead . . ."—to look out for his interests after he was gone, Madison succeeded Jefferson as rector of the University of Virginia. He was interested also, as Jefferson was, in the work of the American Colonization Society for the resettling outside the United States of freed slaves. The modern republic of Liberia is a result of the efforts of this Society. Jefferson never believed that, once free, the Negro and the white man could live side by side. His nature shrank from the prospect of eventual assimilation.

Madison's closing years, like those of Jefferson and Monroe, were troubled by financial difficulties. Long years in the public service brought all three men into unbelievably straitened circumstances. Jefferson was completely bankrupt and appealed to the state to permit him to hold a lottery for the disposition of his holdings so that creditors could be paid. Fortunately, the home and burial plot are today in the possession of an association which will keep them for the enjoyment of posterity.

Monroe lost his home, Oak Hill, and it is today in private hands. Madison suffered the humiliation of being turned down for a loan by the very Bank of the United States the bill for whose rechartering he had signed. His home also is today in private hands.

If inquiry were to be made as to whether the American people appreciate such personal sacrifices on the part of their public men, it is doubtful if the findings would reveal awareness with respect to this on the part of as many as one per cent of the people.

James Madison was a man of exceptionally small stature, and his close association with the six-foot-three-inch Jefferson made for a strange pair. The duration of their friendship attests to its genuineness, and in their last years was a great consolation to both men. On June 28, 1836, Madison died at beautiful Montpellier in the fullness of years.[5]

[5] Montpelier in Hanover County, Va. should not be confused with Montpellier, the Madison estate in Orange County.

5

★★★★★

JAMES MONROE

☆ ☆

		Electoral
VOTE OF 1816:	James Monroe, Republican	183
	Rufus King, Federalist	34
		217
VOTE OF 1820:	James Monroe, Republican	231
	John Quincy Adams, Republican	1
		232

☆ ☆

TO VIRGINIA'S ARISTOCRATIC NORTHERN NECK—THE AREA THAT HAD produced the Washingtons, the Lees, the Fairfaxes, the Carters— the nation again turned to select its fifth President. But with him the "Virginia dynasty" came to a close.

A very normal man, with a very normal boyhood, of ordinary talents, of high patriotism and sincerity, from good and ambitious parents, and with the good fortune to have been alive during momentous years, James Monroe made a quite successful President. He was another Jefferson devotee, and built his boxwood-surrounded home near his friend's Monticello. Called Ash Lawn today, it, too, is a tourist stop.

In his own state Monroe actually worked against ratification of the new national Constitution, so it is evident that he was not by temperament a believer in a strong centralized government. His name, of course, is indissolubly associated with the famous Doctrine—a thesis that was simply included in one of his messages to Congress and has no legislation or other formal pronunciamento to back it. Time alone has most assuredly established its validity. Yet the real force of the Doctrine comes from what the Secretary of State, John Quincy Adams, declared it to be, and not what Monroe at first thought it should be. It is a mark of Monroe's love for his country—the mark of good statesmanship—that he yielded to others when he saw that their position was more tenable than his own.

Monroe was plainly ambitious to succeed Jefferson as President; but he had to wait eight years, during which he served Madison as Secretary of State and even, for a time, as both Secretary of State and Secretary of War, acquitting himself well in these posts. When, at the end of the eight years, he was the logical choice to succeed "the great little Madison," the opposition party had become so moribund that his election was almost a walkaway, and his Administration became known as "The Era of Good Feeling." By the time of his re-election in 1820, there was no opposition party left whatever, and Monroe received every electoral vote but one—that of a New Hampshire elector who, tradition had it for a long time, did not want any other President than Washington to be elected unanimously; but who, it is now fairly well established, did not vote for Monroe simply because he did not like him.

Before Monroe's second term was over, the Era of Good Feeling had disappeared. A new era with new political faces and parties and new national aspirations, hatched already in Jefferson's time, had grown to adulthood; and it was only the interval of John Quincy Adams's four years in the White House which prevented it from at once coming raucously into its full inheritance.

In Westmoreland County, at the present settlement of Monroe Hall, where the elder Spence Monroe had his plain home, James was born on April 28, 1758. The mother was Eliza Jones, and both families had attained some degree of prominence in the colony. James had the advantages of a private tutor and of attending William and Mary College for two years. He happened also to be a schoolmate of John Marshall. His college work was interrupted because the young Monroe could not resist an urge to join a regiment in the opening of what was to become the great war for the independence of the American colonies. He was only eighteen when he became a lieutenant, was wounded at Trenton, fought at White Plains, Harlem Heights, Brandywine, Germantown, and Monmouth. After 1780, before the war was over, he began the study of law under Jefferson's guidance.

His first venture into politics was in 1782 when he obtained a

seat in the Virginia Assembly; he was sent to Congress the following year. In 1786 he again was in his state's Assembly, serving
four years. Although he failed in a try for the First Congress
under the new Government, he was named in 1790 to a vacancy
in the United States Senate. Here he was noted for a regrettable
personal attack on Hamilton.

In 1794 Washington appointed Monroe as Minister to France,
but he was recalled in 1796 because the Administration was displeased with him. The basic reason for this is simply that he was
of the pro-French party in America (a reason for Washington's
sending him to France), while the Administration, and especially
the State Department, was preponderantly pro-British. There
was, however, as much sense to Monroe's appointment to the
French ministerial assignment as there would have been had Franklin D. Roosevelt during the late 1930's sent a pro-German ambassador to one of the European capitals.

Monroe hated monarchy and was an out-and-out Jefferson
convert, at least during these years. He was foredoomed to failure
in the Paris mission, especially as the governments of France were
changing almost from month to month. It was a similar instability
in France almost two hundred years later that proved to be an
enormous obstacle to the stabilization of Europe.

The people's answer to the recall of James Monroe was his
election as the Governor of his native state for three years.
Monroe published a defense of his labors in Paris which was a violent denunciation of the conduct of foreign affairs in the Washington Administration, and the criticism was not lost on Washington himself.

But Monroe was sent to France again, by President Jefferson
this time, to help the American Minister there in the negotiations
for the purchase of New Orleans and related matters. The *fait
accompli* which greeted him as he arrived in France, produced by
Napoleon's decision to sell the entire Louisiana tract, is well
known. Monroe and Livingston, the American Minister to
France, exceeded their instructions when they agreed to buy it all;
but it became one of the most profitable and far-reaching pieces of
"insubordination" in all history.

Monroe went also to Madrid to see what he could do about
the Floridas which the United States desired, especially West

Florida, which Americans insisted was part of Louisiana. He got nowhere. Since he also had been appointed Minister to Britain, he returned to his post in London. Here he tried to obtain a treaty to assure America of a cessation of the depredations on shipping that eventually led to the War of 1812. Again his task was hopeless; and the treaty he did obtain was not even sent to the Senate for consideration; Jefferson just dropped it. Once more the people showed what they thought of their traveling patriot by giving him another term in the Virginia Governorship in 1811. From here he went into Madison's Cabinet.

One of the factors which contributed to the Era of Good Feeling was Europe's having at last achieved peace with the defeat of Napoleon at Waterloo in 1815. An economic depression, the kind which invariably seems to follow after a war, seized the country during the years 1819–21, but was soon dispelled. The nation was growing too fast to be held back by any such phenomenon for long, and this resurgence naturally made for good feeling also.

Early in his Administration Monroe made a tour of the country which was eminently successful. Most Americans had never seen the face of a President before, so that even in Federalist New England the President was enthusiastically welcomed. This trip took him as far west as Detroit. In a second trip he visited the Southern states.

The rise of Andrew Jackson, the statesmanship of John Quincy Adams, and the Presidency of James Monroe are all intertwined; and, since all three men became President, it is somewhat difficult to restrict the recounting of the events of the period to any particular biography. The acquisition of Florida, for example, was realized by Jackson's military expedition against the Seminole Indians there (and against the British Empire as well), by Monroe's Presidency, and by John Quincy Adams's superb handling of the entire matter in his State Department. West Florida had been annexed in Madison's Administration by a *coup d'etat*. East Florida, where the Seminoles were crossing the line to make raids on Georgia, had been coveted by the United States for a long time and was a kind of natural possession anyway. Jackson, who was sent down to quiet things, and who never failed to make what drama he could out of any situation in which he was involved, drove the Indians back, executing two Britishers in the process. As was always the case where Jackson was involved, the Government stood aghast and the people loved it. Adams in his dealings with the Spanish minister asserted that Spain, having sovereignty over territory contiguous to the United States, owed it to America to govern her province peacefully, and emphasized that if she could not do this, the United States would have to do it. This resulted in Florida's acquisition by the United States in 1819 for $5,000,000.

But the act of the most far-reaching consequence in Monroe's Administration was the Missouri Compromise. When Monroe first took office, there was a certain Eastern-Western cleavage in the nation, resulting from, among other things, Henry Clay's internal improvements program. Monroe did not believe that the national Government had the power to build roads and canals unless a Constitutional amendment existed enabling it to do so. For this reason many states undertook their own improvement programs, as New York did in constructing her famous Erie Canal.

But when Monroe left office, it was realized that this sectional cleavage was mere child's play compared with a truly serious separation defining itself between North and South. Missouri with her slave constitution had asked for admission into the Union. With jarring suddenness, the American people—North and South —saw that they were confronted with a menace to their way of life, far greater than the jealousies and insults of foreign powers. Slavery, terrifying, Jefferson said, as "a fire bell in the night," was going to have to be dealt with.

The Missouri Compromise was a stopgap solution to all this, offered by Henry Clay. By means of it Missouri would be admitted with slavery but all other territory in the Louisiana Purchase lands north of Missouri's southern boundary would forever be barred to slavery. Maine was then cut off from Massachusetts and admitted as a free state to keep the number of free and slave states even. (Illinois, Alabama, and Mississippi had already joined with their respective economies.) Clay's bill, of course, was only a compromise, and a temporary one at that. As a matter of fact the Supreme Court in less than forty years was to declare the Act unconstitutional. The surgings of civil agitation were increasing. The explosion into civil bloodshed was not far away.

For more reasons than those of sentiment alone, it should be mentioned that Lafayette, upon invitation of Congress, paid the United States a visit in 1824. He and his son George Washington Lafayette were lionized everywhere, and many old friendships were renewed. Many places in the Eastern United States today bear plaques commemorating the marquis' visit. Congress voted him a purse of $200,000 and 23,000 acres in the new territory of Florida. While all this munificence was being dispensed, Jefferson's last years were clouded with worry about how his daughter and grandchildren were going to live, and Monticello was being put up for auction. Madison was likewise plagued. Monroe's turn was to come.

Monroe had extraordinarily capable men in his Cabinet—John Quincy Adams, William H. Crawford, John C. Calhoun—all Presidential material. Clay was offered a post too, but he declined. Monroe was an impressive-looking man, six feet tall, but he was in no sense handsome. His wife, the former Elizabeth Kortright, was a beautiful woman, and was the mother of his two daughters.

When Monroe left office, he belonged to an era that was already past. It is significant that he was the last President to wear a cocked hat. Even his party was dead. The Jacksonians who came after him were the "democratic" half of the Democratic-Republicans, as Monroe and his colleagues were the "republican" half. The party of Thomas Jefferson, who would have been outraged by the conduct of Jackson and his followers, was as defunct as the Federalists. It had served its purpose. A new force—the force which represented the raw West, which had been hammering at the door for admittance for a great while—was, under an unlettered and peremptory advocate, to be granted its entrance.

Like his predecessors in office, Monroe became an officer of the University of Virginia. In his last years he also took part in a convention for revising the constitution of his native Virginia. He was able to live for only a few years in his beautiful Jefferson-designed Oak Hill mansion, near Leesburg, Virginia. He died at the home of his daughter in New York City in 1831, on July 4th. On the one-hundredth anniversary of his birth, his remains were re-interred in Hollywood Cemetery, Richmond, where a rather barbaric tomb has been erected.

If, during the study of Monroe's two terms, we have had to

face up to the issues of the bondage of the American Negro, the imminent bondage of the Presidential office to political manipulators, the bondage of the American people to visions of one El Dorado after another, then another event of this Administration—the establishment of the first free high school in the United States —is perhaps of great enough significance to have counterbalanced them.

6

JOHN QUINCY ADAMS

☆ ☆

	Electoral [2]	House of Rep.
VOTE OF 1824: [1] John Quincy Adams, Republican	84	13
Henry Clay, Republican	37	0
Andrew Jackson, Republican	99	7
William H. Crawford, Republican	41	4
	261	24

VOTE OF 1828: *See* under Jackson

☆ ☆

IF AMERICA HAS HAD A "ROYAL" FAMILY, IT HAS BEEN THE ADAMS family. They have conducted themselves regally, governed disinterestedly, and demonstrated unalloyed patriotism.

It began with the pre-Revolutionary activities of cousins John and Samuel, followed by the Presidencies of John and his son John Quincy. There followed the services of one of the latter's sons, the first Charles Francis, as Minister to England during the Civil War; he was also the candidate for Vice-President with Van Buren in 1848. There was Thomas Boylston I, President John Adams's other son, who was Chief Justice of the Massachusetts Supreme Court. There were Brooks and Henry II, writers and incisive critics of the American scene. There was John Quincy III, Massachusetts legislator and candidate for Vice-President in 1872. There was the third Charles Francis, Secretary of the Navy in the Hoover Administration; Hoover says in his *Memoirs* that had he known of his great qualities he would have named him Secretary

---

[1] Although this is the first election in which popular vote figures were preserved, they are not given because completely unreliable.
[2] Six states still chose their electors by the legislature; the remaining chose them by popular vote.

of State instead. The United States has been singularly fortunate in having been served so long and so consistently well by one family.

It is a tragedy that America will not seek out this type of service today. The people are not interested in it unless some glamour-tag comes with it. And because the people do not seem to be interested, candidates often are not.

The election of 1824 demonstrated, as nothing else theretofore had, that true democracy is undependable and that the people are not always correct about what is to their advantage. The reason for this is understandable: the people have only a fragmentary or insufficient knowledge of the forces which move society and actuate human endeavors. It can be truthfully said that the public often votes in ignorance. Because the Founding Fathers knew this, they did not want the all-important function of President-electing to be performed by the people directly, and hoped that the device of the Electoral College would save the people as well as the ruling interests from a bad choice.

When, for the second time in American history, there was no majority in the Electoral College, and the choice of a new President fell in 1824 to the House of Representatives, the vote of that body, although contrary to the wishes of the rank and file, was a vote for sound statesmanship. The cries of the Jackson people—the *vox populi*—that their candidate had been cheated of the election made John Quincy Adams's re-election impossible. But there is hardly a single student of history today, hardly an informed person in government who would not agree that when Adams was rejected for Jackson in 1828, it was a sad day for the American nation. *Vox populi* was wrong, as wrong as it ever was at any time in any nation's life.

John Quincy Adams was probably the greatest Secretary of State the American nation ever had. His services after he left the State Department were anticlimactic; he had his real career before he became President. For training in the great work of his life he had an apprenticeship that was without equal before—or since. Even Herbert Hoover's long sojourn in foreign countries was not more valuable to the nation. Adams grew up in the atmosphere and environment of the Revolution: his whole life was connected with the beginnings of the American republic.

While his father was away at the Continental Congress, the seven-year-old John Quincy and his mother Abigail watched the Battle of Bunker Hill raging from a neighboring hill. When the boy was eleven he accompanied his father to Europe on the latter's diplomatic mission. On his father's second trip, a year and a half later, he again went along. His schooling took place in Paris, Leyden, Amsterdam, Leipzig, London. When only fourteen, he became private secretary to the American envoy to Russia. He studied the Russian language, which was undoubtedly useful when, many years later, he became himself the American envoy to Russia. He studied also French, German, Dutch, and Italian, as well as Latin and Greek. In later life he actually read the Bible through in several of these languages. He absorbed knowledge everywhere, and was as a youth a good deal like Madison—precocious and serious. He was with his father again at the peace-signing in 1783 when the Revolution was formally terminated.

Although, as the son of the American Minister to the Court of St. James he enjoyed privileges and opportunities denied to other American youths, young Adams wished to be independent and earn his own living. By his own choice, therefore, he left Europe and entered Harvard University; he graduated in two years with high honors. Three years' reading of law completed his education, and he established his offices in Boston at the age of twenty-three.

Adams had, of course, always aspired to a career in public life. He took another step towards such a career by writing a series of articles in the newspaper in answer to Tom Paine's *The Rights of Man*. These articles were so well thought out that they were attributed to his father. The gift for writing remained an Adams family characteristic.

The young Adams did not have to wait long for recognition. In 1794 he was appointed by President Washington to be American Minister to Holland. He was only twenty-seven years old when this honor came to him, and he was to remain in Europe, this time for six years, the greater part of it spent in Berlin.

After the elder Adams became President, qualms about the propriety of his son's remaining in the foreign service were quickly put to rest by George Washington. He wrote to his successor in the Presidency: ". . . I give it as my decided opinion

that Mr. [John Quincy] Adams is the most valuable public character we have abroad, and . . . he will prove himself to be the
ablest of all our diplomatic corps." Washington's insight was corroborated, the young man remained in Europe; it was not till
1801, after his own defeat for re-election, that President Adams
recalled his son. A few years before this, while on diplomatic
business in London, John Quincy had married Louisa Catherine
Johnson, European-born daughter of the American consul in
London. According to her erudite grandson Henry Adams, the
younger Mrs. Adams somehow never really became quite Amer-
icanized.

After his recall from his post as Minister to Prussia, Adams was
elected to the Massachusetts Senate. There he was referred to by
his party as "too unmanageable." He failed in a try for Congress;
but in 1803 the legislature sent him to the Senate in Washington.
They soon discovered that he was unmanageable there too. When
he thought it more in the interest of the nation to vote with the
Republicans, he did so; and when he voted for Jefferson's embargo, the New Englanders' exasperation with him was such that
they named his successor long before his term expired. Rather
than finish his term under such an onus, Adams resigned. Years
later, after he had left the White House and his district asked him
to be its representative in Congress, he set forth his terms, which
were the only terms upon which he ever served his country;
namely, that as a public servant he would be accountable to no
party, no section, no person; just to himself—and, it is clear, to
his scrupulous God.

When President Madison offered Adams a place in the Supreme Court, he declined it, stating that he did not feel he was
fitted for such a post, even after the Senate confirmed him. But
when he was offered the position of American Minister to Russia,
he accepted. This stay in Europe was to last almost eight years, five
of which were spent in the Russian capital.

John Quincy's most notable effort during this period was his
contribution to the Treaty of Ghent, which terminated the War
of 1812. Henry Clay and Gallatin also were among the commissioners who, by England's own admission, were a far better
corps of men for the negotiations than England had sent. The
compelling logic that Adams was to use for the rest of his life in

dealing with public matters was displayed in all its brilliance in the Ghent Treaty. One incident pertaining to the Indians, of itself of no particular historical importance, is interesting as a sample of Adams's discerning thinking. At Ghent Britain wanted a barrier of an independent Indian nation between her North American possessions and the United States, that is, a barrier created from the Northwest Territory. Adams inquired how, if the Indians were not then an independent nation, England could presume to speak for natives within the domain of the United States. And if they *were* an independent nation, where, Adams asked, were England's credentials to treat for them? Of course, England had to retreat from this position.

During the negotiations, Henry Clay, who was responsible for the war as much as anybody, grew restive and wanted to continue hostilities so that the Untied States could come out the victor, and a real power; but Adams had his way and secured America an honorable peace without any further *faux pas*, as his father had done before him with France.

After the signing at Ghent, Adams, having had enough of Russian winters, went to London as American Minister. As his father before him and his son after him had done, he represented the United States at the Court of St. James at an unfavorable time. John Adams was the Minister immediately after the Revolution. Charles Francis Adams was the Minister during the critical days of the Civil War. During none of these three periods was England particularly friendly with the United States.

At last came the zenith of Adams's career—his tenure as Secretary of State. We should add in passing that Adams had nominally become a Republican since the Federalists deserted him, and Monroe gave that as one of the reasons for his choice of Adams for the Cabinet. In reality Adams belonged to no party; party affiliations as such were throughout his life uncongenial to his temperament.

The new State Secretary obtained Florida for America without loss of either American life or American dignity. He obtained an agreement with England on joint occupation of the Oregon country, which eventually led to America's acquiring title to the Pacific Northwest. The formulation of the great Doctrine that was to allow America to develop without fear of foreign intervention then followed.

The Monroe Doctrine was enunciated because of two threats. One was from Russia which had envious eyes on the Oregon country and wished to extend her possessions from Alaska through this rich fur-trading section. Secretary Adams told the Russian minister that America "would distinctly assume the principle that the American continents were no longer subjects for any new European colonial establishments." Russia's immediate interest ended.

The other threat came from the so-called Holy Alliance and was occasioned by the new South American states, Mexico included, which had revolted from Spain and set up, Brazil excepted, independent republics of their own. The Holy Alliance was a federation of European monarchs, led by the Russian Tsar, whose avowed aim was to preserve monarchy and monarchical holdings wherever they existed. The Alliance, dismayed by what had been going on in Latin America, began considerations for recovering the lost colonies by force.

England, whose countless struggles to keep the balance-of-power on the Continent has cost the world so much in life and treasure, was alarmed at the plans of the Alliance. The astute English foreign minister Canning proposed to the United States that the two countries unite in declaring a "hands off" policy in the Western hemisphere for all European powers. The idea of the Doctrine originally, then, came from Canning—a fact little known to most Americans.

Monroe, conferring with his predecessors Jefferson and Madison, welcomed their approval of Canning's proposition. Said Jefferson: "Our first and fundamental maxim should be, never to entangle ourselves in the broils of Europe; our second, never to suffer Europe to meddle with cis-Atlantic affairs." Monroe, with the backing of his two mentors, then presented the proposal to his Cabinet. But John Quincy Adams's astuteness was equal to Canning's. He at once recognized England's real motive: she was not concerned with the freedom of the new republics stretching from Mexico to the Cape, but with her own security. She feared Spain might cede her old colonies to France, and England could not permit at any cost a revival of a French colonial empire and

French sea power. Canning, in short, wanted to use the United States to preserve the balance-of-power in Europe.

Adams agreed with Britain that Spain should not recover her colonies and that no other European power should seek to achieve a transfer of their sovereignty. But he insisted to Monroe that for the maintenance of American prestige the declaration of such a policy should come from America unilaterally; England could act separately on the issue if she wanted to. Adams's wishes prevailed, the Monroe Doctrine was enunciated as he envisioned it, and Britain had to declare her own policy separately.

Thus a proposition initiated by a British statesman became a fundamental American dogma, and America avoided the danger of becoming, as Adams said, the "cockboat in the wake of the British man-of-war." Canning naturally did not like America's separate affirmation of the Doctrine. The action of the United States had not only left him without the ally he wanted against the rest of Europe but also, he realized, banned *his* country, as well as those against whom he originally had planned the edict, from further colonization schemes in the Western hemisphere. The action had created an American hegemony over the new Latin-American republics; it had made America a rival of England for the goodwill—and commerce—of that part of the world. This was not what Canning had wanted. England's historic cry of "Export or die" had to influence Canning's actions just as it influenced the actions of his many predecessors, not to mention his successors, down to our own day.

The America of today is not the America of John Quincy Adams's day: technological advances, of course, have made her a global power. Her defensive waters extend considerably beyond the offshore limits of the early 1800's and into areas the fate of whose peoples are, therefore, interwoven with the fate of Americans themselves. All this has made it necessary for the United States to make a more modern and expanded application of the Monroe Doctrine, just as she has had to do with her Constitution. Nevertheless, it is well to review the specific tenets of the Monroe Doctrine. It is in two parts. Part I says that

We owe it therefore to candor, and to the amicable relations existing between the United States and those powers [*i.e.,* the

European powers], that we should consider any attempt on their part to extend their system to any portion of this Hemisphere, as dangerous to our peace and safety. . . . But with the Governments who have declared their Independence, and maintained it, and whose Independence we have, on great consideration, and on just principles, acknowledged, we could not view any interposition for the purpose of oppressing them, or controlling in any manner, their destiny, by any European power, in any other light than as the manifestation of an unfriendly disposition toward the United States.

Part II reads:

Our policy in regard to Europe, which was adopted at an early stage of the wars which have so long agitated that quarter of the Globe, nevertheless remains the same, which is, not to interfere in the internal concerns of any of its powers; to consider the Government *de facto* as the legitimate [government] for us; to cultivate friendly relations with it, and to preserve those relations by a frank, firm and manly policy, meeting in all instances, the just claims of every power; submitting to injuries from none.

That, in essence, is the Monroe Doctrine.

However, respecting the recognition of *de facto* governments, Jefferson had pointed out that America could not conscientiously deny to any power that recognition which it so ardently desired when it threw off the yoke of its European sovereignty.

Further, respecting the important Part I, American Presidents today point out that the nation needs friends both in Europe and Asia if it is to survive.

But, happily, all this does not concern John Quincy Adams.

The day came when Adams was to be elected President to succeed Monroe. It had become customary for the State Secretary to be promoted to the Chief Magistracy and Adams's ambition was quite natural. However, there were four candidates in the field, all nominal Republicans—Adams, Crawford, Clay, and Jackson. None had received an electoral majority, and it was left to the House of Representatives to decide the election. It is true that Jackson received the largest number of popular votes, but it must be said that it is doubtful that he would have if only he and Adams had been running, or only he and Clay. Since Clay's ideals were more in line with Adams's, he threw his weight in Adams's direction. This insured the latter's election. When Clay was appointed Secretary of State in the new Government, the Jackson people were sure there was "a deal"; they never stopped shrieking for revenge until they had it. However, John Quincy Adams never made a deal in his life. In fact, his naive impartiality was so genuine that he actually wanted to have Jackson and Crawford in the Cabinet also.[3]

Adams's congenital distaste for political maneuvers, coupled with the avenging aggressiveness of the Jackson forces, made his Administration a continuous heartache. One of the few pleasant things that can be said about John Quincy's Presidency is that old John Adams lived to see his son receive the honor of being elected President.

The President's daily program was unbelievable. Here is an excerpt from his diary:

> I am . . . compelled to take my exercise, if at all, in the morning before breakfast. I rise usually between five and six; that is, at this time of year, from an hour and a half to two hours before the sun. I walk by the light of moon or stars, or none, about four miles, usually returning here in time to see the sun rise from the eastern chamber of the [White] House. I then make my fire, and read three chapters of the Bible, with Scott's and Hewlett's Commentaries. Read papers till nine. Breakfast, and from nine till five P.M. receive a succession of visitors, sometimes without intermission—very seldom with an interval of half an hour—never such as to enable me to undertake any business requiring attention. From five to half-past six we dine; after which I pass about four hours in my chamber upon some public business, excepting when occasionally interrupted by a visitor. Between eleven and twelve I retire to bed, to rise again at five or six the next morning.[4]

In the mid-term elections anti-Administration forces were elected to the Congress. The handwriting was on the wall. Clay and his followers had formed a new party, the National Republicans, and Adams ran the second time under that label, while Jack-

---

[3] Jackson in the War Department, of course.
[4] From the famous diary published as *The Memoirs of John Quincy Adams* (Charles Francis Adams, Ed.); J. B. Lippincott Company, 1874/77.

son called himself simply a Democrat. One cannot resist quoting
from an American writer on the defeat of 1828:

> Adams was lost, but to understand Amercian history it is neces-
> sary to know what was lost with him. He had a vision of the
> possibilities of America that recalls the vision of Washington. An
> intensely religious man, Adams believed that God intended to
> produce a new and happy civilization when He endowed one
> nation with the riches that had been lavished upon the United
> States. This seemingly endless store of land, timber, minerals,
> water-power, could be developed in such a way as to make
> America the wisest as well as the richest of the nations—and this
> was the end and meaning of Adams's ambition. By keeping the
> Western lands in the hands of the National Government, by se-
> curing its gradual and economic development, and by using the
> wealth derived from the careful disposal of this land for public
> improvements and public education, Adams wished to create a
> United States that would be free from poverty and ignorance
> and from all temptation to the grosser forms of greed. . . . But
> the Jackson men saw something more attractive in these lands
> than ages upon ages of physical, moral, and political welfare:
> they saw plunder.[5]

When John Quincy Adams failed to be re-elected, something
went out of the idea of America, something that has never returned. The Presidents were vanishing who could talk about the
theory of government, who knew of the vicissitudes of ancient
societies, who were acquainted with the writings of Locke and
Rousseau and Voltaire and Montesquieu, and who believed that
beneficent administration meant beneficent administration for all,
not for a section, not for a group.

One part of his career was still left Adams before his death on
February 23, 1848. Without conducting a campaign, which had
been his fixed policy all his life in "running" for office, he entered
Congress as a representative from his Plymouth district, and this
district returned him election after election. He became an anti-
slavery Congressman, although not an abolitionist, and fought for
years for impartial application of the right of petition; in other
words, for the right of anti-slavery groups to be heard in Congress

[5] Herbert Agar: *The People's Choice*, pp. 100–102; Houghton Mifflin Company.

as well as all other groups. When, in 1844, Adams's efforts to quash the prevailing "gag rule" were successful, he confided to his diary the most sanguine thanks to Almighty God. Because of his heroic efforts on behalf of the sanctity of the First Amendment, "Old Man Eloquent" became his newest designation.

Adams, like Jefferson and others, knew that the clouds of slavery hovering over the nation decade after decade would eventually bring the violent storm. He knew also, as other realistic people knew, that the Union might have to be preserved by war. He declared that the sword which would sever the shackles of disunion would sever the bonds of the slave at the same time. He opposed the annexation of Texas. He saw no Constitutional authority for incorporating an independent nation into the national domain, and, of course, he dreaded the enlargement such annexation would bring to the mighty slavocracy.

One day, as he was sitting in his chair in the House, he was stricken, and was carried to the Speaker's Room. Two days later, he died there.

It is one of the regrettable tricks of Nature that she so seldom blends superior talents and personable qualities in the same individual. John Quincy Adams illustrated this as much as did his father. He could have been a personal emissary from On High, yet the voter would not have been attracted to his personality. He was short, pudgy, bald; he had a shrill voice. He was very censorious of others.

Most of the time Adams expressed his irritations by means of the daily entries in the now famous diary, probably the most valuable ever written in America. Begun in Europe when he was still a boy, it is of the most inestimable value to the historian, greater than either his father's or George Washington's, useful as these are. Many events in the early days of America are outlined in all the vibrant detail of immediacy that history books do not give; and the entries reveal the real Adams as his deeds or the words he uttered do not.

He was by nature an ascetic, and a lover of literature and the fine arts. He did not have a Dolley Madison who by her glamour and vivacity might offset his dour demeanor. He was a poor companion. At Ghent, when Clay and his cronies would retire from their card games in the early hours of morning, Adams would already be arising for his daily walks and Bible reading.

But the Adamses, father and son, were like that. Their natures corresponded with the rock-ribbed terrain of their native New England—forbidding, unfanciful, the essence of solidity. Though they had in them too the essence of devotion, they could not unbend. Their Puritan natures frowned on displays of emotion and camaraderie; but they recognized the value of such traits and in their diaries deplored the absence of them in their own constitutions. Washington, aloof though he was, could nevertheless radiate warmth and recruit loyalties. Lincoln, too, although the depth of his feelings for others has sometimes been questioned, could accommodate himself to the moods and notions of others and even, if necessary, feign affection in order to get results. In the business of human relations it is a most needful thing to realize that people invariably *feel* the events and issues of life. And in no other field is it so necessary to know this as it is in politics, especially in the politics of the emotional American people.

To his native Quincy, where he was born July 11, 1767, John Quincy Adams was taken for burial. His tomb, which contains also the remains of his wife and parents, has become a place of pilgrimage.

7

★★★★★★

ANDREW JACKSON

☆ ☆

VOTE OF 1824: *See* under John Quincy Adams

		Popular	Electoral
VOTE OF 1828:	Andrew Jackson, Democrat	647,000	178
	John Quincy Adams, National Republican	509,000	83
		1,156,000	261
VOTE OF 1832:[1]	Andrew Jackson, Democrat	661,000	219
	Henry Clay, National Republican	⎰ 554,000 [3]	49
	William Wirt, Anti-Mason	⎱	11
	Other		7
		1,215,000	286 [2]

☆ ☆

THE ELECTION OF ANDREW JACKSON TO THE PRESIDENCY WAS A milestone in American life. The "revolt of the masses" takes various forms. Sometimes it is a bloody revolution; sometimes a bloodless *coup*. Sometimes the people will be content with a kind of barbaric hero by means of whose unconventional acts and periodic iterations of devotion to the popular cause they feel a vicarious enjoyment of revolution.

The adulation of Jackson in his own time is easy to understand. Today we take a more temperate view. For Jackson's greatness stems not from any extraordinary contribution he made to republican government, nor even, as most people believe, from any unusual concern with democratic processes; he was a doer, rather than a deliberator. It stems, first, from his audacious resolve to be

---

[1] Statistics vary; author is using those of Marquis James: *Andrew Jackson*, p. 872; The Bobbs-Merrill Company.
[2] By the time of this election only South Carolina still appointed its electors.
[3] In a few states the National Republicans adopted the Anti-Masonic ticket, hence the need for combining the Clay and Wirt vote in the table.

himself; and, second, from his entrance on the national scene at a particular period in America's development.

That the people wanted Jackson, and elected him, is plain. His impressive and even magisterial appearance, his military exploits, his identificati n with the frontier and the common man, his unconventional conduct, his fearlessness, his opposition to the "money power,"—this was the material which made him.

Jackson's election was possible also because of the remarkable change which was coming over the Electoral College system; more and more people were voting directly for the electors as property, religious, and other former qualifications were being removed as a prerequisite to manhood suffrage; and the electors were bound in honor, if not by law, to vote for the candidate of the party under whose label they had themselves been elected.

When one adds to these changes the abandonment of the Congressional caucus as the means for agreeing on a candidate to bring before the people, and the substitution of the political convention as we know it today—another change made in Jackson's time—it is easy to see why the selection of American Presidents was becoming not more but less discriminating a process all the time. For the anomaly of the convention system is, that while more voices are heard in the candidate-selecting debates than in other types of conclave, the chances of getting the best man in the country for the job are slimmer. The compromises which party bosses must agree upon in political conventions are often not the estimable kind that councils of statesmen or more experienced people might be likely to make.

The naming of Jackson was inevitable. The West had to have, sooner or later, its grand chance in the national elections. It had its own candidate to offer, one who was rough-hewn like itself. Moreover, the country was tired, after forty years of electing Presidents, of having had nothing but Virginia and Massachusetts magistrates to look at. "It was time for a change."

The American people have seldom had much to say directly in determining who shall be their President; but in Jackson's two elections they really spoke. However, what the people did not realize when they sent Andrew Jackson to the White House was, that although democracy may have been served by the election process, the democratic process was distinctly not served by having a man like him at the nation's helm. For, although he was a people's idol, his methods were arbitrary and therefore contrary to democratic processes. That in part is the enigma of Jackson. He was a democrat-autocrat. He was violent, revengeful, generous, impatient—a product of his time and his place. Impassioned as all his words and deeds were, we must judge them in the light of those tempestuous years which his own definite limitations reflected.

It was under Jefferson that the American nation experienced its first wave of democracy; it was under Jackson that it experienced its second. Probably under Franklin D. Roosevelt it experienced its third, but it is only Jackson's and Roosevelt's Administrations that are comparable. Jefferson himself was always the aristocrat. He cherished democracy as a way of life, but this does not necessarily mean that he cherished all the citizens of a democracy. Jefferson hated uncouthness as much as he loved equality. He hated mobs, passions, snap judgments. He believed that urban life, which so many millions of men must follow, fostered such things. Jackson, on the other hand, had no theories about such matters nor did he care to speculate about them. He was motivated by feelings in raw form, feelings which were strongly black or white, seldom gray.

Orphanhood and the frontier made Jackson what he was; he shows no other influences. His beginnings were as drab as Lincoln's. The son of Irish immigrants, he was as sensitive about his early life as was Andrew Johnson, and as combative. He was the only man ever to become President who was wholly a first-generation American: all his forebears were foreign-born.

Frontier life at the close of the Revolution was anything but conducive to cultural pursuits. To a high-spirited fourteen-year-old absolutely alone in the world it could have meant complete destruction. The fact that Jackson came through such a life, which included the gambling and cockfighting phase, in which he squandered a £300 inheritance he received from his grandfather, still ambitious enough to study law, showed that here was no ordinary youth.

Andrew Jackson, Sr. and his wife Elizabeth Hutchinson migrated to the Waxhaw settlement in South Carolina with two small boys. The elder Jackson died soon after his arrival, and his son Andrew was born at the settlement on March 15, 1767, after the father's death. When only thirteen, the boy enlisted as a mounted orderly in the Revolutionary War. This was in 1780 when Cornwallis was inflicting heavy American losses in the Carolinas. Jackson, at this early stage in his life, displayed both the physical and moral fearlessness for which he became so noted in his later years. Ordered by a British officer to clean his boots, Jackson refused and demanded to be treated in a manner befitting a prisoner-of-war. The officer struck him with his sword and Jackson bore the scar from the blow all his life. When one considers, besides, that both his brothers lost their lives in the war and that his mother died nursing soldiers, his intense hatred of the English is in part explained. All Jackson's hatreds, as a matter of fact, went back to events in his childhood and early life.

The Age of Jackson, as this time in America's history is called, is but a formal name for what was in effect the gawky adolescence of a young nation. The Eastern seaboard, already somewhat effete with two hundred years of civilization, had lost to the frontier its grip on the national life. This was coincident with the emancipation through suffrage of the American man. Criminality came with the frontier as well as rugged individualism; Jackson himself suffered all his life from the gunshot wounds of his early years. When he was almost forty, he killed a man for referring disparagingly while drunk to Jackson's marriage; and once in a Nashville tavern, when he fought the famous Benton brothers,[4] friends had to step in and carry the bleeding Jackson away to save his life. Reference has already been made to the unwarranted execution of two Britishers by Jackson during his campaign in Florida[5] against the Seminoles. When he ran for President in 1828, there was a campaign poster published in Philadelphia called "The Coffin Handbill." This handbill pictured eighteen coffins with an account of the eighteen men it was claimed Jackson had put to death at various times in his life. Whether Jackson really had eighteen men killed will probably never be known for a certainty. But if the assertions in this character assassination of Jackson were untrue, it seems strange that so vengeful a man as Jackson did not

[4] One of them later became a Jackson-supporting Senator from Missouri.
[5] The city of Jacksonville, in that state, is named for him.

bring the publishers of them to trial; stranger still that a man like this ever became President of the United States.

One way the hero's reputation came into being, of course, was through war. Jackson offered his services when the War of 1812 broke out, and his name is always associated with New Orleans where, although outnumbered two to one, he won his famous but needless battle against the British. The American losses amounted to only 13, the British 1,971, including their three highest-ranking officers. As usual, Jackson got into trouble with the civil authorities when he declared martial law and even arrested a Federal judge for resisting his orders. When the judge was out of jail and again on his bench, he fined Jackson $1,000. Thirty years later, when Jackson was in need of money, Congress refunded him this fine which with interest had increased to $2,700. After the Battle of New Orleans, Jackson was appointed commander of the Southern Division of the Army.

When Jackson was inaugurated the first time, the influx of his followers into the capital city was likened by many contemporaries to the descent of the barbarians upon Rome. It is not in fact a beautiful story, this first appearance of Demos at an induction of its hero. Contemporary diaries and notebooks have given us graphic accounts of this inaugural reception, where the rank and file without qualification were welcome, and the White House furnishings were treated as if they were the equipment of a stable.

Another problem which penetrated the age, and touched on Jackson's life as well, was the situation of the American Indian. Thomas Jefferson had an unusually great sympathy for the problems of the Indians; Jackson had little. The truth is that Jackson, like so many other politicians, was not really interested in the Indians' land rights. Jackson was a planter; he was as desirous of pushing the Indian into the trans-Mississippi West as his land-hungry fellow-Westerners were.

We have noted before the accounts of the punitive nature of Jackson's campaign against the Seminole Indians in Florida. He was just as punitive in warring against the Creeks and led an army of Tennessee volunteers against them in retaliation for their massacre of the people at Fort Mims, Mississippi. He defeated them at the Battle of Horseshoe Bend in 1814, almost wiping them out,

and forcing them to cede 23,000,000 of their acres. When he became President, Congress authorized him to relocate the Indians
in what eventually became known as Indian Territory, still later
a part of Oklahoma. To this section the Five Civilized Nations
eventually moved. The Indian phase of America's western expansion is not attractive. The Black Hawk War, fought during Jackson's time, and in which the young Abraham Lincoln was a
captain, is indeed a blot on American honor.

The Industrial Revolution, which began even before the American Revolution, was making its tremendous force felt during the
Jacksonian era. The invention of Hargreaves's spinning jenny,
Cartwright's power loom, Whitney's cotton gin, Cort's rolling
mill, McCormick's harvester, Watt's steam engine, Stephenson's
locomotive, Fulton's steamboat, Faraday's dynamo-electric machine, Morse's telegraph,—these were transforming the nation into
something Washington and Jefferson had not dreamed of. New
England's shipping business was giving way to manufacturing,
with the attendant need for protective tariffs. Sociologically and
politically, the consequences were the enlargement of the ever-
widening chasm between North and South.

In 1828 the so-called "Tariff of Abominations" was enacted, a
protective measure for the North's industries. The South, of
course, opposed this tariff. Its attitude—an attitude which became
traditional with the South almost to the second half of the twentieth century—was that it was more in their interest to buy wares
from Europe where they were cheaper than from the North
whose tariff walls made for higher prices and inferior products.
Under its favorite son, John C. Calhoun, who had resigned the
Vice-Presidency in Jackson's first term and become a bitter enemy
of the President, South Carolina passed its Ordinance of Nullification. This act promulgated the theory that a state had a right to
refuse to obey a Federal law when such a law contravened its
original and inalienable right as an independent political entity.
Jackson who, as one historian put it, "would meet [any] dilemma
more than halfway and spit in its face," threatened to use military
force to compel South Carolina to obey and to hang Calhoun "as
high as Haman." At a dinner attended by both him and Calhoun,
he gave a toast, possibly the most famous toast ever given in the
United States—"Our Federal Union—it must be preserved." Cal-

houn responded—"The Union, next to our liberty, most dear," posing in that short sentence the issue of state's rights which was increasingly to harass the nation.

Jackson's proclamation to the people of South Carolina, warning them of the supremacy of the national Government and of the absurdity of nullification, is considered his greatest state paper. Actually, Jackson was in sympathy with the South's tariff views; but the rebellion he sensed was lurking in South Carolina's position he courageously faced up to at once and even sent two warships to Charleston harbor. The result was that South Carolina suspended her nullification ordinance and Congress passed a more favorable tariff bill.

Jackson was admitted to the bar in North Carolina at the age of twenty—due primarily to the ease with which a license to practice could be acquired in that time. He moved to that part of the state later to become the separate state of Tennessee; here he made a living not only in the law but as a trader in horses, slaves, and land and in a general store he operated for a time. From his plantation, "The Hermitage," outside of Nashville, he shipped his cotton and tobacco down the rivers to the Gulf. Thus he became affluent and was as much identified with the propertied class as were the bankers against whom he raged.

In one of his transactions the notes he had endorsed went to protest and the creditors insisted Jackson make good, not in land or produce but in dollars. An innocent victim in this case, he lost $7,000. This loss infuriated him against all banks and he was determined some day to have revenge. Thus began his war on the second Bank of the United States; he did not rest till he had destroyed it, although that particular bank had nothing to do with his loss.

Nicholas Biddle, the young president of the Bank of the United States, was right when he said that Jackson's attack on his bank was not "a cabinet measure, nor a party measure, but a personal measure." Many Jackson supporters did not go along with the President on the bank issue. The Bank had provided a stable currency for the turbulent, developing nation. Everywhere, including Europe, its drafts were honored; its notes never fell below par.

It was not necessary to destroy the Bank, but it did have its faults and these faults made it unpopular, especially in the West where its competition with state banks made it hard for local people to obtain credit. However, when Jackson, with his peculiar talent for making a personal grievance a popular grievance, spoke out against the Bank, it was foredoomed to death.

James Madison, whose party had been opposed to a United States bank, came at last to feel that such an institution was necessary to the national growth and himself signed the bill for the Second Bank's charter. The first Bank of the United States had been allowed to die with the expiration of its charter in 1811. Then came the War of 1812; and America needed a national bank's help. The nation had to turn instead to state banks which often were uncooperative, especially since the moneyed classes opposed the war.

In both United States Banks the Government owned part of the stock but had practically nothing to say as to administration. Some of the Second Bank's advocates admitted that it had too much power and that such an institution, independent of both Federal and state control, was an anomaly in a political system like America's. Further, the Bank had branches from whose profits it benefited but whose losses it would not redeem. Thus when the Baltimore branch failed during the depression of 1819, the head office in Philadelphia refused to indemnify the losers. When, in 1829, another business recession was on, Jacksonians felt they could point fingers at the Bank as the great ogre which produced all their woes.

Nicholas Biddle, called by an English traveler the most perfect American gentleman he had ever seen, typified for the Jackson people the quintessence of patrician snobbery. To his period he symbolized a way of life which the elder J. P. Morgan a century later would symbolize for his. Of course, the great barons of finance may, like everyone else, be civic-minded or not, depending on personal election. When they have a genuine sympathy for the underprivileged, they are rarely lauded for it. But when they possess merely a conscienceless respectability, they are singled out for all manner of public opprobrium—together, often, with those who do not deserve castigation. It was to those among them who lacked a social consciousness that the twentieth-century A. W.

Mellon referred at the time of the great economic crash of 1929 when, speaking of their losses, he said, "They deserved it."

One more thing gave the Bank a bad name: its perquisites to people in government and other prominent places. Daniel Webster, for example, who with Henry Clay supported the Bank, received a regular retainer from it.

In the end, although Congress voted to extend the Bank's charter, Jackson vetoed the bill and it died in 1836 never to be revived. Biddle organized a new bank under a Pennsylvania charter, but the Panic of 1837 caused it to close its doors.[6] Jackson, after his victory, removed all Government funds from the Second Bank and distributed them in numerous state banks. A wildcat era of state banks then ensued, to be followed by the Panic of 1837. But before this panic began, there was such a surplus in the national treasury that for the first and only time in America's history the entire national debt was paid. The excess funds were distributed as gifts to the states.

The keystone of all Jackson's actions was his intuition: he was at the mercy of everything he felt; little else seemed to motivate him. He was bored with ceremony, annoyed with convention, impatient of logic. The standard way of doing things meant nothing to him, including the standard way of interpreting the Constitution. He insisted that he upheld the Constitution, but he did so by his personal standards and he intimated that the Congress and the Supreme Court might possess their peculiarities of interpretation too. "John Marshall has made his decision; now let him enforce it!" was probably his second most famous utterance.

As Cabinet meetings bothered him, he often dispensed with them and depended for help on a "Kitchen Cabinet," a collection of sycophants which, in some ways, resembled the Brain Trust of Franklin D. Roosevelt's time. This group did not disagree with him on his pet projects, among which was the social acceptance of a tavern-keeper's daughter, Peggy O'Neale, who had married his Secretary of War. Because the wives of the other Cabinet members did not accept her, Jackson made Peggy's battle his battle and injected the silly affair into the Administration out of all proportion to its importance. His war for Peggy and his war

[6] Biddle died in 1844, much of his personal fortune gone.

against the Bank had their origin in the same peculiar cranny of his emotional make-up.

Jackson's political experience, while varied, was of little value. As a young man he was appointed district attorney for his area, and later spent six years on the bench of the Supreme Court of Tennessee, where his services were inconspicuous. He was also sent as a delegate to the constitutional convention which paved the way for admission of Tennessee into the Union. Here his liberal views first became known as he opposed the insertion into the constitution of a requirement that all state officials believe in God and in the divine authority of the Bible. He was his state's first Congressman, United States Senator twice, and Military Governor of Florida; however, in each of these posts he spent only a very short time. In the Senate he was not at home and resigned both times, the first time after only six months' service. In the House he strongly opposed the Administration of President Washington and even, when Washington signed Jay's treaty, favored his impeachment.

Jackson did not care too much about being President in 1824 and openly acknowledged his unfitness; but when Adams defeated him that year, he wanted revenge and the Tennessee legislature promptly nominated him for President the year after his defeat. His treatment of Adams was anything but sportsmanlike. In Monroe's time, when Jackson's adventure in Florida was creating such a furor, and Cabinet members were all for censuring or dismissing him, it was Adams who defended Jackson. When Adams was defeated for re-election, Jackson did not pay him the respect of a social call nor did he permit him to have the White House, as had been the custom, for a final reception for his friends. Consequently, Adams, imitating his father's example of a quarter century before, did not ride with his successor to the inauguration ceremonies. After Adams returned to Congress, he wrote:

> Though I had served him more than any other living man ever did, and though I supported his Administration at the hazard of my own political destruction, and effected for him at a moment when his own friends were deserting him what no other member of Congress ever accomplished before him—an unanimous vote of the House of Representatives to support him in his quarrel with France; though I supported him in other very critical periods

of his Administration, my return from him was insult, indignity, and slander.[7]

The reason for Jackson's affronts to Adams was that he held him responsible in part for the slander used in the campaign of 1828 against his wife, the beloved Rachel, for whom he had an almost divine adoration. Rachel Donelson Robards was a divorcee but when she married Andrew Jackson neither she nor the bridegroom knew that the divorce decree had not yet been granted. The couple remarried sometime afterward. The incident, which seems to us in this sophisticated age stressed out of all proportion to its importance, was a serious matter in those times, and Jackson had many a fight over loose talk about his or his wife's "adultery"—including a gunfight with the Governor of Tennessee. Character vilification is always a shabby affair in politics, and Jackson's rage at his detractors seems justifiable to us; he wins our sympathy, especially as we find no evidence that he ever resorted to any smear technique himself. Adams was actually not guilty of smear either, but by his silence he gave the impression that for political reasons these tactics within his party had his tacit approval.

In the interim between Jackson's election and his inauguration, his beloved Rachel died, and the glory of all Jackson's victories seemed to go to the grave with her. She never was enthusiastic about her husband's public life and complained once that in their thirty-odd years of marriage Andrew had not spent one-fourth of the time under their roof. Her life was one "long flight from fame." She had no children of her own, but she was a mother to every waif and orphan who came her way, several of whom were at the Hermitage continuously. She was quite stout, a devout Christian, and smoked a pipe. It was her nephew whom the Jacksons adopted as a baby and who became the spendthrift Andrew Jackson, Jr. The Jacksons adopted an Indian boy also, a victim of the Creek campaign, and Jackson truly loved these boys, for he had a strong parental instinct. To the day of his death on June 8, 1845, Rachel held her husband's heart in thrall; he lies buried beside her on the Hermitage grounds.

[7] From the diary, published as *The Memoirs of John Quincy Adams*; J. B. Lippincott Company.

In his later life Jackson's temperament cooled a great deal, so that some of his friends could truthfully say they never saw him in a passion. However, he knew he had an ability and a reputation for rage, and did not hesitate to exploit both when it suited his purpose. Friends would see him storm about before a certain person, and then suddenly become calm as soon as his visitor departed, just as if nothing had happened; it was a performance, designed to get results.

Jackson was tall and gaunt with a long, thin face topped by an immense crop of hair. His features, while not attractive, were said to be impressive with their intense, blue eyes. He was a dramatic person in a dramatic period of transition in American national life; and without being either a student of life or an advocate of any great constructive project, won large groups of people to him. He had an intuitive talent for identifying himself with the wants and desires of the people. Franklin D. Roosevelt was the only other President who was able to manage a similarly strong identification with the public. Neither of these men were good administrators; dazzling, exciting men often are not. In fact, much of the attractiveness of popular heroes is possible because their personalities are not burdened with the laborious qualities which accompany a striving after a perfectly solid administration.

Apologists for Jackson point out that their hero was an honest and patriotic man. But other American Presidents were, at least, honest and patriotic men, including Grant and Harding. They point out that, an orphan of immigrant parents, Jackson rose to the highest position in the land. But so have countless of the world's famous ones—tyrant as well as benefactor—risen from obscurity to renown. Americans are prone to laud accomplishment irrespective of how it is realized, of what might have been lost in realizing it, and what world background was indispensable for the performer of the extraordinary act. One recent historian, who rates Jackson as "excellent" and John Quincy Adams as "mediocre," declares that Jackson's "central contribution was to plant a strong democratic impulse in the American breast." But the democratic impulse is inherent in all men's breasts; all people, of whatever nation, hate tyranny, love liberty, desire a decent living, and yearn for benevolent government. Jackson's central contribution, rather, was in showing that the people will acquiesce in revolutionary changes—even if it means abandoning formerly sacred precepts—when traditional methods become fossilized, and are identified too long with one segment of society.

Andrew Jackson adapted himself to his expanding, expansive times and was fortunate enough not to have to face the inevitable economic depression which he passed on to his successor. He did indeed retain his immense popularity to the end of his days. There appeared in Jackson's nature also a true and genuine reverence for God, a qualifying factor in this turbulent career, so characteristic of the years of turbulence in which it flourished.

★★★★★★★★

8

MARTIN VAN BUREN

☆ ☆

		Popular	Electoral
VOTE OF 1836:	Martin Van Buren, Democrat	763,000	170
	William Henry Harrison, Whig	⎰	73
	Daniel Webster, Whig	⎱ 735,000	14
	Others		37
		1,498,000	294

VOTE OF 1840: *See* under William Henry Harrison

VOTE OF 1848: *See* under Zachary Taylor

☆ ☆

AT THE BANQUET AT WHICH JACKSON GAVE HIS FAMOUS TOAST ABOUT the Federal Union, so characteristic of him, and Calhoun gave his reply, so characteristic of *him,* Martin Van Buren also gave a toast, calling for "Mutual forbearance and reciprocal concessions . . ." In that toast Van Buren characterized himself more eloquently and tersely than any biographer could have done.

John Quincy Adams called him *l'ami de tout le monde—*"the friend of all the world"—and thereby subtly characterized not only Van Buren but all politicians. Certainly nobody could be more conscious of this than Adams who, holding public service to be the noblest of human callings, was frustrated in all his constructive efforts as President because he was himself not *un ami de tout le monde.*

It was in the Jackson Administrations that the repugnant spoils system was first put into practical application in the Federal government; and Van Buren as an officer in those two terms has rightly borne a large share of the censure for institutionalizing the system. Some writers say that Van Buren has been unjustly maligned in this respect, since he did not originate the spoils system. Nevertheless, he was educated and nourished in the New York school of "machine politics"; and from the time he was a young man who visited with old Aaron Burr, he never lost sight of what would be required of him as to the practices, loyalties, and expedients necessary to success in politics. "We give no reasons for our removals," he once replied to one who complained that a certain useful public servant was being replaced by a party worker.

When he became President, Van Buren did his best to rise to the dignity of his great calling. But he had hardly been installed in office when the dreadful Panic of 1837 exploded before him. Although he had nothing to do with the ensuing depression (unless campaigning for Jackson can be construed as a significant contribution), he was blamed in part for it and voted out of office.

Thomas Jefferson also believed in "rotation of office" and was the first President to practice it, but he did so on a very moderate scale; he felt that, personally, he could not head a government if the majority of its members did not have his political convictions. However, he did not believe with the Jacksonians that the test of party service came before a test of talents; nor could he ever even have insinuated what Jackson openly advocated, that the "duties of all public offices are, or at least admit of being made, so plain and simple that men of intelligence may readily qualify themselves for their performance . . ." Although consonant with certain aspects of Jackson's personality, this was more likely simply a rationalization of an expedient system. Owing largely to Jackson and Van Buren, the national scene was to present a picture of incompetents in the highest places, and the energies of good Presidents would be sapped by a constant clamoring for jobs. Lincoln in his most trying days was harassed by it. Perhaps Garfield actually lost his life because of it; it was an office-seeker who shot him down. William Henry Harrison's precarious health was so further weakened by the importunities of people seeking places in the Government that he is often counted a fatality of the spoils system. The Civil Service Act of later years did bring some relief from this political curse.

Van Buren received his early training in New York City, where he had gone in 1801 to study law, but he was born in the little Hudson River town of Kinderhook, on December 5, 1782. The son of a tavern-keeper, Abraham Van Buren, his people had

been in the United States for a hundred and fifty years. Maria
Hoes was his mother, and a distant relative, Hannah Hoes, became his wife and the mother of his four sons. She died while still
a young woman, so that Van Buren was a widower for all of his
national public life. Although the family had been in America for
a long time, Dutch was still spoken in the home and most of the
family social contacts were with other Dutch families.

Van Buren was successful in his profession, so that he was able
to indulge in his favorite pastime of politics; and after starting out
as a surrogate for his home county, he went to the New York
Senate in 1812 and again in 1816, when he was also appointed
Attorney-General for New York. In 1821 and 1826 he went to the
Senate in Washington and in 1828 was elected Governor of his
state, serving only two months before going into Jackson's Cabinet as Secretary of State. Long before this, his shrewd political
insight gave him a sense of the way things would be happening,
and he recognized that his fortunes would be insured by following
the Jackson movement.

Van Buren's principal political connection before coming into
the Jackson Administration was a junto called the Albany Regency, a political force which lasted clear into Cleveland's Administration. This group, which was something like the modern
Tammany Hall, contained several future Presidential candidates.
William L. Marcy, a future Secretary of State, and originator of
the slogan "To the victors belong the spoils," was a member.
Thurlow Weed, New York's great political boss and not a member of the Regency, made the comment that he never knew a
group of men who possessed so much power and used it so well.
Of course, Weed also believed in the spoils system, calling it a
"brilliant feature of excellence in our benign form of government . . ."

It is interesting to observe how Van Buren voted when he was
in Washington. First of all, he did not conduct himself as most of
the other members of his Party were conducting themselves with
respect to John Quincy Adams. He never accused the latter's
Administration of any wrongdoing; as Senator, he even voted for
Clay's confirmation as Secretary of State. He voted against Federal aid for the Cumberland Road, against the occupation of Oregon, and against all internal improvements, thus placing himself in

opposition to Clay and his "American system." However, he tried to check the extension of slavery, especially in the new Territory of Florida. He began the fight to do away with imprisonment for debt. It is evident that a duality in Van Buren's nature enabled him to rise above politics to statesmanship when a crisis demanded it.

After resigning as Secretary of State, he was sent by Jackson in 1831 to England as Minister. He was now to suffer the embarrassment of not being confirmed by the Senate (Calhoun's machinations), even though he had by then been widely entertained in London and had dined with the King. Jackson, who personalized everything that happened to his friends and his Administration, felt insulted by Van Buren's non-confirmation and became determined to make Van Buren his successor in the White House. He accordingly dictated his nomination for Vice-President in 1832, running with Van Buren at that time. By 1836 it was a foregone conclusion that Jackson's wishes would prevail and that Van Buren would be elected President that year.

The Whigs, who succeeded the National Republicans, could not agree on a candidate. Clay had long been the leading Whig, but his political battle scars made him ineligible. Clay was a personable and charming figure, had speaking ability, political experience, and a great following. Lincoln, in his early career, had called him "my beau ideal." He was a useful statesman, had, through his slavery compromises, rightly earned the title of "The Great Pacificator," and might have made a good President. So important was his influence that Van Buren, while he was out of office and seeking to repair his political fences preparatory to running for the Presidency again, called not only at the Hermitage to pay his respects, but at Clay's home in Kentucky as well.[1]

It was during this period that the first important third-party movement got under way in the United States—the Anti-Masonic Party. This party had a considerable membership, ran a Presidential candidate in 1832, and had some names on its roll which were to become important names; members included William H. Seward and Millard Fillmore, a later President. The Party's title was a misnomer because it was not nearly so anti-Masonic as it was anti-Jacksonian. By 1836 this party had merged with the Whigs,

[1] Clay's beautiful home Ashland, at Lexington, Ky., is now open to the public.

and William Henry Harrison, one of the candidates that year, received the blessing of the anti-Masons. Daniel Webster and two other Whig candidates also ran against Van Buren. The hope of these Whigs was to prevent a majority in the Electoral College and bring the House of Representatives, where the Whigs and other anti-Jacksonian elements had mustered a majority, to name the President—one who was a Whig. They almost succeeded; Van Buren's plurality was only 27,000. But the contest for Vice-President, for the first and only time in American history, had to be decided by the Senate because no candidate had received a majority. The Senate elected Richard M. Johnson, a Senator from Kentucky, one of the original War Hawks, who happened to be married to a Negro wife.

The Panic of 1837 was the first serious economic depression the American nation experienced; the Government did nothing about it but let it conclude by itself. It lasted for seven years, when changes occasioned by the Mexican War and related matters brought prosperity again. The people were in great distress during the Panic. At the end of Jackson's term there were 788 banks in the nation; in the Panic 618 of them failed. Six months after Van Buren was in office, nine-tenths of the factories were shut down. Long speculation and unwise credit expansion affected the country exactly as a similar kind of dissipation was to do in 1929. And just as Herbert Hoover in the years following 1929 had to stand up personally against the lashing of the storm produced by the excesses of previous years, Van Buren had to do the same thing in his time under the same circumstances—but with an important difference: Hoover was busy his entire term trying to succor the nation while waiting for natural laws to do their curative work.

In his first message to Congress, wherein he considered at length the nation's economic crisis, Van Buren said:

> The framers of our excellent constitution, and the people who approved it with calm and sagacious deliberation . . . wisely judged that the less Government interferes with private pursuits, the better for general prosperity. It is not its legitimate object to make men rich, or to repair, by direct grants of money or legisla-

tion in favor of particular pursuits, losses not incurred in the public service. This would be substantially to use the property of some for the benefit of others.

Van Buren's statement is explained by the fact that both before and after the Age of Jackson it definitely was not considered the Government's business to control economic processes; that attitude comported with the philosophy the early patriots embraced.

In this same address to Congress, which was meeting in special session, Van Buren made such a frank and unflinching presentation of the money situation of the country that his address has been called one of the great American state papers. It was an appeal to the people, no less than an exhortation to the lawmakers. The Panic had caused the state banks, now the sole repositories of the public funds, to suspend specie payments. Van Buren asked if this system was safe. Did not the public welfare demand that the revenues of the Government be deposited with public officers instead of private institutions where they might be used again for speculation? Was it not less expensive to have the care of the public money with customs officers and postmasters than with profit-making organizations? So, after several attempts, Van Buren's independent Government treasury was established with sub-treasuries in the principal large cities—a principle that is still part of the finance policy of the nation. Clay and Webster opposed it; they were still for a new "United States Bank."

Along with the monetary difficulties, a crop failure in 1835 contributed to the Panic of 1837. There was the unbelievable situation of Europe actually shipping grain to the United States. It was also in 1835 that a second Seminole War broke out under the chieftain Osceola. It lasted seven years and Van Buren was censured for the expense of this long war.

Modern economists say that Jackson's money policy also was responsible for the depression. In 1836 Jackson had ordered that no more paper money be accepted by the Government for payment of public lands sold; people had to give specie. This decree created a great scarcity of hard, acceptable money, and added to Van Buren's woes: it seemed that nobody could blame Jackson for anything.

Van Buren's inability to gain re-election in 1840 was inevitable. "Van, Van is a used up man," the campaigners droned away and whooped up the companion chant, "Tippecanoe and Tyler too." Reason had nothing to do with any of this, of course. Van Buren accepted his defeat philosophically and made a social call upon the President-elect.

Van Buren would have liked the nomination again in 1844; but it happened that he took a courageous stand against a popular issue of the time, the issue of Texas. He opposed the annexation of this republic on the grounds that it would mean war with Mexico, thus taking the statesmanlike position on the matter that John Quincy Adams took. The Democrats could not risk running a candidate who took so sensible a stand on the issue of war. After all, it was a whole generation since the War of 1812 had been concluded. Memories were short, the inconveniences of that long-ago war had been forgotten, and it was claimed that "this situation was different." The expansionists were busy indoctrinating the people with Manifest Destiny, the Will of God, and all the rest of the abracadabra available to charlatans for the mystification of a too-credulous humanity. Polk, the expansionist, was called for, and elected—together with the war.

In 1848 Van Buren rather reluctantly accepted the nomination of a new anti-slavery party, the Free-Soilers; and while he did not win, he took enough votes away from the Democratic candidate to insure the election of the Union-loving Zachary Taylor.

Van Buren had great skill in getting on with men. He had no difficulty in keeping the friendship of political opponents like Adams, Clay, and Calhoun. Washington Irving, who was at the American legation in London when Van Buren arrived at that city, wrote with great enthusiasm of his geniality. He was a small man, only five feet six inches tall, a *bon vivant,* and was much criticized in his time for his fine living.

Van Buren was disappointed in both Pierce and Buchanan, two of his Democratic successors, and only when Lincoln assumed the guidance of the nation did his faith in White House leadership revive, and his own health improve. His long life spanned the beginnings of the great Victorian Age. He saw Jefferson come to power in 1800 and he lived to see Lincoln rise to power in 1860.

He did not permit himself to fall into the financial difficulties of some of his predecessors and so spent his long period of carefree retirement at his home called Lindenwald, where he died July 24, 1862. He was buried in the cemetery at Kinderhook.

9

WILLIAM HENRY HARRISON

☆ ☆

VOTE OF 1836: *See* under Van Buren

		Popular	Electoral
VOTE OF 1840:	William Henry Harrison, Whig	1,275,000	234
	Martin Van Buren, Democrat	1,129,000	60
	Other	7,000	
		2,411,000	294

☆ ☆

IF THE AMERICAN PEOPLE CAN BE CHARGED WITH HAVING A NATIONAL sin, it could be their predilection for oversimplification in considering any problem, or event. The campaigns of Andrew Jackson were outstanding examples of the people's tendency toward oversimplification. It was not necessary for Jackson to demonstrate that he was a sound candidate. He could tell the people in their own vernacular that he was *for* them and *against* somebody else who was their oppressor; that sufficed.

After the Jackson victories, the Whigs decided to take a leaf out of the Democrats' book of experience. If the Democrats could oversimplify, so could they. If the Democrats could produce a champion who spoke the popular language and dispensed with "highfalutin" trappings, they could produce one too. The fact that both Andrew Jackson and William Henry Harrison lived in fine plantation houses with carriages and servants made no difference. If doubts arose, they could always put a coonskin cap on their man and circulate stories about his frontier life.

The Whigs knew they had to do that very thing in 1840 if they were to win. They therefore took the aristocratic, Virginia-born Harrison, advertised him as a man of the soil, and circulated stories of his fights with the Indians and his pioneer's life at his home at North Bend, Ohio. Further, this frontiersman was the son of Benjamin Harrison, signer of the Declaration of Independence; that also was thought of as making the Whig candidate a perfect patriot.

William Henry Harrison was born to distinguished Tidewater Virginia gentry on the James River at Berkeley.[1] Berkeley and Brandon, on opposite sides of the James, were the ancestral seats of this old family, and included between nine and ten thousand acres. The lord of Berkeley, father of the ninth President, who was Governor of Virginia as well as a Signer, was Benjamin Harrison V; his wife was the well-born Elizabeth Bassett. William Henry was educated by private tutors and at Hampden-Sydney College. He started out to study medicine; gave medicine up to enter the army.

Despite his affluent background, it was easy to manage the transformation of Harrison into the people's man the politicians desired. Although Van Buren, his opponent in 1836 and 1840, was only a poor tavern-keeper's son who had to get everything he had through hard work, it was also quite simple to publicize Van Buren as the bloated aristocrat who sat at his faultless dinners in the warm White House while the people suffered in the panic-ridden winter of 1838.

That is practically all there is to the Presidential career of William Henry Harrison. When he was born, on February 9, 1773, the Boston Tea Party was almost one year away, and when Yorktown fell he was still a growing, rather frail boy. What he absorbed in his youth, therefore, was not so much the atmosphere of revolution as that of nationalism, which came into full bloom with the War of 1812 in which he took part.

Harrison served as aide-de-camp to General Anthony Wayne and in 1794 took part with him in the Battle of Fallen Timbers, by which victory, terminating in the Treaty of Greenville, the Indians agreed to the existing borders of the Northwest Territory. In 1798 Harrison resigned from the army and settled at North Bend. The same year he was appointed Secretary of the Northwest Territory; he was chosen its first delegate to Congress.

[1] It is interesting that the first Thanksgiving in America is claimed to have been celebrated at Berkeley, one year before it took place at Plymouth, Mass. See Clifford Dowdey: *The Great Plantation,* pp. 34–35; Rinehart & Company, Inc., 1957.

In 1800, after Indiana Territory had been separated from the Northwest Territory, Harrison was appointed Governor of Indiana and for the next twelve years was at this post. Here he was given authority to sign treaties with the Indians and effected the transfer of millions of acres of their lands to the Government. Inevitably, this led to trouble. Tecumseh and his brother, the Prophet, maintained that past cessions of land were invalid. Doubtless the moral support of the British during these times made them bolder than they would otherwise have been. At Tippecanoe Creek, in October 1811, there was a battle; a force assembled by Harrison threw back an attack by a group under the Prophet, and Harrison thereby became the Indian-fighter hero the Whigs so sorely needed. Tippecanoe, in more than one sense, was not a decisive victory; sometimes it is called the opening battle of the War of 1812. As chief-of-command in the Northwest during the War of 1812, Harrison defeated Tecumseh at the Battle of the Thames, the battle which cost Tecumseh his life.

After resigning his commission in the army a second time, it was only natural for the hero of Tippecanoe to seek a new life for himself in politics. In 1816 he entered the House of Representatives as a follower of Henry Clay. In 1819 he was in the Ohio Senate. In 1824 he was in the Senate in Washington. In 1828 he went to Colombia as the first American Minister there and was promptly recalled by the new Jackson government for purely political reasons, a move which Van Buren, Jackson's Secretary of State, distinctly deplored.

It was in 1836 that Harrison was first put forward as a candidate for President. By the time 1840 came around, he was already a man whose real vigor was gone; he entered the Presidency, only to succumb to pneumonia one month later on April 4, 1841—the first President to die in office. Plagued by office-seekers from the very first, he even resisted them in his delirium on his deathbed. His wife, the former Anna Symmes, although unable to attend the inauguration because of poor health, nevertheless outlived her husband by nearly a quarter of a century.

One can only guess what the fortunes of the nation would have been had Harrison lived. Of one thing we can be sure: there would have been a third Bank of the United States. His Cabinet appointments were excellent and these men would possibly have been a bulwark against serious mistakes. Harrison's nature was one which would also have insured a better working relation with Congress; there was not the testiness in him that there was in his successor, Tyler.

Harrison was passionately devoted to the principles of republican government and got himself into serious trouble during his stay in Colombia because of his beliefs. Simón Bolívar, the great South American liberator, was the head of the Colombian government while Harrison was there, and was being feared in both the Old and New Worlds for his imperialistic ambitions. Harrison took it upon himself—after his successor had arrived—to write Bolívar a letter admonishing him not to abandon the tenets of democracy and bidding him follow the example of George Washington, not the footsteps of Alexander the Great. The letter, although a sincere and friendly one, created consternation when its contents became known, and Harrsion was all but asked to leave the country. The chagrin of this episode, the farcical nature of his dismissal as Minister by Jackson, and the further insults from Jackson who also compelled him to wait for months before a boat could be made available to take him back home—all this made the Colombian experience an unhappy one for both Harrison and the United States.

Overlooking the Ohio at North Bend stands an imposing memorial built over the mausoleum which is the last resting-place of the ninth President.

10

★★★★★★★★★

JOHN TYLER

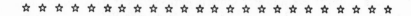

VOTE OF 1840: *See* under William Henry Harrison

☆ ☆

AFTER THE CONTROVERSIAL AND IMPERIOUS JACKSON CAME TO THE Presidency, it was inevitable that the politics of the entire nation would for a long time center around the issue of him alone. Not only did the hostility to him come from the Northern mercantile interests, but from the conservative Southern aristocrats as well. How could a proud, patrician, almost feudalistic society, such as the *ante bellum* South was, accept someone whom they thought of as a barbarian, who as late as the year before his death spelled Canada as "Canedy"?

In addition, although he called himself a Democrat, Jackson cared nothing about the theory of States' Rights, which was the mainspring and life's blood of his Party; and to Southerners such an attitude was comparable to mortgaging one's eternal soul. The Southern conservatives, therefore, as the Southern conservatives of the twentieth century were so often to do when the exigency left them no alternative, made common cause with the conservatives of the North. They became known as States' Rights Whigs. In 1840 they joined with the Northern Whigs to put a Presidential ticket in the field; but it was an unnatural alliance. After Jackson died, there was nothing left on which the two factions could unite; in fact, all their essential differences came out to torment them both. It is this situation which explains Tyler's term as President and which made his Administration the near-fiasco it became.

The fathers of both Harrison and Tyler were associated in the early days of the Republic. Both opposed ratification of the

Constitution; both believed it encroached too much on states' rights; both were Governors of Virginia. The elder John Tyler's last public office was as a Federal District Court judge.

John Tyler the President was born March 29, 1790, at the family homestead Greenway in Charles City County, Virginia. It was on the James River, only a short distance from Berkeley, the Harrison mansion. His mother was Mary Armistead. With a "blue blood" background of this kind, and with his father in public life, it was only natural that the son would study law and go into public life also. At the College of William and Mary, from which he was graduated, and of which he later became chancellor, he revealed a great interest in history. Like Jefferson, he loved music and poetry, and also played the violin. In 1809 Tyler was admitted to the bar. In 1811 he took his seat in the legislature and was annually re-elected to that body until 1816 when he was sent to the House of Representatives in Washington.

In Congress Tyler was a "strict constructionist"; that is, he believed the Constitution meant to give the Federal Government the powers it stated and no more. The doctrine of implied powers —that is, additional powers which the believers in a strong central government felt were *implied* in the Constitution—was viewed by him, as it was by nearly all other Southerners, as destructive of their rightful liberties. He was against rechartering the Second Bank, internal improvements as espoused by the Clay-Adams school, a national bankruptcy act, the Missouri Compromise. His social philosophy was therefore as clear as anybody's could be. That the "loose constructionist" Whig Party would have wanted to run a man like Tyler for Vice-President can be attributed only to the desire to capture Southern votes.

In spite of the role he played for the Whigs, Tyler had shown prior to coming to the Presidency that he was a man of courage, independent in action, and unafraid of public opinion. In the Senate, when a vote was taken on Jackson's "force bill" against South Carolina, and Southern Senators absented themselves so as not to be put on record one way or the other, Tyler remained in his seat and cast the one and only *nay* against the measure. Although he disapproved of the Bank of the United States, he disapproved also of Jackson's arbitrary transfer of the Government deposits from that institution to those of Jackson's own choosing.

All these indications of Tyler's independent thinking should have been a warning to the Whigs; but they disregarded these signs because nobody dreamed that Harrison might die in office. Between his terms as Congressman and his election as Vice-President, Tyler held several other public offices. He had tried in 1824, unsuccessfully, to win the race for the United States Senate. He then re-entered the legislature of his state, was elected Governor twice, and then sent to the Senate in Washington where he demonstrated the abilities which made him so "available" to the Whigs in 1840.

Although Tyler was nominated for the Vice-Presidency by the States' Rights Whigs as early as 1836, it was only four years later that both branches of Whigs named him. It was over the inflammatory issue of Texas that the States' Rights Whigs later returned to the Democratic fold—Tyler with them.

After his accession to the Presidency upon Harrison's death, the first President ever to achieve office in such a way, Tyler became the first President against whom impeachment proceedings were ever introduced in Congress. It is significant that his difficulty with that body was similar to that of Andrew Johnson, who actually was impeached. Tyler resembled Johnson also in that he was by conviction a member of one party, while temporarily accepting the designation of another. The vetoes of Tyler angered Congress as much as the vetoes of Johnson did. Tyler opposed the whole program of Clay, who was the national Whig leader, and should have been heeded to some degree at least. Two different bills for chartering a reorganized Bank of the United States, designed so as not to betray the prerogatives of the states, were also vetoed by him. In addition, he vetoed tariff and other bills, and in all his conduct showed himself the strict constructionist that he was. Popular feeling against Tyler was bitter as a result of his stubbornness. He was burned in effigy, and the White House was stoned; yet the President refused to change his position. In 1841 his entire Cabinet except for Webster resigned. Webster had some work with the British to finish, and when that was done, he resigned also.

But the issue which was to agitate Tyler's term more than any other was that of Texas, the great southwestern region—comprised not only of the present state of Texas, but of parts of Okla-

homa, Kansas, New Mexico, Colorado, and Wyoming as well—
which was to bring the nation to war as John Quincy Adams and
Martin Van Buren had predicted. Before Texas revolted from
Mexico, Adams was in favor of purchasing it. In fact, Adams believed that the United States should eventually take control of the
whole of North America—in a peaceful fashion. This was his
conception of America's grand destiny. Adams seems to have experienced a different emotion entirely from the desire for expansion of his time, or the imperialist feelings current in McKinley's time.

The pattern of the Americanization of Texas was a familiar
one. American citizens had followed it with West Florida and
would follow this pattern later with respect to the Hawaiian
Islands. Heavy infiltration of Americans—at the invitation of Mexico herself—from 1821 on created a climate that could no longer
be called Mexican. Mexico became alarmed on seeing that Americans outnumbered Mexicans in Texas and in 1829 began to
restrict immigration. Next, her President abolished slavery in the
entire province; this the Southern settlers considered an outrage.
Sentiment for the secession of Texas from Mexico grew. In 1836
Texas did declare her independence in a bloody revolution, and
Jackson's friend Sam Houston became its president.[1] Various attempts to annex it to the United States met with failure, principally because the North knew what annexation would mean—
the extension of slavery and the upsetting of the delicate voting
balance in Congress. Tyler favored annexation; Jackson did also.
Tyler declared he was opposed to the perpetuation of slavery,
but that he was opposed also to the imposition of restrictions upon
its extension: it was a matter of states' rights. This was the position which many other prominent Southerners held.

Jefferson, Madison, Washington, and other Southern planters
were opposed to slavery, and the record reveals plainly how the
first two felt about emancipation. In his will Washington provided
for the manumission of all his slaves after his wife's death. Years
before that, he had stopped buying them. And Jefferson had said:
"Nothing is more certainly written in the book of fate than that
these people [the slaves] are to be free."

[1] This was the revolution which produced the saga of the Alamo and of the
death of Davy Crockett.

But in 1793 something happened which changed everything. Eli Whitney invented a gin for seeding cotton rapidly. Coincident with the Industrial Revolution, the cotton gin related perfectly to England's hungry spinning jennys; and the South became England's cotton field, in return for which it hoped to get England's tariff-free wares. The leisurely life of the planters-become-exporters thus was extended and the slave system with it; but realistic Southerners knew it could not last. Yet jealousy of the North's prosperity and resentment at the North's pontification was such that they became more and more sensitive about the sanctity of their "peculiar institution." They could see nothing but that Northerners were seeking to bring down the standard of living for Southern whites by wrecking the Southern economy. In the North, where there once were 50,000 slaves, emancipation had been completed by 1800. As far back as 1774, Connecticut and Rhode Island had prohibited the importation of slaves; and generally the new state constitutions adopted after the Revolution prohibited slave traffic. Had the cotton gin not come into existence, it is entirely probable that the issue of slavery would have gradually resolved itself in the entire South and become abolished as world opinion more and more came to condemn it.

By 1844 action on Texas was urgent. Both England and France were making overtures to the new Texas republic; and what the United States had sought to avoid by the purchase of Louisiana and the enunciation of the Monroe Doctrine seemed to threaten again. Also, there was an economic depression all through Tyler's term—a continuation of the Panic of 1837; and the acquisition of Texas was looked upon by Southerners as well as by some Northerners as a new program which somehow might change their fortunes.

It was not possible to get a two-thirds vote in Congress to achieve Texas annexation by treaty, so Tyler recommended that the end be realized by a joint resolution of both Houses. This was done and Tyler had the satisfaction of having his Administration achieve this political victory a few days before he left office. His successor Polk was unequivocally committed to further annexations, so that Tyler experienced the additional pleasure of anticipating that expansionist.

Tyler would have liked a nomination in his own right in 1844

—by the Democrats, this time—but that was not to be and he supported Polk, especially as he saw the aged Jackson supporting him; and he turned his back on the Whig Party whose White House representative he had been as a matter of convenience. When the dreaded conflict which slavery precipitated at last came, Tyler headed a peace mission to Washington in a last-minute effort to head off hostilities; but the Lincoln Administration was not interested in the proposals offered. He returned to Virginia, was elected to the Confederate Congress, but died January 18, 1862, before taking his seat. His grave is in Hollywood Cemetery, Richmond, where James Monroe and Jefferson Davis also lie interred.

Tyler was twice married, first to Letitia Christian who died after he became President, and second to Julia Gardiner. Each wife bore him seven children, and one of his sons became chancellor of the College of William and Mary, as he himself once had been. There are many descendants living.

****

11

JAMES KNOX POLK

☆ ☆

		Popular	Electoral
VOTE OF 1844:	James K. Polk, Democrat	1,337,000	170
	Henry Clay, Whig	1,299,000	105
	James G. Birney, Abolitionist	66,000	
		2,702,000	275

☆ ☆

"PERSONALITY" IS ONE OF THE FAVORITE WORDS OF THE AMERICAN people. Character analysts know that if anything can imbue a man with personality it is the presence in him of a genuine interest in people. In a leader a lack of such interest would be fatal.

In studying a life like Lincoln's, no matter how much of the commonplace is reflected in it, our interest is sustained; not because Lincoln was a common man—he was most uncommon—but because his interest in people makes us identify ourselves with him. Polk's life confirms this thesis; despite his brilliant accomplishments, he emerges as vapid. Issues, and his personal absorption with them, meant more to him than did people.

This colorless man was in retirement in Tennessee when he was nominated for the Presidency by the Democrats. He had been a Jackson supporter, member of the legislature of his state, Congressman, Speaker of the House, and Governor of Tennessee. When he was Speaker, he was the recognized leader of the Administration forces in the House.

In 1844, when Tyler was willing to run but was not wanted because of his "difficult" nature and former Whig associations, when Van Bureau was willing but also was not wanted because he had let it be known that he opposed the annexation of Texas, Polk became the Jackson-supported candidate the Democrats needed. He was the first "dark horse" candidate to reach the

White House. This is remarkable because only the year before his nomination he had been defeated for re-election as Governor of his home state, and in the campaign immediately preceding that had been defeated also.

Part of Polk's desirability came from his being a resident of the "frontier" country of Tennessee where he had lived since he was eleven. He was born in historic Mecklenburg County, North Carolina,[1] on November 2, 1795, son of a prosperous farmer, Samuel Polk. He was sent back to North Carolina to complete his schooling and was graduated from the University of North Carolina; he won first honors in mathematics and the classics. Polk began his law practice in Tennessee. After he entered politics and the Jackson camp, he bore the catchy sobriquet "Young Hickory."

Not only was Polk's nomination unreasonable: his election was also. Nearly all the national men of ability were in the opposition Party—Clay, Webster, Greeley, John Quincy Adams, Seward, Lincoln; but with its President, Tyler, and its chief leader, Clay, political enemies, the Whigs had no leadership. The aging Clay made a last attempt to capture the Presidency and would have won it but for the third-party candidacy of the Liberty Party's James G. Birney who, although unable to win himself, took enough votes away from Clay to give Polk the election.

The contest was waged on the issues of Texas and Oregon; in a word, expansionism. Clay, wishing to offend neither North nor South, dodged this issue, and it cost him votes. But regardless of whether the campaign had this annexationist issue or not, the people wanted, above all else, a diversion from the long depression caused by the Panic of 1837, and the Whigs under Tyler had not been able to give it to them.

For some time new states had been coming into the Union by twos, one slave and one free; and the agitation for Texas and Oregon corresponded with this program designed not to upset the balance-of-power in the representation in Congress. In Jackson's time Arkansas and Michigan had been admitted together. During the Panic new admissions lagged; then Florida and Iowa, Texas

[1] The inhabitants of this county were said to have declared their independence of the British crown in 1775, some time before the Thirteen Colonies did so.

and Wisconsin, joined the Union. When Polk left office, there
were fifteen slave states and fifteen free.

With the incorporation of Texas into the national domain,
Mexico severed diplomatic relations with the United States. Polk
now made it clear that the acquisition of California was to be the
prime goal of his Administration.

When Jefferson was President, he had sent two of his fellow-
Virginians, Lewis and Clark, out to explore the Missouri River
to its source, define the northern boundaries of Louisiana, open up
the fur trade to Americans, chart the new country, and record
what scientific data they could. Congress authorized $2,500 for
this exploration; it turned out to be one of the most profitable
appropriations Congress ever made. The two men left Missouri
in 1804 and eventually descended the great Columbia River to
the Pacific.

The entire Oregon movement constitutes a great American
epic. Hundreds of families traveled in ox-cart caravans over the
Oregon Trail (a different one from that blazed by Lewis and
Clark), fighting disease, privation, Indians, wild animals, and cold.
The British also were in Oregon, and in 1818 it was agreed with
England to occupy the country jointly for an indefinite time.
John Quincy Adams had always believed in the importance of
Oregon and wanted to come to an agreement with England over
the possession of it as soon as possible; but England had always
insisted on the Columbia River as the southernmost boundary of
her portion. When England expressed a willingness to compromise on a parallel of latitude north of the Columbia but south of
the Alaskan border, a boundary line with which many Americans
were satisfied, Polk seized the opportunity. So it was that in 1846
America's territorial limits for the first time officially extended to
the Pacific. However, the entire Oregon question was not settled
easily; in fact, for a time it looked as if the United States might
have a two-front war to fight, against Britain and Mexico as allies.

Polk was willing to liquidate all outstanding Mexican differences as peaceably as possible. He wanted to buy California and
New Mexico and the indications were that he was not going to
quibble about price. But Mexico would not sell. It was clear that
Polk would now wait for some other means to obtain the two
territories. The means eventually presented themselves in the dis-

pute over the southern boundary of Texas which that state insisted was the Rio Grande by agreement with Santa Anna, an agreement which Mexico claimed had no validity. Polk ordered General Taylor to enter the disputed area, whereupon a Mexican force attacked, causing sixteen American casualties. "The cup of forbearance has been exhausted," said the President in asking Congress for a declaration of war; and Congress passed a resolution recognizing that a state of war between the two countries existed "by the act of the republic of Mexico . . ." U. S. Grant, who served in this war, deplores it in his *Memoirs*. Abraham Lincoln, who was serving his only term in Congress at the time, devoted one of his very few speeches there to decrying the Mexican war.

Another voice spoke against the war also—that of the now experienced Henry Clay. Over a generation had passed since the time when, as an energetic young Congressman, he was an agitator for a war of conquest against England and was dissatisfied that the War of 1812 had ended with no territorial gains. Now things were different—Clay had abandoned youthful enthusiasms. However, his mature advice was now to be rejected. The new war was to come. And he was to lose his namesake son in battle.

That Polk was insincere about the cause of the war is proved by the fact that, as was subsequently learned, his original war message, before the Rio Grande affair took place, was on the basis of unpaid claims against Mexico and her spurning of the emissary America had sent down with an offer to buy the desired lands. Of course, it can be said in mitigation that Mexico was a feeble government and was not administering the Southwest in a progressive way, not making it possible for the riches of the country to be opened up for development; and that the area was little more than a string of adobe missions lying in a lethargic *mañana* land. By the very nature of the American entrepreneur temperament, such a situation was intolerable. When this inviting situation was added to the expansionist ambitions of a young and growing country, it became impossible to avoid either invasion or other means of land cession. But to other countries such rationalization was ridiculous: to them it meant nothing but old-fashioned depredation.

Military operations in the Mexican War were conducted by Generals Scott and Taylor and were terminated by Scott's cap-

ture of the Mexican capital on September 14, 1847. The exploits
of Col. Stephen W. Kearny should not be forgotten, for it was he
who laid claim to New Mexico and California. Kearny's enemies
were climate and terrain rather than military forces, but his accomplishment was distinctive nevertheless.

By the Treaty of Guadalupe Hidalgo, Mexico ceded the
United States the areas it wanted—California, the vast New Mexico
territory which was to create several new states, and the extension
of the Texas border to the Rio Grande. One-half of Mexico's
territory was involved in this transfer. Mexico was paid $15,000,-
000; in addition, the United States agreed to pay certain claims
against Mexico, specifically, most of the American claims origi-
nating before the treaty date. Including Oregon, the expansionist
Polk had added 800,000 square miles to the area of continental
United States.[2]

Polk was a very hard worker; he was absent from Washington
no more than six weeks during his entire term. He was also pompous and suspicious and demanded of his Cabinet appointees that
all disavow any Presidential aspirations while serving in his Administration, a most amazing request for a President-elect to make.
In his diary he writes: "I prefer to supervise the whole operations
of the Government myself rather than entrust the public business
to subordinates and this makes my duties very great." With his
lack of humor, his formality and unimaginativeness, it is little
wonder that when Polk died on June 15, 1849, only three months
after he left office, he was not mourned as a President ordinarily
would have been.

Although Polk was an expansionist, it is not fair to say that he
was a sectionalist. We do not know what he would have done if
the critical internal decisions regarding Kansas, Nebraska, and the
Fugitive Slave Law, by which his successors were challenged, had
been his to make. Being a Southerner, Polk naturally had Southern
sympathies; however, he was not for expansion because he was
interested in slavery expansion but because he was a typical
nationalist. The moral aspect of slavery did not trouble him as

[2] It is interesting to observe that these conquests were not the end of Mexico's being annoyed by the territorial ambitions of her northern neighbor.
As recently as 1931 there was agitation in the U. S. Senate for the acquisition of Lower California, which was referred to as a natural "Achilles' heel."

it did so many other Presidents, despite his strong Presbyterian church affiliation. Although he did advocate extending the Missouri Compromise line all the way to the Pacific Ocean as a means of averting domestic strife over the matter of introducing slavery into the territory acquired from Mexico, he opposed the Wilmot Proviso which, had it not failed in Congress, would have barred slavery forever from this area.

The Fabulous Forties, as this period often is called in American history, over most of which Polk had presided, was a seething time for the young nation. Gold was discovered in California in 1848 and the migration of Easterners to that latest El Dorado is another American epic around which legend and drama have woven a tradition.

1848 saw also the arrival in America of the incredible Andrew Carnegie, and the death of America's richest man, John Jacob Astor I, whose fur trading post in Oregon helped make that country so desirable. But another significant event, seldom mentioned as important in the annals of the United States, was the great German immigration which resulted from the failure of the revolutions of 1848. In 1845 the potato famine in Ireland caused the beginning of great Irish migrations to the United States.

The Victorian Age was coming into a glorious period both in Europe and in America during the Forties. The period signified empire, cultural development, and further first fruits of the Industrial Revolution. Regular transatlantic steamship service became a reality. The first telegraph line was established; railroads were forming elaborate networks over the nation. A renascence of cultural life was taking place on both sides of the Atlantic. Among those who were creating literature in England and America were Emerson, Longfellow, Poe, Whittier, Tennyson, Thackeray, Dickens, Thoreau, Channing, Eliot, Lowell, Whitman, Carlyle, Bryant, Dana, Irving, Macaulay, Fitzgerald, the Brontes, Holmes, Disraeli, Hawthorne, Mill, the Brownings, and Darwin.

There is no evidence that any of this rich legacy was ever created for James K. Polk. He emerges in history texts as simply another President in the roster. He did not absorb anything of the humanities and he did not bequeath anything. When an epidemic of cholera swept the South, Polk was among its fatalities at the early age of 53. At his bedside when death came were his mother, the former Jane Knox, and his wife, the former Sarah Childress. The State of Tennessee had the remains of the eleventh President and his wife interred on the grounds of the state capitol. Polk left no descendants.

★★★★★★★★★★★★

12

ZACHARY TAYLOR

☆ ☆

		Popular	Electoral
VOTE OF 1848:	Zachary Taylor, Whig	1,360,000	163
	Lewis Cass, Democrat	1,221,000	127
	Martin Van Buren, Free-Soiler	291,000	
		2,872,000	290

☆ ☆

THE WHIG PARTY ELECTED A PRESIDENT ONLY TWICE. BOTH TIMES the nominees were national heroes and both times the incumbents died in office. It was enough to make any political party feel it suffered from a jinx.

However, it was the nation, not merely a party, that suffered from the jinx: the monster of Slavery and Secession—from which the nation suffers even today. As in 1848 a natural cleavage into liberals and conservatives was not possible among the electorate because of the issue of slavery, so in later years it was not possible because of its aftermath—fratricidal war, bitter memories of reconstruction. As the South voted sectionally then, so it voted sectionally well into the twentieth century.

Certainly the United States has lived with this problem for a long time. Did this problem not exist, it is entirely possible that the Presidential elections of 1884, 1892, 1912, 1916, and perhaps even 1948—years with conservative trends—might have produced different victors.

Taylor was the first President whose public career had been exclusively in the army prior to coming to the White House; Jackson and William Henry Harrison had held civil posts as well as military. Taylor was the son of a Revolutionary officer, Col. Richard Taylor, and of Sarah Strother, and was born in Orange County, Virginia, November 24, 1784. Like the Washingtons,

Lees, and Custises, his family was related to most of the well-to-do and cultured families of the time, so that Zachary was not without "background." In fact, his army opportunities were partly due to the intercession of another relative, James Madison.

Zachary Taylor was only nine months old when his father moved his family to Kentucky, then still part of Virginia. Col. Taylor was appointed Collector of the Port of Louisville and later entered the legislature. Zachary was educated by a private tutor, and had no other formal schooling.

Taylor's boyhood was a time of much Indian fighting; one of his brothers was killed by an Indian. When he was 22, Zachary joined the army. In the War of 1812, he was a captain and was sent to Fort Harrison on the Wabash where, with only fifty men, he defeated a force under Tecumseh. He was immediately promoted to major. Later, as Colonel Taylor, he fought in the wars against the chief of the Sauk and Fox tribes, Black Hawk. The young Captain Abraham Lincoln served under Taylor. Later Taylor was sent to Florida in the Second Seminole War—the costliest Indian war the United States ever had. He defeated the Indians at the Battle of Okeechobee in 1837. He was assigned an impossible task after this—that of moving the unwilling Indians from Florida into the area set apart for them on the Western side of the Mississippi. The stories in connection with these removals are unpleasant; the United States never was able to move all the Indians out and there are, of course, Seminoles in the Everglades to this day.

After his efforts in Florida, Taylor was transferred to the army's Southwest Department and stationed in Louisiana. There he bought a plantation near Baton Rouge. This was his first home, and he became the owner of some 300 slaves. It was as a resident of Louisiana that he was elected to the Presidency, although Taylor always considered Kentucky his home state.

We have already outlined the causes of the Mexican War. There were two lines of attack in this war. The one from the north was under Taylor. The other led out from Vera Cruz on the east coast where General Winfield Scott and his troops landed, the Mexican capital their goal. The Administration considered the latter campaign the more important because Mexico City could be more easily reached by Scott than by Taylor, and because Scott's army could live off the land it conquered. After winning the battles of Palo Alto and Resaca de la Palma, Taylor began the invasion of Mexico; after three days' fighting he captured Monterrey. He was guilty of disobeying orders there when he gave generous armistice terms to the Mexicans, and President Polk criticized his action sharply.

Polk never lost sight of the political implications of any of the military actions of this war. He was jealous of Taylor and Scott, both of whom were Whigs, and he did not want the exploits of either to accrue to their respective Presidential possibilities; he knew only too well how the public made and loved its heroes.

The Mexican general Santa Anna learned of the plan of the American War Department to transfer the bulk of Taylor's troops to Scott, and set out after Taylor in the belief that he would have an easy victory over the reduced American force in the north. At Buena Vista, with only 5,000 men, Taylor defeated Santa Anna and his 20,000 men in a brilliant victory. Polk's fears were now realized: Taylor became a national hero. This was in February of 1847. In March Scott took Vera Cruz and in September he hoisted the Stars and Stripes over the halls of Montezuma in the Mexican capital. The war was over.

New York's political boss Thurlow Weed early saw Taylor as Presidential timber. He sought out the latter's brother for information about the General and learned that, although Taylor appeared to have absolutely no Presidential ambitions, he had some strong prejudices—all Whiggish. The shrewd Weed declared that Taylor's prejudices were quite as valuable as policies and set out to make this man President. Taylor did not seek the Presidency and admitted he had only general ideas about the nation's problems.[1] But, once elected, he sought the Presidency of a nation and not of a party; in this approach to his duties he was remarkably like Washington and Eisenhower. Many great military men are remarkably unpolitical.

The most important events of Taylor's Administration were the Gold Rush of 1849, the entrance of California into the Union as a free state, and the slavery legislation which is known as the Compromise of 1850. This last compromise superseded the Missouri

---

[1] Because it did not bear postage, Taylor refused the Whigs' letter of notification; hence he did not know officially of his nomination until sometime after other parts of the country knew.

Compromise of 1820. As in the earlier compromise, something was offered to both North and South; but the new compromise was in the North's favor on two very important counts. It permitted the principle of "popular sovereignty" in the lands acquired from Mexico; but inasmuch as these lands were not suited to plantation life nor, in some places, to cotton growing at all, it was quite unlikely that any new states could be added to the South's slavery empire. The new Compromise also postponed secession for ten years, during which time the North's already superior economic power might be further strengthened, and her eventual victory in any contest with secessionists, should the issue of secession have to be resolved in battle, definitely assured.

As early as August 1846, American conquerors entering Los Angeles had proclaimed the annexation of California. Even before that, the South looked toward that land as a possible addition to its cotton-slave dominions. However, in 1849 California held a constitutional convention in which the delegates, comprising Northerners and Southerners, voted overwhelmingly to outlaw slavery. Slavery, as a lost cause, can be said to date from that event.

On a hot July 4th in 1850, at exercises held at the site of Washington Monument, President Taylor became ill with what seemed to be cholera morbus. His condition worsened steadily and on July 9th he died in the White House. His death hastened the domestic crisis; for, although not a great man, he was in every sense a *national* man, and as such possessed greater qualities of leadership than did any other single Chief Executive between Jackson and Lincoln. Although a Southerner and a slaveholder, he cherished the Union and said he would hang rebels more quickly than he had hanged spies in Mexico. Polk in his diary calls him "narrow-minded," "bigoted," "partisan," "without resources," and "unfit for command"; but it is doubtful that a man with all these failings could have inspired the loyalty which Taylor seems to have inspired in the military. His tastes and virtues were simple; personally he was actually unkempt, and often directed military operations looking more like a farmer than a general. U. S. Grant, who served under him, is said to have dressed in a slovenly fashion in imitation of his idol. In no way profound, Taylor was genial, generous, in every sense unpretentious, and supremely patriotic. Like many another military man, he deplored the suffering caused by war: "My life has been devoted to arms, yet I look upon war at all times, and under all circumstances, as a national calamity, to be avoided if compatible with the national honor."

It is interesting to note that all the great Civil War figures—Grant, Lincoln, Lee, and Jefferson Davis—at some time served under Taylor. It is difficult to understand why a great historian like Beard never recognized Taylor's real worth. The educator, Horace Mann, while admitting that he had not voted for Taylor, nevertheless declared his election "the greatest godsend of our times . . ." Before he became President, some of the opposition bruited it about that Taylor was deficient in adequate command of the mother tongue. All one needs to do to refute this point is to read the General's beautiful letter of condolence to Henry Clay upon the loss of the latter's son at the Battle of Buena Vista—a classic of its kind.

Taylor's wife, the former Margaret Smith of Maryland, was as undesirous of the limelight as was the publicity-shy Rachel Jackson. She was at her husband's side throughout all his campaigns and was a devout churchwoman. There is no truth to the rumor, so long persistent, that she smoked a pipe. She was the mother of one son and five daughters, but there are no descendants living in the male line today. One of her daughters married Jefferson Davis, which displeased Taylor very much. The Taylor family lies buried in Zachary Taylor National Cemetery, outside Louisville, Kentucky, where a suitable monument has been erected.

Zachary Taylor had declared that he could save the Union without shedding a drop of blood. Among his plans, in case of rebellion, was one to blockade the Southern ports. It is regrettable that he did not have the opportunity to put his plans on trial. Had he lived, it is almost certain he would have been re-elected.

13

★★★★★★★★★★★★

MILLARD FILLMORE

☆ ☆

VOTE OF 1848: *See* under Taylor

VOTE OF 1856: *See* under Buchanan

☆ ☆

FILLMORE, WHO AS VICE-PRESIDENT SUCCEEDED TO THE PRESIDENCY upon the unexpected death of Taylor, was, among other things, one of the three handsomest men ever to become President. Of better than average height, he was of impressive appearance and possessed an urbanity commensurate with it. His parents were Nathaniel Fillmore and Phoebe Millard; he was the second of nine children in a poor family and was born January 7, 1800.

Millard Fillmore's life is a classic American success story. He was born in a log cabin at Summer Hill (then called Locke), Cayuga County, New York. He had very little education, and, as is so often the case with the eldest of many children on a farm, had no end of chores to perform. At fourteen he was apprenticed to a clothmaker; he had to walk most of the one hundred miles to where his employer had his business. As happened so often in those difficult pioneer days, the employer mistreated his charge. Millard refused to stand for it, and walked the one hundred miles back to his home.

Fillmore was an ambitious youth and learned quickly; not only that, he showed signs of brilliance. His father, who recognized this, appealed to a local judge to let the boy study law in his office. The judge agreed; and by teaching school and doing surveying work Fillmore enabled himself to complete his studies. He was admitted to the bar at twenty-three; soon after he became a member of a law firm in Buffalo.

However, Fillmore was very much attracted to public life.

First he was elected to the New York State Assembly. Later he served two terms in Congress. While a New York legislator, it is interesting to note, he took a leading part in developing the public school system, and was responsible for the enactment of the law abolishing imprisonment for nonpayment of debt.[1]

In 1848 the Whig Party was looking for a Vice-Presidential candidate. The Clay element in the Party had been offended by the nomination of Taylor for the leading place on the ticket, and Fillmore was chosen in an attempt to conciliate this element. Although he was little known, and had been defeated for Governor of New York, he was at the time of his nomination Controller of New York State. Without doubt his handsome appearance and genial manners were thought of as balancing Taylor's ordinary looks and slovenly manner of dress.

On entering upon his duties as Vice-President, Fillmore exhibited the greatest humility. He admitted to the members of the Senate that he would need help in presiding over that body. In the late eighteen-forties, when slavery was disturbing Congress on such an extensive scale, Fillmore's qualities were useful; Southerners especially held him in high esteem. Unfortunately, Fillmore was an outstanding example of what was wrong with the Whig Party: the time for conciliation over the South's "peculiar institution" was nearly past. Only a forthright stand would now be effective. A Jackson or a Taylor would have provided the kind of leadership needed in the crisis.

When Fillmore took up his duties in the White House, an almost impossible task awaited him. Taylor's Cabinet resigned in a body and Fillmore had to make all new appointments to his official family. Meanwhile the Compromise of 1850, which had been debated while Taylor was still alive, was about to become law. The three titans of the era—Webster, Clay, and Calhoun—were speaking their final pieces in their respective pleas in the Senate for and against the legislation. "I speak today for the preservation of the Union," intoned the frustrated Webster. In the campaign two

[1] Legislation against the cruel incarceration of persons who could not pay their bills was being demanded more and more by the people. Not only did this sort of penalty belong to medieval times, but it did not make sense for the most obvious of reasons. The plight of Robert Morris, who did so much to finance the American Revolution, thrown into debtors prison in his last years, was something many Americans could not forget.

years before, Weed had suggested Webster for the Vice-Presidency; but, like other Senatorial giants who have considered the second-place position beneath their talents, Webster declined, only to see that, if he had not done so, he would have been granted the greater office. Tired and disillusioned, he asked for support of Clay's latest compromise with all his fervor of speech. Thomas Carlyle wrote of his "mastiff mouth" and of his eyes like "dull anthracite furnaces."

The Compromise was enacted. Soon after, the three titans died. A new and stricter fugitive slave law was part of the Compromise and when Fillmore signed it, he knew he was signing his political death warrant. It is an interesting sidelight on the character of Taylor and Fillmore that, although a Southerner and a slaveholder, the former opposed the Compromise as being too favorable to the South; and that the latter, a Northerner and opposed to slavery, signed it because he thought it the best way to preserve peace and the Union. It is an example of rare honesty, in both men.

The new Fugitive Slave Law was unenforceable. It imposed penalties for sheltering fugitives or aiding in their escape; fugitives were denied trial by jury or even the right of summoning witnesses; and there were other evil features in it. Ralph Waldo Emerson called it, "This filthy enactment," and added: "I will not obey it, by God."

Three other events in Fillmore's short term are worthy of note. Commodore Matthew C. Perry was sent to Japan to open up that virtually unknown country to the trade of the West; this sort of thing had always been England's peculiar province in the past. Then there was the Kossuth affair. Kossuth was a Hungarian revolutionist who came to the United States, actually making the voyage on an American man-of-war. He was received with honors and entertained by American statesmen. The incident is interesting as the first example of American intervention in European affairs; it implied that the United States had the kind of responsibility to Europe it was not ready to fully accept until 1917. Plainly, the independence of Hungary was not directly America's affair, and her concern with it was a violation of the Monroe Doctrine; but a dependency wishing to cast off the yoke of a mother country could not help but win a sympathetic response from the United

States. The President himself considered it entirely improper for him to say or do anything which could be construed as an interference with respect to the internal affairs of Hungary.

The third important event during Fillmore's Presidency was the publication of Harriet Beecher Stowe's *Uncle Tom's Cabin.* Some people have gone so far as to say that *Uncle Tom's Cabin* caused the Civil War. It was a sensational book. It was not an accurate picture of the South, however, although millions of Northerners believed it was; Mrs. Stowe had never even been in the South before writing the book. It seems incredible that her book of fiction was read as pure fact; but the times were ripe for the acceptance of *anything* sensational. Very persuasive, perhaps, was the fact that the author came from a noted family; few people thought of questioning anything authored by a Beecher. Yet even *Gone With the Wind* is a more useful account of Southern life in that turbulent period.[2]

Although Southern Whigs wanted Fillmore as their candidate again in 1852, the Northern element whom he had alienated by signing the Fugitive Slave Law was against him. They turned, instead, a third time to a general, the pompous Winfield Scott. But in 1856, when their fortunes were at their lowest, the Whigs once more nominated Fillmore, and so did the so-called Know-Nothing Party.

The latter party was officially called the American Party, the avowed purpose being to keep the United States a nation of "natives." It was a secret society, and a foolish movement. Members, when asked about their beliefs, replied: "I don't know." It was an anti-foreign group, especially anti-Catholic. In 1850, when Fillmore was President, the foreign-born in America numbered about ten per cent of the population of 23,000,000; and the proportion was rising due to heavy German and Irish immigration. When to this segment were added approximately three million Negroes, these devotees of a "nativist" philosophy felt that before too long little of the original America would be left. That unlimited immigration to America might have unfavorable effects on the institutions of the United States was to be debated again and again; in an election as recent as that of 1952, the matter was to

[2] Made into a play, Mrs. Stowe's story became the greatest hit of all times; in one city it played for eighty-three years.

emerge in the Presidential campaign and be discussed pro and con with fierce partisanship.

It would be unfair not to recognize that there was a sound reason for the formation of an "American" party in the United States and for Fillmore's preoccupation with such a movement. Many Americans were alarmed over the Kossuth affair. When that patriot did not succeed in interesting the Government in the cause of Hungarian independence, he appealed directly to the people, especially to German-born citizens. He urged them to assume their role as the balance-of-power in choosing the President of the United States—meaning, of course, a President sympathetic to projects like Kossuth's.

A campaign book for 1856 contains a paragraph which reads: "The American party is not founded, as its enemies represent, on hostility to the residence of foreigners in this country, but to their participation in our politics before they have become imbued with American sentiments." It was partly because of this very desire to give foreign-born a chance to absorb the atmosphere and feeling of America that the law was passed during John Adams's Administration raising to fourteen years the length of residence in the country before citizenship could be conferred. But the Know-Nothing Party, much as it vociferated about its principles, would not take a courageous stand on the slavery issue, and for this reason it disappeared from the national scene.

The Know-Nothings only once ran a candidate for the Presidency, in 1856; Fillmore carried one state in that election. When he first went to the New York legislature, it is interesting to note, he ran as an Anti-Mason under the sponsorship of Thurlow Weed. To run for public office as both an anti-Mason and an anti-Catholic in one lifetime is an interesting feat indeed—especially in those times, when feelings ran high on a variety of issues and people freely gave expression to these feelings. This feat is perfectly indicative of Fillmore's character, and of his position today. Although he had few thoughts of self-interest, Fillmore's lack of forthrightness has caused historians to treat him on the whole with indifference, and so the American people have virtually forgotten him.

One thing more should be said about Fillmore's character. Oxford University wanted to confer an honorary degree upon him, but he declined on the ground that he was not entitled to receive such a degree—an example of honest modesty rare in public life.

Fillmore went back to Buffalo upon retiring from the Presidency and became that city's leading citizen. He was also the first chancellor of the University of Buffalo. In 1861 he entertained the Lincolns on their way to the inauguration. However, he supported McClellan in 1864; after Lincoln's death, he sympathized with Andrew Johnson.

Fillmore was twice married. Abigail Powers, the first Mrs. Fillmore, mother of his son and daughter, died soon after her husband left the White House. Some years later he married Mrs. Caroline McIntosh, who survived him. The line of descent of Millard Fillmore has concluded. He died March 8, 1874, and was buried in Forest Lawn Cemetery, Buffalo, where the Republican women of the area have erected a memorial to him and his family. The destruction of Fillmore's papers, carried out in accordance with his son's will, has long been considered by historical writers as an act of purest vandalism.

14

FRANKLIN PIERCE

☆ ☆

		Popular	Electoral
VOTE OF 1852:	Franklin Pierce, Democrat	1,601,000	254
	Winfield Scott, Whig	1,386,000	42
	John P. Hale, Free-Soiler	157,000	
		3,144,000	296

☆ ☆

POINTING OUT THAT A CHIEF EXECUTIVE WAS INCOMPETENT IS NOT A pleasant task. However, by no stretch of the imagination could Franklin Pierce ever be termed anything else.

In his youth Franklin Pierce had every advantage. His mother was Anna Kendrick and his father Gen. Benjamin Pierce, soldier of the Revolution and twice Governor of New Hampshire. Franklin, one of eight children, was born at Hillsborough, in that state, November 23, 1804. He attended all the "prep" schools which certain classes still consider of great importance in any upbringing. Later he attended Bowdoin College in Maine where he formed a lasting friendship with Nathaniel Hawthorne, and met Jane Appleton, his wife-to-be.

Pierce was a lively, gay, and magnetic young man of medium height and, like most attractive people, never knew what it was to lack friends or a good time. He was not intellectually gifted; he enjoyed more than anything else the campus drills which he himself conducted. When, at the beginning of his third year at Bowdoin, he saw that he ranked lowest in his class, he began, with the help of his friends, to apply himself seriously to work. At his graduation he was fifth in his class, giving at his commencement a discourse on Locke. Pierce began the study of law and at twenty-three was admitted to the bar.

At twenty-eight he was elected to Congress; at thirty-three to the United States Senate. Before his term as Senator had ended, he resigned and returned to Concord, New Hampshire, to resume the practice of law. He declined various offices in political life, among them that of Attorney-General in Polk's Cabinet, because of his wife's delicate health.

After he left Washington, Pierce resolved not to re-enter public life unless it was to accept his country's call to arms. This call soon came, with the Mexican War. Pierce enlisted; soon thereafter President Polk tendered him a commission as brigadier-general. Pierce was wounded in this war.

The Presidential campaign of 1852, like that four years previously, was characterized by the candidacies of Mexican War heroes. The Democrats, after 48 fruitless ballots, selected Pierce. The Whigs named Winfield Scott, known as "Old Fuss and Feathers," an aide to every President from Jefferson to Lincoln. Pierce defeated Scott, and it is perhaps regrettable. It is safe to say that either Scott or Hale could have confronted the serious issues of the time at least as well.

In his inaugural address Pierce came out unequivocally for the annexation of Cuba, as his predecessor Polk had done. His running-mate even took the Vice-Presidential oath of office there. The South, of course, was interested in Cuba; for, with the addition of another slave state, they felt sure their section would be dominant in the affairs of the nation. President Fillmore had opposed the annexation of the island. When Spain refused to sell it to the United States, three American diplomats in Europe issued a statement, called the Ostend Manifesto, stating that it would be the policy of the United States to obtain Cuba peacefully, if possible, and by force, if necessary. The future President James Buchanan was one of these diplomats. It is incredible that three men who had no right to do so could have declared such a policy and had it published. The world capitals were shocked; America was regarded as a nation of highwaymen. The State Department was compelled to disavow the policy.

It is easy to see what might have happened if the world had not been shocked. America might have found an excuse to go into Cuba; it might have pretended that a native uprising was putting American lives in danger; or the Government and the newspapers might have created a story about Spain's being a backward government tyrannizing the inhabitants of Cuba and then claimed that it was America's "Christian" duty to bring the Cubans under her protective wing.

Politics do not adjust to justice. Governments fulfill ambitions by making justice adjust to politics. We are used to thinking only of England or Russia or Germany as being guilty of imperialism. The American situation was called "expansionism" or, to put the sanction of Providence on it, Manifest Destiny. However, whatever its policy was called, America was an imperialist nation, and clearly made land grabs right up to the Spanish-American War.

In the second year of Pierce's Administration the United States bought 45,000 square miles of land in the Southwest from the rather poor government of Santa Anna for $10,000,000. This large tract was purchased for the purpose of building a railroad to the Pacific via a southern route, with the interests of the South in view. Known as the Gadsden Purchase, this was the last territorial addition made to the continental United States before Alaska was acquired.

The matter of a transcontinental railroad brings us to the most serious event in Pierce's Administration—the incendiary Kansas-Nebraska Act. *Uncle Tom's Cabin* may not have caused the Civil War, but it is entirely possible that the Kansas-Nebraska Act, which Pierce signed, did. Senator Stephen A. Douglas of Illinois, later Lincoln's opponent for the Presidency, sponsored this bill. It was reported that he, together with others, was interested financially in acreage in Kansas and Nebraska because it was almost a certainty that the railroad to the Pacific would go through this area; they wanted territorial government developed here in anticipation of that event. It was purely an opportunistic arrangement from first to last.

In violation of the Missouri Compromise, the Kansas-Nebraska bill, which allowed both Northerners and Southerners (the latter with their slaves) to settle in the two territories, became law. Later, when the territories were to apply for admission as states, it was intended to let the inhabitants themselves vote whether they were to be slave states or free. This was the "popular sovereignty" principle which applied to the conquered lands from Mexico and was part of the Compromise of 1850. The territory affected by the Kansas-Nebraska bill was that unorganized part of the Louisiana Purchase lands north of the 37th parallel, excepting Iowa and

Missouri. The struggle for the passage of this bill was epic. Senatorial stalwarts like Charles Sumner, Salmon P. Chase, Sam Houston, Thomas Hart Benton staked their all in opposing it. Trouble began as soon as Pierce signed the Act. Kansas had civil war.

At this point, we first hear of John Brown, the fanatical Abolitionist who had grandiose ideas about freeing the slaves. He thought of himself as a special liberator destined to perform God's will.[1] He could not see that it would have been more in the public interest if he had thought of himself as a special steward for his twenty children. At Pottawatomie, in Kansas, Brown and his raiders killed five innocent men in their beds; but Brown went free. "They that take the sword shall perish with the sword"; and some years later we see that Brown too perished by violence.

All this might have been averted if Pierce had not been so strong a partisan of the Kansas-Nebraska bill. He proved to be naive in his belief that by leaving the disposition of the slavery question in the hands of the voters themselves the problem would be definitely settled. Pierce did not understand the social forces of his times; indeed he did not possess the mental equipment to grasp any part of their significance.

After war came, Pierce was bitterly critical of the Lincoln Administration, advocated a cessation of hostilities and a return to the *status quo ante bellum,* but the North never really trusted him again; they thought of him only as a Copperhead. So strong was the feeling against Pierce that when his friend Nathaniel Hawthorne dedicated a book to him, Emerson in anger tore out the dedicatory sheet, and Harriet Beecher Stowe upbraided the book's publishers.

The attachment of the gay, extroverted Pierce and the shy, sensitive Hawthorne for each other is one of the curious friendships that occasionally occur among people in public life. Perhaps it can not really be explained. It should be realized, though, that Pierce did give recognition to the intuitive and religious compulsions of life, and it possibly explains his studies to master John Locke. At any rate, the friendship of the two men was lifelong, and Pierce was alone with Hawthorne when the novelist died.

Pierce's Administration was one of great prosperity for the

[1] On the body of Lincoln's assassin, Booth, was found a diary in which Booth wrote of himself as an instrument of God's punishment.

nation and paved the way for the election of another Democrat—
James Buchanan. It is interesting to observe that the Bessemer
process of steel manufacture was perfected during this time by an
Englishman, a fact that certainly had a profound influence in making the American nation, in possession of one-half the known coal
reserves of the earth, the world's greatest industrial power. While
Pierce was President the Republican Party was founded at Jackson, Michigan; created out of defunct Whigs, Know-Nothings,
Abolitionists, Free-Soilers and others, it formed an omnibus anti-
slavery bloc in 1860. At the same time Stephen C. Foster was composing his native American ballads; and Otis invented the modern
elevator.

After Pierce left office, he went back to his old convivial habits. His domestic life was filled with tragedy and sorrow. All three
of his sons died in boyhood. When he was elected President, one
was left, an eleven-year-old. Two months before the inauguration, this boy was killed before Pierce's eyes in a railroad accident.
If, as has been said, Pierce's life contained too much light-hearted-
ness, certainly that was more than balanced by his later griefs.

His children, his wife, and his close friend Nathaniel Hawthorne gone, Pierce died at Concord, October 8, 1869, and was
buried in that city.

15

JAMES BUCHANAN

☆ ☆

		Popular	*Electoral*
VOTE OF 1856:	James Buchanan, Democrat	1,838,000	174
	John C. Frémont, Republican	1,341,000	114
	Millard Fillmore, Whig and Know-Nothing	874,000	8
		4,053,000	296

☆ ☆

LIKE HIS PREDECESSOR IN OFFICE, JAMES BUCHANAN, ONE OF THE most misunderstood of Presidents, was called a "sectional" President, the implication being that his sympathies were primarily with one section of the country, namely, the South. Northerners seldom consider that Lincoln also was considered sectional—by the South.

Buchanan was born in a log cabin at a spot called Cove Gap, in Franklin County, Pennsylvania. His father, a shrewd Irishman, had a trading post near there; and a few years later, as their finances improved, the family moved a short distance away to the growing town of Mercersburg to which the natal log cabin was moved and where it is now preserved.

James was born April 23, 1791, the eldest son of eleven children of James Buchanan and Elizabeth Speer. Both the mother and father were hard-working Scotch-Irish Presbyterians; the father prospered as a merchant and in land transactions. When the younger James was sixteen, they were able to send him to Dickinson College, at Carlisle.

At first this naturally intelligent boy did not do well at school for the simple reason that he spent his time in all kinds of mischief. At the end of his first year, his father received a letter from the college stating that it was only because of their high regard for the senior James that the boy was not expelled from school.

Years later Buchanan explained that he traveled in bad company because he did not wish to be thought of as a "softie." The young Buchanan returned to college through the intercession of others, improved, and was graduated first in his class.

Buchanan's people were Federalists and, as might be guessed, opposed to the War of 1812. Nevertheless, young Buchanan, already admitted to the bar, volunteered for service in the war.

Soon after, he became interested in politics. His unusual success in his profession was due not only to his knowledge but to his ability as a speaker; through study he had developed considerable oratorical talents. In 1814 he entered the Pennsylvania legislature, as a Federalist, and served two terms. In 1821 he went to Congress and served in the House for ten years. Here he was remembered as having declared that slavery was "a great political and a great moral evil." Since the Federalists had about died out, he became a Democrat and a Jackson follower.

Buchanan's greatest services were in the State Department. For this he had had fine preparation. He was appointed in 1832 as Minister to Russia; upon leaving this post the Tsar paid him the compliment of saying he hoped the Government would send him another Minister like Buchanan. Van Buren wanted him as his Attorney-General, but Buchanan declined. Polk made him Secretary of State, in which post he arranged for the settlement of the Oregon dispute. He was clearly an expansionist. He openly advocated the acquisition of Cuba. After the end of the war with Mexico, he wanted to annex all of that nation lying west of the Sierra Madre Mountains. But the Mexican undertaking was Polk's pet project; Buchanan's wishes about Mexican annexation were disregarded.

After his efforts as Secretary of State for Polk, Buchanan retired to Wheatland, his beautiful estate outside Lancaster, Pennsylvania; Pierce called him out of retirement to become Minister to England. Buchanan accepted, but it had been plain for a number of years that he had considered himself the top man for the nomination for President. In 1856, when his chance came and he became the nominee of the Democratic Party, he was already sixty-five years old.

It is a matter for speculation whether Buchanan would have

won if it had not been a three-party contest. With the reappearance of Millard Fillmore on the national scene, the combination of Frémont and Fillmore made Buchanan a minority President. It is certain that most of Fillmore's votes would have gone to Frémont, who was the first candidate the new Republican Party had ever put up for President. Frémont was a colorful figure; he had been instrumental in the seizure of California, although he had been court-martialed for disobedience. He later gave Lincoln a good deal of trouble.

In his inaugural address Buchanan was emphatic in indicating that he was a strict constructionist. This boded ill for the Abolitionists. While the Kansas-Nebraska dispute was on, he was fortunately out of the country, so that the people and the Party did not feel that he bore any particular battle scars to make him ineligible for the high post to which they now were calling him.

Buchanan was to know no peace while he was in the White House. Two days after his inauguration the Supreme Court handed down its sensational Dred Scott decision. Buchanan completely concurred. This decision declared that the states alone could legislate with respect to slavery and that Congress had no right whatsoever to forbid slavery in the territories; this automatically opened up all the territories to slavery. It ruled also that a Negro was not a citizen, whether bond or free, and that, Negroes being property, they could not plead their cases in the courts of the land. The decision of the Court was seven to two, a majority of the bench being slaveholders. Roger B. Taney was Chief Justice and wrote the opinion.

Following this came the incredible Lecompton Constitution affair and the damaging effects it had on Buchanan's name in the North. At Lecompton, Kansas, a convention was held, presumably representing the majority of the residents of that state, at which a pro-slavery constitution was adopted. Following this, Kansas applied for admission as a state. It was obvious at that time that Kansas contained a larger number of Northern immigrants than it did Southern; but Buchanan, influenced by his pro-Southern Cabinet, urged the admission of Kansas and the acceptance of the Lecompton Constitution. Senator Stephen A. Douglas then broke with the President, condemned the Lecompton Constitution as a violation of the "popular sovereignty" principle then prevailing by reason of the Compromise of 1850 and the Kansas-Nebraska Act. In a popular referendum, the voters of Kansas overwhelmingly rejected the Lecompton Constitution, adopted an anti-slavery constitution, and compelled the Buchanan Administration to admit Kansas into the Union as a free state.

Then came the Panic of 1857 which did Buchanan no good. The following year the Lincoln-Douglas debates in Illinois highlighted the growing tension over the slavery issue more and more. And after John Brown's raid at Harpers Ferry for the purpose of inciting a slave rebellion, the South's fears became worse, even though Brown was hanged. Abolitionists, clergymen, and "do-gooders" articulated inflammatory incriminations with ever-mounting zeal. Minnesota and Oregon also came into the Union as free states. Cabinet members resigned one after another. President Buchanan's Party split into three virtually separate movements, each with its own Presidential ticket in 1860. Buchanan's choice for the Presidency, John C. Breckenridge, a pro-slavery man, was defeated, and an anti-slavery man, Abraham Lincoln, won the election. In February 1861 the dreaded thing happened: the Confederacy was formed.

In his message to Congress in 1860, the outgoing President, probably knowing that the worst was at hand, said that there was no constitutional right allowing any state to secede from the Union, but that, at the same time, no state could be compelled to remain in the Union—which amounted to saying nothing at all. In his heart he blamed the North for inciting the rebellion: he stated that Northern writers and statesmen were too extreme, not conciliatory enough. He was correct up to a point. Thousands of clergymen, for example, who might have devoted their efforts to preaching patience, brotherliness, and understanding, as the Master taught them, simply poured oil on the fires of suspicion and hatred. In this respect they were much like many clerics in the first World War two generations or so later, who, like John Brown, thought that helping to create hatred for the enemy was doing God's will.

As the problem of slavery came to a head during the Buchanan Administration, one must inquire here why the South was on the defensive about what it maintained was its way of life. Involuntary servitude was being abolished in the Western world. Mexico had abolished it in 1829; Britain in 1833; France in 1848; Portugal in 1858. The whole system was outmoded, and the South was aware of it. The South knew it was clinging to a way of life that the power of world opinion would compel her to abandon sooner or later.

On both sides of the Atlantic the American slavery question in all its economic, social, political, and traditional aspects has been exhaustively considered. It was a mighty complex, the attempted eradication of which could only have terminated in an eruption. However, there was another factor—a psychological one—as powerful as any of the social ones, and that was the North's "holier than thou" pose which struck the Southerner as, at the least, ludicrous and offensive.

The war could possibly have been averted, but Buchanan could not do it. He was not direct enough; he could not rise to the occasion; he lacked the courage necessary at crucial times. At first he refused to send any reinforcements to the Federal forts in Charleston harbor, in South Carolina, the state most violently anti-North, and the state sure to be the first to leave the Union if a break-up should come. Then his tactics changed and he sent a ship to the aid of Fort Sumter, but it was too late. He tried to follow whatever course would make it as easy as possible for his successor to handle the crisis. Throughout the war he supported the Lincoln Administration. He was a man of unimpeachable honesty and patriotism; it was unfortunate that the years of his tenure in the White House were not years of quiet and prosperity when he would have shown to better advantage.

America's only bachelor President, Buchanan was engaged to marry in his youth. Because of a lovers' quarrel, the young woman broke off the engagement and in the following months she died suddenly. Young Buchanan was disconsolate: "I feel that happiness has fled from me forever," he wrote. He never had a second love.

He was devoted to his mother, as the eldest son so often is, and admitted he owed much to her. He was devoted also to a favorite niece who presided over the White House while he was President and made his Administration a great social success. The Prince of Wales, later Edward VII, was one of his guests.

On June 1, 1868, James Buchanan died and was buried in Lancaster where his grave, the only one in the plot, gives the onlooker a feeling of utter loneliness.

★★★★★★★★★★★★★★★★

16

ABRAHAM LINCOLN

☆ ☆

		Popular	*Electoral*
VOTE OF 1860:	Abraham Lincoln, Republican	1,866,000	180
	Stephen A. Douglas, Northern Democrat	1,375,000	12
	John C. Breckenridge, Southern Democrat	847,000	72
	John Bell, Constitutional Unionist	587,000	39
		4,675,000	303
VOTE OF 1864:	Abraham Lincoln, National Unionist	2,330,000	212
	George B. McClellan, Democrat	1,836,000	21
		4,166,000	233

☆ ☆

WE COME NOW TO ONE OF THE MOST DIFFICULT PERSONAGES IN ALL history to describe, much less explain. In the subject of this biography we find greatness, and we find too its frequent counterpart—enigma.

What makes a man great? Certainly making history is not enough. Napoleon, Caesar, Genghis Khan, Hitler, many others, have made history.

There is one element of character which probably more than any other is the test of whether a person is truly great or not. That characteristic is Magnanimity. It implies largeness of mind, nobility of spirit; a nature in which there is no pettiness, a nature that forgives enemies, that gives up profit and advantage in order that the greater number may benefit. It bespeaks, in short, a concern for others greater than the concern for one's self.

A man's words alone will not show whether he possesses magnanimity. Even a man's acts will not always show it, for a man may perform certain good acts from a purely selfish motive. It is in the larger view of a man's whole life, seen in retrospect, in the natural difference between isolated acts of goodness and an entire life, that we may discover whether he possessed magnanimity. Whether a man in public life has lived a truly good life or merely performed good acts for expedient reasons is not an easy thing to tell at first; the perspective of time reveals a just balance.

And so in the heat of the day many people judged as great will diminish when partisan passions have cooled; and others in low esteem or ignored in the busy affairs of men will emerge into greatness when future generations have achieved a just, objective vision.

A clue to Lincoln's character has been given us by a Southern writer: "He loved mankind, and that meant all men. He was for the underdog, for the poor and downtrodden, white or black, and it did not make any difference to him whether they lived in the North or the South. It is the one quality that made him a great man . . ."[1]

Magnanimity is a quality that may be cultivated, and an individual may decide for himself whether he will give his life to the dedication it requires. "Good nature," an important trait often confused with magnanimity, is, however, independent of it. Lincoln had both. One may be born with good nature, and Lincoln was. To act in accordance with this trait was as natural to him as buzzing is to a bee. It was at times quite impossible to insult him. During the Civil War some men in his own Administration tried to insult him and got no reaction. This could have been partly due to his inurement to privation, a concern with the essentials of life that prevented much worry about "name-calling."

Perhaps the most telling and succinct account of Lincoln's character has been given by Herndon:

> He was morally and physically courageous, even-tempered and conservative, secretive and sagacious, skeptical and cautious, truthful and honest, firm in his own convictions and tolerant of those of others, reflective and cool, ambitious and somewhat selfish, kind to all and good-natured, sympathetic in the presence of suffering or under an imaginative description of it, lived in his reason and reasoned in his life. Easy of approach and perfectly democratic in his nature, [he] had a broad charity for his fellow-men

[1] W. E. Woodward: *A New American History*, pp. 507-508; Rinehart & Company, Inc.

and had an excuse for unreflective acts of his kind, and in short he loved justice and lived out in thought and act the eternal right. . . . I do not say that he never deviated from his own nature and his own rules. His nature, the tendency of it, is as I state. . . . Lincoln struggled to live the best life possible. This I know.[2]

Samuel Lincoln, the original migrator to America, came from Hingham, England, to Hingham, Massachusetts, in 1637. His descendants migrated to New Jersey, Pennsylvania, and Virginia.

Abraham Lincoln was the name also of the President's grandfather. It was he who migrated from Virginia to Kentucky in 1782 with his wife and five children when Kentucky was still a part of Virginia. He was killed by the Indians a few years later.[3] It is his son Thomas who became the father of the President.

Both Lincoln's parents were born in Virginia. William H. Herndon, Lincoln's law partner in Illinois, who spent a great part of his life doing research on Lincoln's life and ancestry, and on whose material most of the old biographies of Lincoln are based, states that there is reasonable doubt as to whether Thomas was really the father of young Abe. In fact, Herndon goes into elaborate detail to show why Americans could rightly harbor such a doubt.

Thomas was married to Nancy Hanks, daughter of Lucy Hanks and a Virginia man. Herndon's stand that Nancy was illegitimate is now claimed to be disproved. The first child of Thomas and Nancy was a girl named Sarah. She was two years older than Abe. Besides another son who died very young, there never were any other children born to Thomas through either of his marriages.

On a large but poor farm, known then, as it is now, as Sinking Spring Farm, Abraham Lincoln was born February 12, 1809. This was near Hodgenville, Kentucky, in what is now Larue County.

Although the young Lincoln was born in a log cabin at Nolin Creek, he did not live there long. His father, who was losing his lands because of the careless way in which property titles had

---

[2] Letter to Jesse W. Weik, November 21, 1885; original now in the Library of Congress.

[3] Kentucky was known as much as the place of "the dark and bloody ground" as it is known as the Blue Grass State. It was known as "the dark and bloody ground" among the Indians themselves because of the constant warring between the Iroquois and Cherokee tribes for its possession.

been established in that wild country, moved to another sizable farm on Knob Creek; there young Abe lived until he was seven years old.

Thomas Lincoln moved to Indiana in the fall of 1816, and there, near the town of Gentryville, in what is called the Pigeon Creek country, in Spencer County, he made a clearing on a new farm, and, with his young son's help, built a cabin home of the type generally found at that period which could be erected in about four days. Neighbors doubtless helped Thomas with construction. The floor was of packed earth.

In 1818 Nancy died and was buried in a crude box constructed by her husband. The twelve-year-old Sarah tried to keep things going in the home; Thomas Lincoln went back to Kentucky for a visit. When he returned, he brought with him a new wife, a widow named Sarah Bush Johnston, whom he had known earlier. She had three children of her own; these, together with some much-needed furniture, joined the Lincoln household.

Extreme want ceased to be feared after Thomas's second marriage. In this Indiana place, in new surroundings, the young Lincoln grew into manhood. Long before he reached twenty-one he had grown to his full height of six feet four inches. Although he was never a heavy man, and, even, some people thought, looked rather consumptive, he had unusual strength, could wrestle well and, what was most necessary in those pioneer days, knew how to handle an axe.

During both the Kentucky and the Indiana years Lincoln had as companions two cousins of his mother, the youths John and Dennis Hanks, both older than he. He had also Sarah Bush Lincoln's children to grow up with after his father remarried. Lincoln's stepmother was still living at the time of Lincoln's death, and Herndon visited her to get a statement. She corroborated the stories about her son's superiority and honesty, adding that he never gave her a cross word nor a word that was not the absolute truth.

Much has been written in recent times concerning the influence of environment. Lincoln's case contradicts some of the theories in these studies. Despite pressure from every quarter toward shiftlessness or at best the average, Lincoln was uncommonly ambitious. He was hungry for books. He could not get enough of them. He read and reread. He had less than a year's schooling in his whole life; he was literally self-taught in everything.

The foundations of his character were not set by the church, which Lincoln rarely attended, but by what he absorbed from a few, central books—the Bible, *Robinson Crusoe*, Aesop's Fables, Weems's *Life of Washington*, a history of the U.S.A., *Pilgrim's Progress*, and one or two others. From a justice of the peace he borrowed the *Revised Laws of Indiana* which whetted his appetite for the profession that was to launch him on his career—law.

Abe, by his own admission, as well as that of others, did not care about physical work. His first employers sometimes complained that he did not earn his wages. In a way we are loath to censure Lincoln; he continuously needed time for reading or studying—and for practicing speech-making. He was an unusually fine mimic and would, on occasions, repeat sermons he heard at church to his associates with appropriate gestures. All through life he had a reputation as a storyteller. Often, dignified officials would be annoyed when he bade them listen to some story or joke when they were anxious to get down to serious business—especially as the stories many times had an uncultivated, bucolic twist. Thomas Lincoln always was disappointed that his son spent so much time on "eddication" instead of doing the work that was immediately necessary. We hear conflicting stories about Thomas; neighbors testified that he loved his children; yet at times he was harsh with Abe and even cruel.

Lincoln was in his middle twenties before he paid any attention to girls. He had a gaunt and awkward frame, heavily-lined, leathery skin, and large ears; it is more than likely that he did not consider himself a romantic figure. He had other, redeeming qualities. He neither smoked nor drank liquor. All testify that he never used profanity. He was gentle and kind, for which reason, probably, he never cared about hunting and fishing. At school he reproved his classmates for tormenting animals and even wrote a paper about it.

There were important defects in Lincoln's character, however, and a portrait, to approximate fidelity, must take account of them. Outside of a certain love for literature, it would be correct to say that, for the most part, he seemed to be indifferent to the arts. This was the despair of his wife and of his colleagues in both the

law and Government. It was Lincoln's great qualities as a leader—
and his great magnanimity—which rescued him from a dullness
that might otherwise have been as total as Polk's. He also was
unsystematic in his work; and although a successful lawyer, and
even a famed one, not the superior kind one would be led to
expect in a man of his abilities.

In 1830, Thomas Lincoln moved once more. This time it was
to be Illinois, at a place some miles west of Decatur on the Sanga-
mon River, not far from Springfield, which was to become the
capital of the state. As usual, the Hanks boys moved there also.
This was Lincoln's fourth and last home under his father's roof.
He stayed a year to build fences and help with the crops; then
took a flatboat trip to New Orleans. This was his second trip to
that city. When he was nineteen and lived in Indiana, his employer had sent him to New Orleans with a load of produce. That
was his first glimpse of a large American city. The second time he
saw, among other things, the slave market and how it worked.
One of the Hanks boys reports that it was then he said: "If I ever
get a chance to hit that thing, I'll hit it hard."

Upon his return from his second New Orleans trip, Lincoln
decided to settle in New Salem, a town with a population of one
hundred. He had a job there as a storekeeper which lasted only
about a year; it was interrupted by Lincoln's answering the call
for volunteers in the war against Black Hawk. Lincoln was given
a captaincy, stayed in the Army for eighty days, and saw no fighting. It is difficult to imagine the soft-hearted Lincoln shooting
anybody, considering that he even objected when his playmates
molested a turtle.

In 1832 the young man ran for the Illinois legislature as a
Whig, but was defeated. In need of money, he opened up a store
with a fellow called Berry. The store failed. Berry was always
drunk; Lincoln always read and had almost no business sense. It
was Lincoln who after many years paid the debts of both partners.

Among the other jobs Lincoln held in New Salem were that of
postmaster and deputy county surveyor. In 1834 Lincoln again
ran for the legislature, and this time he won. He was elected to
four consecutive terms; his experience in law-making was to prove
invaluable. In addition, he studied law, tutoring himself. In 1836
he received his license to practice and moved to Springfield which

was to be his real home. In 1837 he entered in a law partnership with Stuart; in 1841 he entered one with Logan; and in 1844 he formed the partnership of Lincoln and Herndon, which was never dissolved.

Except for a term in Congress, to which he was elected in 1846, the remainder of Lincoln's life prior to his becoming President was spent practicing law in Springfield, and raising his family. He was also making friends throughout the State. However, Lincoln's opposition to the Mexican War while a Congressman made him few friends; by prior agreement, he did not seek a second term. Throughout his two years in Congress he voted consistently with the Whig minority. He approved the resolution of thanks voted to Zachary Taylor for his Buena Vista victory; that resolution included a description of the Mexican War as "a war unconstitutionally and unjustly begun by the President."

Lincoln's relations with women do not show that he possessed the gallant attitude of Washington. He liked them; but he himself suggested on several occasions that he did not understand women; he appeared to hold them in awe. The story of Lincoln and Ann Rutledge is now considered to be pure fabrication. Lincoln did know a young woman by that name, but there was no romance involved. It is partly because of Herndon's fostering of the Rutledge story that Lincoln's wife and son came to distrust Herndon as they did.

In 1838 it looked as though Lincoln might marry one Mary Owens, but for various reasons they decided against marriage. Then, in 1840, he became engaged to Mary Todd, a high-spirited, cultured girl from Kentucky whom, tradition long had it, he actually deserted at the altar. This also is now believed to be a myth, and biographers believe it was, more simply, a broken engagement. In 1842 Lincoln did marry Mary, when he was thirty-three. In between the first planned wedding and the second actual wedding Lincoln suffered great mental anguish. He actually had to leave the State and recover at the home of his friend Joshua Speed, in Kentucky.

After Lincoln returned from his Congressional term, he settled down to practicing law in earnest and became, for the first time, financially independent. The state judicial circuit in which he lived, which included fifteen counties, made it necessary for the court to move from county to county to hear cases. This was called "riding the circuit," and Lincoln was one of the riders. Some writers declare that these years of circuit riding, which Lincoln seems really to have loved despite the inconveniences involved, were the only really happy years of his life.

Lincoln was soon recognized as one of the leading members of the bar. However, public affairs would not let him rest. In 1854 he made a speech at Peoria, Illinois, which made him famous. He explained his opposition to the hated Kansas-Nebraska Act which Douglas had authored. He was not in favor of new slave states being admitted, but new free states. He stated that it was only in free states that poor people might better their condition.

In 1856 Lincoln joined the new Republican Party, which had been formed during the Pierce Administration. In 1858 Lincoln received that party's nomination for United States Senator. It was then that the famous Lincoln-Douglas debates throughout the state took place, Douglas being the candidate of the Democrats. It was just before these debates that Lincoln said: "A house divided against itself cannot stand." Although Lincoln received the majority of the popular vote, Douglas was sent to the Senate because, in those days, it was the state legislatures which named Senators. As the year 1860 neared, Lincoln became more and more disturbed about the national situation. If, as a young man, he showed no particular "sense of destiny" with respect to himself, his thoughtfulness now definitely betrayed a feeling that somehow he would be called upon to play an important role in the crisis that was coming.

Early in 1860 Lincoln was invited to New York City to give the Cooper Union address. His speech made a great impression; the Republicans named him that year as their candidate for President. He was elected in a four-cornered contest, receiving a majority of the electoral vote, but only 40% of the popular vote. On February 11, 1861, he bade a sad farewell to his friends in Springfield, telling them he might not see them again. He never did.

To tell of the remainder of the life of Abraham Lincoln is to tell of the Civil War. Why did this war come to the American people? As always, the majority of the people did not want war. Actually, the Southern states, had they had an opportunity to vote on it, would not have favored secession from the Union; historians are rather sure of that now. However, there were radicals seated in important places on both sides. By the time Lincoln was elected, feeling had run so high that the South felt his election meant only one thing—the end of their way of life. They seceded.

Eleven states left the Union and formed the Confederacy with Jefferson Davis as their president.[4] Richmond was made the capital. Texas' founder-Governor, Sam Houston, who strongly opposed his state's decision to break away from the Union, was forced to resign. In spite of all this war might yet have been averted if South Carolina had not fired upon Fort Sumter on April 12, 1861, when the demand of the Confederacy for its surrender was refused by the Union commander. That act of violence, it seemed, had to be answered with violence. At once Lincoln called for 75,000 volunteers.

Threats of secession by Southern states had been rife before, during the eighty-odd years since the Revolution had ended. However, nothing had ever happened that could be construed as a rebellion except the local incident known as the Whiskey Rebellion in 1794, when Pennsylvania farmers refused to pay the Federal tax on whiskey. At that time President Washington called out 15,000 militia against the disobedient, arrested a few, and released them later. But no armed resistance against the national Government had ever been made; least of all, no American political entity had ever fired upon a Federal installation.

Some historians believe that Lincoln was hasty in calling for troops. Congress alone has the power, after all, to declare war, according to the American Constitution. Congress was not in session when the firing on Fort Sumter occurred. There is still doubt as to why Lincoln did not call Congress into session right away, instead of waiting until July, after the call for troops. Was he afraid that, because it was still predominantly Democratic, Congress would delay, and even refuse to give him the powers needed to deal with the emergency?

Between the Fort Sumter firing and the calling of Congress Lincoln did several things which, strictly speaking, were unconstitutional. A blockade of Southern ports was ordered; the regular army was enlarged; expenditure of money was ordered without

---

[4] Davis was born in Kentucky, about eight months before Lincoln, but with an upbringing entirely different from Lincoln's.

authority from Congress; the writ of habeas corpus was suspended. This last meant that anybody, anywhere, could be arrested on even the slightest suspicion and thrown into jail for an indefinite period without any hearing whatsoever. The suspension violated a right which free men had had for six hundred years. Almost everybody today agrees that, in this action at least, Lincoln was in error. Congress alone had the right of suspension; and morally, perhaps even Congress did not have the right.

At last the first real clash of Northern and Southern forces took place. This was on July 21, 1861, and is called the First Battle of Bull Run. The North thought that it would be an easy success for its forces. Congressmen in high hats and all sorts of well-wishers and watchers went along drinking and making speeches. Before the day was over, the North—army, Congressmen, and all—was in complete rout. When they counted over 3,500 dead and wounded, not even knowing what the number of missing were, North and South knew they were in for something that was going to be far from an easy success for either side, and that the conflict would not be settled in a short time.

The year 1862 was a sad one for Lincoln. His son Willie died in the White House; it was the second son he had lost. Then, although the Battle of Antietam was a Northern victory, it was a costly one in lives. General McClellan, in charge of Eastern operations, was a disappointment to the Administration and was relieved of command. The Peninsular Campaign, aimed at capturing Richmond, was bogged down completely. The South defeated the Union at Fredericksburg; defeated it again at the Second Battle of Bull Run. Enlistments were falling off—this made it necessary to pass a draft law later. In the mid-term elections that fall, the anti-Administration candidates won many Congressional seats. Lincoln was being ridiculed in the newspapers. His own Secretary of War called him a "gorilla." His Secretary of the Treasury was planning to succeed to the Presidency in the next election. In France, Napoleon III was taking advantage of America's internal crisis by challenging the Monroe Doctrine in Mexico. Further, England's sympathies seemed definitely with the Southern cause, and Lincoln was faced with the problem of what moves to make to keep England from recognizing the Confederate States as a sovereign nation.

Nevertheless, in Southern waters and in the West some hopeful events were taking place. Signs pointed to the North's shaking off some of its discouragement regarding the war. In February of the crucial year 1862, Commodore Foote had taken Fort Henry on the Tennessee River, and an unknown by the name of Grant had astonished the nation by capturing Fort Donelson on the Cumberland, a Southern stronghold held by an old classmate of his. A little later, Grant and General Buell won the Battle of Shiloh Church; without Buell, Grant would surely have lost it. Corinth in Northern Mississippi fell soon after, and then Memphis was occupied. Some weeks previously, Admiral Farragut had captured the South's largest city, New Orleans, thus closing the entrance to the Mississippi River. What was happening was that the Confederacy was being squeezed in the Mississippi Valley from both extremes, thus slowly narrowing the theater of war mainly to one section—the East. Despite all this it is important to remember that it was not until 1863 that some sign of the outcome of the war became evident.

Chancellorsville in Virginia was won by the Confederates in May of 1863, with frightful losses on both sides. In this battle the South lost one of its two ablest commanders, General "Stonewall" Jackson. But General Robert E. Lee, the South's brilliant and beloved leader, who was the son of "Light Horse Harry" Lee of Revolutionary fame, and who had turned down the offer at the beginning of the war to command the Union forces, decided to invade the North with his 70,000 men, thereby threatening Washington. At Gettysburg in Pennsylvania a battle was fought on July 1, 2 and 3 against Northern forces of 90,000 under General Meade. The outcome of that battle is known to all. Lincoln was genuinely disappointed that Meade did not follow up his advantage and go after the retreating Lee.

As if to put a seal of finality on doubts as to the outcome of things, Grant, after a six weeks' siege, took Vicksburg on July 4th, thus cutting the Confederacy in two.

The entire world now knew that the Union would win the war; therefore no foreign government would risk recognizing the Confederate States. Fears about the English sympathy for the Southern cause were set to rest. The North had been shipping wheat to Europe in 1862, three times as much as it had ever shipped before, because of crop failures on the Continent. "Wheat was King" now, instead of Cotton.

On January 1, 1863, Lincoln had issued the Proclamation of Emancipation. This paper is not the pure piece of liberation many people have imagined it to be. It was very much a political move. Foreign governments would see that the United States, by proclaiming the slaves freed, was truly engaged in a moral struggle. That the foreign governments should believe this was important to the Lincoln Government in 1862. The act also proclaimed to certain groups in the United States, such as the radical Republicans and certain church groups, that the Government intended to set the slaves free, besides saving the Union.

It is also not generally known that the Proclamation applied only to the slaves in the seceded states; the slaves in the border states of Kentucky, Missouri, Maryland, and Delaware, which did not secede, were not affected by it. Everything was done, from the beginning of hostilities, to keep these four border states from going with their "wayward sisters."

The year 1863 ended with what amounted to complete victory in the West. Although the North suffered a defeat at Chickamauga, the two engagements at Lookout Mountain and Missionary Ridge near Chattanooga were such signal victories that Lincoln and Grant could concentrate all their attention on Lee and the Eastern campaign.

Grant was called East and given full command of the Union armies. He was clearly the leader Lincoln had been seeking for three years. Since the beginning of the war Lincoln had had to direct the entire effort himself; the technique of war actually had to be learned by him—no doubt a difficult achievement for a man of Lincoln's temperament. With the persevering Grant to depend on, many of Lincoln's worries were over.

In 1864 Grant began his plans for wiping out what remained of the Confederate force. In that year were fought the bloody battles of the Wilderness, Spotsylvania, and Cold Harbor, all in Virginia. The losses were so great that the battles might properly be called slaughters. Every foot of ground was contested by the Southerners; the losses of the Union exceeded those of the South. Meanwhile, Admiral Farragut took Mobile Bay and sealed up the last Gulf port the Confederates had.

General Sherman's assignment for the Union was to subjugate Georgia and the Carolinas. His famous march through Georgia, in which he destroyed the city of Atlanta, and the destruction of private property by ruthless bands among his men are well known. There was very little opposition. Sherman himself did not approve of the outright barbarism of his troops. In Columbia, South Carolina, to which city his men set fire, his feeling for the hungry people was such that he gave them five hundred head of cattle.[5]

To General Sheridan was assigned the job of securing the Shenandoah Valley so as to prevent the Confederates there from joining with Lee's army at Richmond.

Meanwhile, the 1864 Presidential campaign was getting under way, and for a time Lincoln actually believed that his Administration would not be returned to power. Chase and Frémont were more than anxious to get into the White House: each hoped to be the nominee of the Republicans that year. The Northern Democrats nominated General McClellan, a man greatly liked by his troops, who exhibited none of the complexity and mysticism which in Lincoln was so disturbing to many. These Democrats said they believed in stopping the fighting, in leaving the institution of slavery alone—and, they claimed, in preserving the Union.

The Administration availed itself of much political strategy in order to maintain power. In 1863 West Virginia had been detached from the "Old Dominion" of Virginia and admitted into the Union as a free state, and the Administration correctly counted on the support of this new state in the campaign. In 1864 Nevada, although containing less than one-sixth of the required number of inhabitants for statehood, also was admitted, mainly because the Administration needed another free state's support.

At last Grant entered Richmond. Caught at Appomattox Courthouse between the forces of Grant and Sheridan, Lee surrendered, April 9, 1865. The war ended. On April 26th the Confederate General Joseph Johnston surrendered to Sherman in North Carolina.

Actually, from the beginning, the South was doomed. Exactly how much could 8,500,000 people, 3,500,000 of whom were Ne-

5 Lloyd Lewis: *Sherman: Fighting Prophet,* p. 508; Harcourt, Brace and Company.

gro slaves, do against 23,500,000 who had wealth, manpower, and industrial production on their side, to say nothing of sole access to material from across the seas?

It is estimated that a total of 600,000 men gave their lives in this contest, and of that number more died of disease and undernourishment than from weapons.

Of the death of Lincoln there is little to say. Every schoolboy knows how in Ford's Theatre, Washington, an actor named Booth shot him, and how he died the next morning on April 15, 1865, without ever regaining consciousness. In 1864 he had been re-elected President; and in his second inaugural address, considered one of the most beautiful utterances in the history of all statesmanship, he had said, "with malice toward none; with charity for all . . . let us . . . bind up the nation's wounds . . ."

In spite of this speech, it is clear that extremists and the vengeance seekers in Congress would never have allowed Lincoln to carry through his policy of bringing the defeated states back into the fold with complete forgiveness. If the assassin's bullet had not killed him, disillusionment with his countrymen might have. Many people in the North, including intellectuals like Emerson, felt that the country had seen enough of Lincoln and were looking forward with definite relief to his exit from office.

Because the telegraph had just come into general use, it was the first time that the death of a great figure was known so soon throughout the nation. The people were thrown into mourning practically simultaneously, and with great suddenness. The route of Lincoln's return to Springfield was approximately the same as the one by which he left Springfield in 1861. In all the large cities of the East his body was taken from the train to lie in state. Some reporters averred that now his face had taken on a look of great peace.

Early in May the body was laid to rest in Oak Ridge Cemetery, where an impressive mausoleum houses his remains, and where his wife and the three youngest of his sons also are entombed.

Lincoln's domestic life was as full of care as his public life. He could never really understand his wife's aristocratic, imperious ways, so different from those of old Sarah Bush Lincoln, the sympathetic stepmother who had encouraged him in his studies, and for whom he had a deep love. Mary Lincoln encouraged her husband also, but partly, it is clear, because she was ambitious for herself. There is, however, no question but that she has been greatly wronged by many writers; much of what has been written about her is as peculiar and mythical as some of the things written about Lincoln himself. She was capable of deep affection, had strong likes and aversions, and enjoyed lasting friendships. Her difficulties were not simply temperamental but also fortuitous, for she had lost three brothers in the Confederate cause. It is believed that Lincoln and his wife truly loved each other, in spite of the friction others observed. Tremendously saddening events had occurred in the lives of each, events that the majority of people would not be able to bear. Mary's mind was indeed sadly affected; she had to be confined for a time in an asylum.

Of Lincoln's four sons, two survived him, but only one, Robert Todd Lincoln, grew to manhood. He was appointed to Garfield's Cabinet. Robert's only son, Abraham, died in youth.

It is beyond doubt that, no matter who would have headed the Union government during the Civil War, the Confederates could not have won. Lincoln's fame, then, rests not so much on his direction of the Northern forces to victory, successful as that was, but on his great qualities as an individual. It cannot be denied that he was a rather poor administrator. Even over his growing sons he had poor control and Herndon complains that they were poorly disciplined. But in the other necessary qualities of leadership—patience, concentration, ability to separate the petty from the important, the willingness to listen to others, the ability to reject the idea that he was indispensable—in all these Lincoln was the acme of what could be desired.

If Lincoln appears mystical, unclassifiable, it is no doubt because, as Herndon said: "He never revealed himself entirely to any one man, and therefore he will always to a certain extent remain enveloped in doubt."

The Gettysburg Address, Lincoln's most famous statement, delivered when he was asked to make "a few appropriate remarks" at the dedication of a national cemetery, is written in as expressive language as has ever been used. The applicability of the message for the age is still being pondered—beyond the beauty of the utterance. Although Lincoln spoke of "government of the people, by the people, for the people," there are those who insist that government of the people does not presuppose government *by* the people. There are also those who maintain that government *by* the people, irrespective of its past susceptibility to error, is infinitely more desirable than the most beneficent of despotisms. Government *for* the people is what citizens have longed for throughout all ages.

Perhaps the answer to all of this lies in the wisdom of the citizens themselves.

Grieved as the American people have been that a fratricidal war ever appeared necessary in their political development, they have nevertheless felt some compensation in the life of Abraham Lincoln, whose grandeur and melancholy will remain as integral a part of the saga of their country as the Union to which he gave his imperishable labors.

★★★★★★★★★★★★★★★★★

17

ANDREW JOHNSON

☆ ☆

VOTE OF 1864: *See* under Lincoln

☆ ☆

IT IS ONLY IN RECENT TIMES THAT ANDREW JOHNSON HAS COME INTO his own. It was known even before he died that the many defamatory things published about him were not true. He left the Presidential office serene in the confidence of "my ultimate vindication."

If it were to be asked of Americans generally which President had the smallest amount of schooling, probably 98% would answer Abraham Lincoln. Lincoln's schooling amounted to about one year; Andrew Johnson never had any at all. His widowed mother was so poor that she could not afford to send him to school even for a few weeks. Johnson was born in a homely cottage in Raleigh, North Carolina, December 29, 1808. His father, who died when Andrew was three, was named Jacob Johnson; his mother was Mary McDonough, although the marriage contract refers to her as Polly. The father was a handyman and the mother a maid in the same tavern.

At the age of fourteen Andy was apprenticed to a tailor; but, together with his older brother who was apprenticed with him, he ran away—a violation of the contract. A reward of ten dollars was advertised for their capture. The boys opened up their own shop at Carthage, North Carolina; then moved to Laurens, South Carolina; then decided to go back home. Andy wanted to make things right with his old employer in Raleigh but he could not get his former job back; the employer would not trust him again.

Mrs. Johnson had remarried, but neither her husband nor the boys were doing any good in Raleigh. They decided to move to Tennessee. Everything was piled into a two-wheeled cart, drawn by an old nag, and with this equipment the four emigrants, taking turns at riding, made their way to their new home which was to be at Greeneville, Tennessee. Here Andy opened his own tailor shop. Here also at the age of nineteen, he married young Eliza McCardle—a marriage so successful that it was said by their friends to have been made in heaven.

Andrew Johnson at the time of his marriage was illiterate. His wife taught him to read and write, and how to do sums. While he was sewing away at garments in his place, he would have people read to him, absorbing every bit of knowledge he could. He read everything that came his way; he had become an ambitious young man. There are indeed certain extraordinary resemblances between Lincoln's life and Johnson's.

Andy Johnson's tailor shop prospered. He turned out good work. He made friends among the townspeople; and soon his shop became a meeting place for people interested in discussing public affairs. Once a week he walked eight miles to a college where there was a debating society, and practiced speaking on public matters. As he prospered he became a slave owner. He and his family would never again know such years as he had lived through in his childhood, among the worst that any American in public life had ever experienced—even worse than Lincoln's.

Johnson was highly sensitive about his early life. Not only did he hate poverty but he hated the wealthy classes who so often made life unbearable for the poor. Throughout his life he opposed people of privilege. His black eyes, his large head and thickset shoulders, all gave force to the savage voice as it lashed out against money barons or hypocrites. Charles Dickens, after calling on him, said that he "would have picked him out anywhere as a character of mark."

The greatest fault Andrew Johnson had was his overly outspoken manner. Although he could be dignified and the essence of decorum at times, he was often tactless and undignified in debate; sometimes he would argue with members of his audience. Because it gave the people an incorrect estimate of his usefulness, this did him much harm while President. And the Radicals, who actually ran the Government in the immediate postwar era, made capital out of this weakness in Johnson's nature.

In 1829, as alderman in Greeneville, Johnson began his long and varied public life. Next he became mayor of his town; then a member of the Tennessee legislature; then State Senator; next Congressman in Washington for ten years; twice Governor of Tennessee; United States Senator from Tennessee; Military Governor of his state, appointed by Lincoln; Vice-President on the Union ticket with Lincoln; then, in 1865, President of the United States. And, in 1875, he served briefly in the United States Senate.

As Governor, no doubt remembering his own lack of opportunity, he favored free education for all citizens. One of the great advantages the North had when war came between the states was its system of free education. In the South education was not free everywhere, and free high schools were an unknown thing altogether.

As we have noted, Johnson owned slaves. Yet he championed the Homestead Act, a bill in Congress which slaveholders almost to a man opposed. Johnson introduced this bill when he first went to Washington, and he fought for it for sixteen years until at last it became law in 1862. This was the first time that public lands were given "free" to American citizens. For payment of a small registration fee, anyone could obtain title to a tract of 160 acres in the West, provided he had lived on it and cultivated it for five years.

The slave states opposed doling out land because it meant the creation of more free states, since the lands were in a climate where cotton was not grown. President Buchanan, who was originally in favor of the Homestead Act, vetoed it on political grounds, and it had to wait for secession to become law. The passage of this act was a very important event in American history and had widespread effects, social and political.

Johnson was a Southerner and he loved the Southern people. But more than the Southerners he loved the American Union and its Constitution, a sacred document to him. In view of that, we can see what a dilemma he was in when, as a Senate member from Tennessee, his state seceded with the other ten. He made a powerful plea in the Senate for preserving the Union, and as late as March 1861 boldly denounced secession to his colleagues. He was the only Southern member of Congress who refused to secede with his state.

Hard as all this was for Johnson, the worst was yet to come. In 1862 Lincoln had appointed him Military Governor of his home state of Tennessee. In 1864 he was Lincoln's choice as his running-mate in the Presidential election. Upon Lincoln's death, Johnson became President.

At the beginning, Johnson's impulsive nature made him in favor of hanging everybody involved in Lincoln's assassination, and dealing harshly with the leaders of the Confederacy. When these initial passions had cooled, he became conciliatory and, in fact, adopted the magnanimous attitude of Lincoln. A French statesman, observing Johnson's methods, said of his policy: "It is simple like everything that is great, it is resolute like everything that is good." Some weeks after Lincoln's death, the President issued a proclamation of amnesty to all citizens who had taken part in the Southern cause excepting only certain military officers, and people of substantial wealth. By Christmas of 1868 everybody had been pardoned, including Jefferson Davis, who had been a Federal prisoner for two years.

But in March 1868 a crisis as great as the Civil War took place in the American Government. The radicals in Congress, led by an astonishing group of hate-mongers, chief of whom were Ben Wade of Ohio and Charles Sumner of Massachusetts, had decided that the Lincoln-inspired policy of forgiveness Johnson was following should have no place in the reconstruction of the Southern states. Even the pictures of these men reveal implacability and fanaticism. They had violently opposed the Lincoln reconstruction program, protested against Lincoln's renomination, and were quite happy when an assassin's bullet seemed to settle their worries for them.

The Southern states had been to a fair degree reconstructed by the time Congress reconvened in December of 1865. The President went so far as to announce to that body that the Union had been completely restored. The wayward states had ratified the Thirteenth Amendment, abolishing slavery from the country, met certain other requirements, set up new state governments, and sent new representatives to Washington. But in Washington these representatives were denied admission. The hate-mongers were intent on punishing the seceded states, and this is how the contest between Johnson and Congress began.

Since the beginning of the Republic, a slave had counted as three-fifths of a person in numbering the population on which a state's representation in Congress was based; this was according to Article I of the Constitution. With emancipation, a slave counted as a full person; and by this process twenty-nine additional Representatives from the South—all Democrats—were added to the House. Consequently, the leadership of the Republican radicals in the national Government was threatened. These radicals did not intend to sit idly by while the initiative was wrested from them by legislators from a section which was supposed to have been vanquished. Some eighty Senators and Representatives from the South were eligible to return to Congress, but these were all to be denied admittance unless their state governments were "reconstructed" in accordance with the harsh provisions of Congress instead of the generous terms of Lincoln and Johnson. Lincoln had taken the initiative in respect to, accepted the responsibility for, and directed the war against, secession. After the death of Lincoln, Congress did not wish to let the Executive again effect this kind of leadership. If that was Johnson's intention, the Radicals would destroy him. Since the Congressional elections of 1866 strengthened the Radical group, they went through with their program.

The South was now divided into five military districts until it complied with the high-handed demands of the Congress. This left the section open for "carpetbaggers" and all sorts of adventurers who came from the North and "advised" the Southerners, taking advantage of both whites and negroes in every conceivable way. In this they had the collaboration of a certain type of Southerner called "scalawags." It was this exploitation, not the Civil War itself, which doubtlessly brought about the Solid South. The South was willing to co-operate with the Lincoln-Johnson type of Republican.

Congress sent to the President a series of reconstruction bills, all of which he vetoed and all of which were passed, over his veto. It enacted the infamous Tenure of Office Act, by which the President could not remove any one of his own appointees without approval of Congress. This and the other measures passed by Congress at this time Johnson held to be unconstitutional. It is interesting to observe that, sixty years later, in 1926, the Supreme

Court invalidated the Tenure of Office Act. Scholars agree today that Johnson was right in all his other veto messages as well.

When, in 1867, the President removed from office his Secretary of War, Stanton, who had joined the Radicals, the House of Representatives voted to impeach him. Never before had a President been impeached in the United States. This meant the President would have to stand trial, with the Senate sitting as jury and the Chief Justice of the United States sitting as judge. In this trial Johnson was acquitted by one vote.[1] However, so certain were the Radicals of winning, that Ben Wade, president pro tempore of the Senate and next in line for the Presidency in case the office became vacant because of such a crisis, was making plans for moving into the White House. The significance of the President's victory can not be overemphasized. The trial of Andrew Johnson was one of the turning-points in American history. The incredible Thaddeus Stevens cried that never again would it be possible in the United States to remove a President except by "the dagger of a Brutus."

When his name was called out at the trial, Andrew Johnson was not there. He did not appear at all. He went about quietly doing his work. One can understand that with his impetuous nature it was difficult indeed for him not to speak out; but his former Attorney-General, Stanbery, who represented him, cautioned silence.

Had Johnson thought of himself, he need not have become involved in this fight with Stevens and his allies. He could easily have gone along with them and been assured of the nomination for President for a second term. The impeachment trial, while acquitting Johnson, ended his influence among the people. The Government was headed by the Congress, not by the Executive, and Congress did not intend to relinquish its power again.

We have seen that the Southern states ratified the Thirteenth Amendment as a prerequisite to being admitted again into the Union. Now, the Radicals, having barred the new Southern representatives from Congress, like kidnapers demanding additional ransom, required that they ratify also the Fourteenth and Fifteenth Amendments, which they proposed. The Fourteenth Amendment

[1] Of seven Republican Senators who voted for acquittal, not one succeeded of re-election.

provided, among other things, that the Negro should be assured the same protection and immunities as the whites, not merely freed from bondage as the Thirteenth Amendment provided. The Fifteenth Amendment was supposed to guarantee him the vote. Both amendments were submitted not because the Radicals were interested in the Negro, but, it was obvious, because they were interested in the continuation of their own power in Government. Their patriotism was a sham.

The two additional amendments were finally adopted, although the Southern legislatures which ratified them were then ruled not by legitimate governments chosen by the people or the interim governments recognized by the Lincoln and Johnson Administrations—these had been ousted—but by carpetbag governments, some of which had a larger number of Negroes in their legislatures than whites.

After this era of revolution, chaos, and hate—which so nearly wrecked the entire American Government—the South was not easily normalized. It had to wait at least until Hayes's time; and the United States is still paying the price for the Reconstruction policies of the North.

One act of Johnson's has been subject to wide criticism. That was his permitting the execution of Mrs. Surratt for Lincoln's murder, for which eight persons were tried and four sentenced to death. Clemency was recommended by the court for Mrs. Surratt, for no evidence could be found against her to warrant the supreme penalty. Johnson signed the death warrants when they were presented to him but did not know of the clemency recommendation until two years after the hangings. It had been purposely withheld from him because the general feeling against Mrs. Surratt, at whose boardinghouse one or two of the conspirators lived, was high, and the Lincoln avengers wanted death for all they thought connected with the murder plot. It is now agreed that Mrs. Surratt was not guilty, and that her hanging was a gross miscarriage of justice.[2]

[2] A photograph of the clemency recommendation together with the story of how it was withheld from President Johnson can be found in Robert W. Winston: *Andrew Johnson, Plebeian and Patriot*, pp. 277–291; Henry Holt and Co., 1928.

Johnson did not believe in interfering with constitutional processes. When the courts decreed something, he accepted it. In this he was different from Lincoln. Lincoln also knew the Constitution and the laws were sacred; but Lincoln felt strongly that the laws were made for the citizens, not the citizens for the laws. Lincoln understood, as probably few statesmen have ever understood, when an exception to the law was the healthier thing. He saved boy after boy from the firing squad during the Civil War, often irritating the War Secretary, Stanton. But Lincoln knew how to take into account that "circumstances alter cases." Johnson, although a generous man, was at heart one whose mind did not look out upon the grand eternal sweeps as Lincoln's did. Lincoln, whose lowly beginnings were equally as drab as Johnson's, nevertheless possessed a genius for profound insight into human behavior that precluded his ever performing an unjust act.

Johnson's accusers on occasion called him a drunkard. We have too many testimonials in his behalf from people who knew him intimately to believe that this was true. He did drink liquor, and made no effort to conceal it. He would have been a curious Southerner and a curious frontiersman if he never had taken a drink. It is interesting that, on the day of his inauguration as Vice-President he was rather tipsy from having taken a quantity of brandy. He had taken the brandy to enable him to get out of a sickbed and take the Vice-President's oath on March 4th. If he had followed his own wishes, he would have taken the oath when he was able to; but Lincoln would not hear of this. Lincoln in those trying times apparently wished to make certain that there would be a duly sworn Vice-President on hand.

Two items in the foreign affairs of the time deserve comment. One is Seward's purchase of Alaska. At first this was ridiculed in various ways—"Seward's Folly," "Johnson's Polar Bear Garden," etc.—not because Alaska was not considered a good buy, but plainly because the Radicals did not want the Johnson Administration to receive credit for a *coup*.

The other event is Seward's ultimatum to France to get out of Mexico. In 1863 Napoleon III, in violation of the Monroe Doctrine, landed an army in Mexico and placed Maximilian, a member of the ancient house of Habsburg, on the throne as emperor of that country.[3] After the ultimatum, Napoleon withdrew his forces. Maximilian, in spite of tremendous European efforts to save him, was executed.

After Johnson left office he tried several times to return to Congress in order to prove once and for all that the people had vindicated him. He had to wait until 1875 for this. In that year, in response to the demands of the people, the Tennessee legislature sent him for the last time to the Senate in Washington. When he got there, only thirteen of the thirty-five Senators who had voted to remove him from office still held their seats. To one of them, Morton of Indiana, he offered his hand, and Morton grasped it. This erstwhile passionate and vindictive man, a member of no church, had instinctively obeyed the Biblical injunction to forgive.

Johnson served but a very short time in the Senate; his death came on July 31, 1875. His wish was granted that he be buried with a copy of his beloved Constitution under his head and the flag of his country as his winding sheet. The place of his interment has been acquired by the Federal Government and is now part of the Andrew Johnson National Monument.

All who knew the Johnson family speak of the wonderful qualities of his wife Eliza. All during his White House term she was an invalid. Her mild nature was a great influence on the gruff, emotional man. In fact, without her, it is safe to say that Andrew could hardly have emerged from his tailor shop. Their three sons all died in young manhood; descendants are living today only through the female line.

Each American Presidency has its usefulness. Andrew Johnson's, through his impeachment and trial, has been to establish the individual regnancy of the Presidential office, because of which the American people cherish it and its incumbent in a way, it is hoped, that the passions of an era will never threaten again.

[3] Napoleon also permitted Confederate ships to be built in French shipyards.

★★★★★★★★★★★★★★★★★★

18

ULYSSES SIMPSON GRANT

☆ ☆

		Popular	*Electoral*
VOTE OF 1868:	U. S. Grant, Republican	3,012,800	214
	Horatio Seymour, Democrat	2,703,200	80
		5,716,000	294 [1]
VOTE OF 1872:	U. S. Grant, Republican	3,597,000	286
	Horace Greeley, Democrat and		
	Liberal Republican	2,834,000	
	Scattered	35,000	63
		6,466,000	349 [2]

☆ ☆

IF EVER THERE WAS A SQUARE PEG IN A ROUND HOLE, IT WAS President Grant. And if ever there was a period in the nation's life that was a low-water mark politically, it was during Grant's two Administrations.

And yet we must face the fact that for some of these periods of bad statesmanship the American people themselves are responsible. The populace in every nation has always loved its military heroes. It was a hero the people gave their vote to in those three elections in which Jackson ran for the Presidency. In 1848, despite the availability of abler men, it was the hero of Buena Vista who was wanted. In 1868 and 1872 the people wanted their hero again; not realizing, of course, that a true hero is far more likely to be an unglamorous person than a glamorous one, more likely to recommend unpopular policies than popular ones.

Let us look again at the election of 1860. If the contest in that year had been between two persons—Lincoln and just one other— the American people would hardly have chosen Lincoln. It is true that today the man in the street says that Lincoln was for the common people; but the facts indicate that the common people

[1] Mississippi, Texas, and Virginia did not vote.
[2] First time that all electors ceased being named by legislatures.

were never sufficiently attracted to Lincoln in any sense to clamor for him. It was only through the purest of accidents that Lincoln ever reached the Presidency at all. He was not of "hero" material.

In 1952 a national hero again was chosen. In fact, Eisenhower was picked by the party managers primarily because he was an idol of the people and therefore a sure vote-getter. While Eisenhower was a comparatively enlightened hero and may even have provided a key to American security in the second half of the twentieth century, the fact remains that most people *feel* their elections: they do not think about them. And that trait is bound to be tragic in its effects most of the time.

Grant should never have accepted the Presidency. He confesses in his *Memoirs* that he did not like to work; he was never even a good provider. He flitted from job to job, failing at each. He had a poor personality; he was not even moderately interested in people. One of his biographers, Woodward, says that he was a zoöphile, an inordinate lover of animals—which always suggests the question whether the person so described is a lover of human beings.

Even as a child in Georgetown, Ohio, where he grew up, and where his parents moved a year after his birth on April 27, 1822, at Point Pleasant, Ohio, Grant showed great love for horses—but hardly any affection for companions. He did not draw people to him; he did not seem to care about them; he did not need them.

The parents of this strange personality were Jesse Root Grant, an opinionated man of a long line of acquisitive Yankees from New England; and Hannah Simpson, as unemotional and undemonstrative a woman as ever lived. As one looks at her picture and sees the utterly matter-of-fact character outlined in her features, one wonders whether she could ever have inspired anybody. The fact that the name of her first-born, Ulysses, was drawn by lot may indicate how little sentiment she had. At the close of the Civil War, when Grant's name was a household word, he paid a visit to his parents. Woodward says: "His mother appeared, in her working apron, her countenance without smile or elation. 'Well, Ulysses,' she said, 'you've become a great man, haven't you?' With that remark she returned to her household duties." [3] All during

[3] W. E. Woodward: *Meet General Grant*, p. 14; Liveright Publishing Corporation.

her son's Presidency, she never once visited him in the White House although she was invited to do so. She simply wasn't interested.

Grant inherited his mother's indifference to human relationships. Fanatically considerate of animals, especially of horses, he was indifferent to human beings, to such an extent, some say, that he cared little for human life in war and thus was able more readily to win battles. During the Battle of the Wilderness he was called a butcher.

Yet on more than one occasion this stolid man wept, for he had a definitely effeminate side to his make-up which is little known to Americans generally and certainly hardly understood even by psychologists. Even into young manhood his face looked cherubic. It is not for nothing that in his cadet years he was at times called "Little Beauty." He was also called Sam in allusion to Uncle Sam, initials for which are the same as his own; also "United States" Grant and "Unconditional Surrender" Grant; to say nothing of the variations he had employed in Hiram Ulysses, Ulysses Hiram, and finally Ulysses Simpson—for all of which changes he had perfectly good reasons. At home he was called Lys. In the neighborhood he was called "Useless."

This unmilitary, even delicate, personality shrank from coarseness of all kinds. Like most men, he had weaknesses, as is evidenced by excessive drinking and cigar smoking, but he hated profanity and obscene stories. It has now been established that Lincoln never said of Grant, as is commonly believed, that he wished he knew what brand of whiskey Grant drank so that he could send some of it to his other generals. We have Lincoln's own statement denying that he said such a thing.[4]

Grant hated his father's business, which was that of tanner. He hated the sight of blood—whether of animals or humans—and he told his father he could not go into the tannery. The elder Grant then interceded with his Congressman to get an appointment at West Point Military Academy for his son. Lys was glad to go for the change of scenery, eager to see the large cities which lay between Georgetown and the Hudson River institution. He always loved traveling.

[4] J. G. Randall: *Lincoln the President,* Vol. III, p. 62; Dodd, Mead & Company.

Grant never liked military life, either at West Point or after he became a General. He admitted that, after having satisfied his desire to see Philadelphia and New York, he had hoped some accident would befall him and make him ineligible for West Point. Why he went there at all is one of those puzzling things in Grant's peculiar life. It may be that when he agreed to go, he already realized that it was the lack of plan with respect to his life which was giving him a "lost" feeling; that maybe it would be wise to accept what somebody else, in this case his father, had offered as a solution.

At a seminary in Marysville, Kentucky, not far from where he lived, and where he had spent a year just before going to West Point, Grant had shown little interest in study and had made mediocre grades. At West Point his grades did not improve. In mathematics he was good; and in horsemanship he excelled. In due course he was graduated; and it was his hope that he would be able to get a job teaching mathematics. However, he went to St. Louis first. There he met Julia Dent, sister of a classmate, and after the Mexican War he married this young woman.

Grant says in his *Memoirs* that he regarded America's war with Mexico "as one of the most unjust ever waged by a stronger against a weaker nation." In fact, he says the Civil War was America's punishment for waging the unjust war against Mexico.

Nevertheless, Grant took part in the Mexican War and there showed that fearlessness and indifference to danger which were to characterize his actions ever afterwards. In the war he had an opportunity to watch Zachary Taylor, and there is little doubt that in that shoddy-looking soldier he saw the prototype of himself. It was in Mexico that Grant developed the habit of drinking for which he was to be a target of criticism all his life.

In 1852 Grant was transferred to the Pacific Coast, and stationed at Humboldt Bay, California. His family did not go with him. With little to do, he began drinking again. He was warned about it, but the drinking continued. He was then compelled to resign his commission. This was in midsummer 1854, after he had served eleven years in the army.

Back in St. Louis, Grant found himself jobless. He tried many things, failed in them, borrowed money, incurred the ill-will of relatives, including his father and father-in-law. It is interesting to note how true to pattern it followed, after he was famous, that the father-in-law became quite proud of his son-in-law, although Grant's character hadn't changed a whit since first he married old Colonel Dent's daughter.

When Grant was called from obscurity to the fame of the battlefield, he was working in Galena, Illinois, for his two brothers who ran a leather store there. The eldest son in a family knows how humiliating it is to accept anything from younger brothers. Yet this is what Grant had to do in order to keep his wife and four children alive. He felt like a plagued man, perhaps rightly so.

Like many others, Grant did not believe that the war between the states would last long. He was for the Union, notwithstanding the fact that his wife, a Missourian, owned slaves. General Lee had freed *his* slaves because he personally hated the institution of bondage; yet he was against the Union when the showdown came. Such were the contradictions taking place over secession. Northerners fought in the Confederate armies and Southerners commanded in the Northern armies. Families and clans were split, some members going on one side and others joining the opposing side; all too often the Scriptural warning that a "man's foes shall be they of his own household" was realized.

In June 1861 Grant emerged from his "do-nothing" life. In that month, after he had been waiting for connections in the War Department in Washington, and with General McClellan, to materialize, the Governor of Illinois called Grant to take charge of some Illinois volunteers and gave him a colonel's rank. By sheer luck—the kind of luck which was to augment Grant's life throughout the Civil War—an Illinois Congressman, who wanted to do something for a resident of his state, recommended that Grant be made a brigadier-general. When Grant heard of his new rank, he was as surprised as everybody else. Thus began the career of this stoic and passive man.

Grant's headquarters were at Cairo, Illinois, and he was under Major General Frémont, the Republican Party's first candidate for President. After Lincoln had dismissed that pompous and officious person, the department was assigned to the cautious General Halleck, who became Grant's new superior.

Grant was a man of action, not one of contemplation. Because of this, he conflicted with Halleck. He had to beg Halleck to let

him attempt the capture of Fort Donelson as he had had to beg
Frémont before that to let him try to capture Paducah, Kentucky. It is hard to see how Grant can be described as physically
lazy in view of this eagerness. Although he did not get permission as regards Paducah, he went ahead and took it anyway, and
by that step attracted Lincoln's attention to him. Although he did
not get permission as regards Forts Henry and Donelson either,
he took the responsibility and, together with Commodore Foote,
brought about the surrender of those two highly important Tennessee forts.

At this point Grant, in his letter to the Confederate General
Buckner, made those two famous statements, quoted so often—
"No terms except unconditional and immediate surrender can be
accepted" and "I propose to move immediately upon your works."

Thus, at the hands of an unknown, one who had never read a
military treatise in his whole life, the morale of the North bounced
back overnight. The government at Washington promptly made
Grant a major-general and placed him in command of the Army
of the Tennessee. Then jealousy came into play and complaints
were sent in about Grant's drinking. Lincoln did not pay much
attention to them. This was in 1862 when things looked very dark
indeed in the other theaters of war and defeat hung everywhere
in the air.

Grant's method for winning battles was that of attrition—he
hammered away at the enemy after he had located him, and never
gave up. In fact, it is proper to say that there was no particular
genius involved in Grant's technique; it often was extremely costly
in lives.

At Shiloh, or Pittsburg Landing, Grant had a difficult time, and
complaints were heard about him again. Had it not been for General Buell's arrival with reinforcements, the battle would have
been lost. Nevertheless, the Confederates had to give ground all
the way to Corinth, Mississippi, where another battle was fought
and won by the Federals. Memphis was a naval victory. Six weeks
earlier the victory of Farragut at New Orleans had come. Grant
confronted the last remaining Southern stronghold on the Mississippi—Vicksburg. Capture of this stronghold was second in importance only to Richmond.

The Union strategy for Vicksburg is an epic in American warfare. Months were spent in preparation and experimentation, and Grant's schemes to capture the fortress high on the bluff two hundred feet above the water have been likened to Napoleon's campaigns. Bayous, swamps, and canebrakes obstructed Grant in the East, a flood-swollen Mississippi in the West. A smallpox and measles epidemic broke out. Grant's drinking became heavy again, and Lincoln sent down Dana, the Assistant Secretary of War, as an observer; however, Dana's reports to Washington were all in Grant's favor. Vicksburg fell after a long siege. Neither the army of the enemy nor the populace had much food, and were eating mule meat. Grant took about 30,000 prisoners in this assault, and his men divided their rations with the hungry enemy. This great victory, on July 4, 1863, coming the day after the victory at Gettysburg, removed all doubts both at home and abroad as to who would be the winner in the American Civil War. The Confederacy had been cut in half.

Vicksburg established Grant's reputation. So elated was the Administration by his victories that he was again promoted; he was also called upon to finish up the work around Chattanooga. Missionary Ridge which, together with Lookout Mountain, was captured by the Federals, was in reality a victory for the soldiers themselves. Grant did not send them up these heights and was disturbed when they went up of their own accord. Success here can be attributed mainly to Grant's good luck.

Congress now created the rank of Lieutenant-General, and gave Grant this designation. He was called to Washington in March of 1864 and made chief-of-command. Grant's plan was to start out in Virginia in May to capture Richmond and end the war. Thus he would tackle the job previously taken up in turn by McClellan, Pope, McClellan again (Antietam with 12,000 Union losses), Burnside (Fredericksburg with 12,000 Union losses, Hooker (Chancellorsville with 16,000 Union losses), and Meade.

It is strange that the Confederacy, knowing as certainly as the rest of the world did that their cause was lost, insisted on contesting every foot of soil they yielded. General Lee, whom the Federals had to pursue until the end of the war, was of an entirely different temperament from Grant; he adopted the military profession because he loved it. In the tactics of warfare he was considered the superior of Grant. He had greater culture, family background, and wealth. He was married to the only child of George Washington Parke Custis, George Washington's adopted son and Martha Washington's natural grandson. That is how he had come into possession of the Custis residential mansion and grounds called Arlington, which was seized during the Civil War and converted into a national cemetery. Lee was sober and Puritanical and, with respect to personality, he suffered from this excess of sobriety and correctness.

There is no need to go into the details of the campaign which led to Appomattox. The fact that it took from June 1864 to April 9, 1865 to accomplish the end is a fact which speaks for itself.[5] In the Battle of the Wilderness the North suffered 55,000 killed, wounded, and missing in six weeks. At Cold Harbor 6,000 Union soldiers died within an hour. Superiority in numbers, bearing heavily on results from the very day Sumter was fired upon, eventually decided the issue.

Grant's terms to Lee were considered generous. The men were allowed to depart for their homes upon signing a parole; officers might keep their side arms; and the cavalrymen could take their horses along for the spring work on the farms. It is not in mitigation of Grant's character to say that his generosity to the defeated was impelled, partly at least, by admiration for the valor of his opponent in a craft they both had chosen. The great contrast between the two Generals in appearance was so outstanding that even the undramatic Grant had to comment about it in the *Memoirs.* Lee with his great dignity, height, and faultlessly correct attire, surrendering to a short, shabbily dressed and uncommunicative Midwesterner—in the history of men there are few such situations. Grant must have been somewhat stunned by it, for Lee had to remind him twice what it was they had come together for.

Grant's selection for the Presidency was inevitable. In 1866 he was created a full general, the first since Washington. Honors came to him fast. Galena and Philadelphia each presented him with a house. He was certainly, publicly, no longer a misfit.

We have stated that Grant did not genuinely care about people. As a result he never was able to inspire his troops as was Washington. He was a poor judge of people and events. When the Rad-

---

[5] These are the dates for the mighty Siege of Petersburg.

icals in Congress, intent on their persecution of the President, and intent on wreaking vengeance on the prostrate South, offered Grant the nomination for the Presidency, Grant resigned the post of Secretary of War which Johnson had tendered to him after he had dismissed Stanton. Grant favored Johnson's impeachment, and tried to help bring it about. On his inauguration day Grant childishly refused to ride with Johnson in the carriage to the ceremonies as had always been the custom.

When he became President, Grant was only forty-seven years old. He had voted only once in his life before, in 1856—for Buchanan. The country was surprised when his Cabinet appointments were announced. The Truman Administration, eighty years later, which was to be termed "government by crony," had adequate precedent in the Grant Administrations. The combination of cronies in places of power, and the President's pitiful inability to suspect any of his appointees of any wrong, at once bred scandal after scandal. The President himself was always rigidly honest. But, as has been repeated, he did not know human nature. He respected wealth, and considered it as a sufficient and satisfactory sign of achievement. Nobody as naive as Grant was in this respect should ever be in charge of the administration of a nation's affairs.

Always plagued by importunate relatives, Grant early in his Administration was lured into a trap by his brother-in-law, led by two high-powered rascals of finance, Jay Gould and Jim Fisk. The aim of these three men was to corner all the gold of the country. The nation was still on a paper money basis, so that gold was merely a commodity the price of which could rise or fall depending on the law of supply and demand. However, to buy up the gold on the market and make it scarce, the wizards needed the co-operation of the Government. They entertained Grant in New York, assuring him that the well-being of the country depended on the Government's not selling any of the gold it owned. Grant was "fixed," his brother-in-law assured his associates; but in the nick of time Grant woke up, ordered his Secretary of the Treasury to "dump" $4,000,000 of gold on the market, caused a severe fall in its price and thus smashed the conspiracy. The day this happened is known in American history as Black Friday; thousands of investors were ruined in this speculative attempt, although Gould and Fisk cleared $11,000,000 for themselves.

There were many other shady deals during the Grant Administration, one of them having to do with the transcontinental railway, completion of which had been achieved in 1869. In this scandal, Schuyler Colfax, the Vice-President, lost his reputation; and he was not placed on the ticket again when the Administration came up for re-election in 1872. Next, the Secretary of the Treasury had to resign under fire in connection with peculiarities of the tax collections. Next, Grant's own secretary was put on trial for being involved in a swindle. Next, the Secretary of War resigned under threat of being impeached. The Speaker of the House, James G. Blaine, later a Presidential candidate, was accused of using his influence for private gain. The Attorney-General was forced to resign. Then the Secretary of the Interior had to resign. The Collector of Internal Revenue was indicted. The Secretary of the Navy was under constant fire for getting rich during his incumbency. Grant's brother-in-law was guilty of misconduct as collector of customs in New Orleans. The American Minister to Great Britain was recalled in disgrace. The Minister to Brazil was guilty of extortion against that very country. Federal judges had to resign or defend their reputations from accusations. It was an unbelievable era.

Disillusioned as the American people were by these happenings, they nevertheless trusted Grant himself. Grant, still the nation's savior, was worthy of their trust, they believed, as long as no personal blemish against him appeared. In 1872, he was re-elected, defeating the erratic Horace Greeley who died a month after his defeat and whose funeral Grant himself attended. Since a leading Presidential candidate never before had died before the electoral vote was formally counted, the Greeley electors who won scattered their votes among several availables as a courtesy gesture when the Electoral College assembled for its formalities.

In 1873 came the financial panic which was to last six years. Yet, it must stand to the credit of the Grant Administration that, during the panic, the fiscal affairs of the nation were put on a sound basis; taxes were reduced, and the income tax law was repealed, never to come back until an amendment to the Constitution legalizing it was adopted forty years later. The Panic of 1873 was of such proportions that the great banking house of Jay Cooke &

Company, the financiers of the Civil War, failed.[6] Congress in its excitement passed an ill-considered inflation bill, but the President rose to the occasion and vetoed it—an act that is a green spot in this Sahara of malfeasance which was the Grant Administration.

Grant had an obsession while he was President—Santo Domingo. Throughout his two terms he tried to get Congress to approve the annexation of that shaky republic. But the Congress thought—we believe wisely—that it was not in the interests of the American people to bring additional Negroes, on a distant island, who did not even speak English, under the American flag. But the island could have been had for the asking. Grant, of course, was interested in the exploitation of it by Eastern financiers; just as the South was interested in Cuba in *ante bellum* days for similar reasons.

At last, Grant, the politicians' President, left office. With his wife and young son Jesse he took a trip around the world. Kings and potentates honored him. He was a celebrity everywhere, both in Europe and in Asia. He was away for two years, and it was the hope of the political managers at home to prepare the ground, while he was gone, for his third term. But everything Grant was to do from now on was to be anticlimactic. The planlessness and fortuitousness of his early life came back to haunt him in his late life.

He wanted the nomination again in 1880; he did not receive it. He was ready to flout the tradition against the third term because he simply needed a job; his finances were in very bad shape, just as they had been in his early years. His salary while President had been raised from $25,000 to $50,000 per year; but he spent a good deal. On his deathbed Congress granted him a soldier's pension. He never fully understood the mystery of money.

To make matters worse, his older son, who seems to have had no more financial sense than the father, influenced the ex-President to join up with yet another money scoundrel, one Ferdinand Ward. The banking house of Grant and Ward was formed. Grant's part in the venture was to lend dignity and a famed name to the transactions. In three years this firm was bankrupt, with liabilities of $16,700,000.

[6] The day the Jay Cooke banking house failed is sometimes referred to as the Second Black Friday.

When the stunned man came to, he set to work to pay off his debts in the same stubborn manner in which he set out to win battles. He went to work on his memoirs. Already he was suffering from cancer of the throat. His time was short. He was taken to Mount McGregor, in New York State, and there he finished the manuscript four days before his death, which came on July 23, 1885. The memoirs were overwhelmingly successful; Grant's family earned a half million dollars from their sale; and they are considered the greatest military reminiscences written after Caesar's.

By popular subscription a tomb of magnificent proportions was erected for Ulysses and Julia Grant on Riverside Drive, New York.

Thus ends one story of an American hero.

✭✭✭✭✭✭✭✭✭✭✭✭✭✭✭✭✭✭✭

19

RUTHERFORD BIRCHARD HAYES

☆ ☆

		Popular	*Electoral*
VOTE OF 1876:	Rutherford B. Hayes, Republican	4,034,000	185
	Samuel J. Tilden, Democrat	4,286,000	184
	Peter Cooper, Greenbacker	82,000	
	Others	9,000	
		8,411,000	369

☆ ☆

IN THEIR BIOGRAPHY OF PRESIDENT HAYES, ECKENRODE AND WIGHT have this to say: "Rutherford B. Hayes has not appeared in the eyes of history as large of stature as he really was, because he was a normal man, and we instinctively believe that normality is mediocrity. Nearly all the other figures of the age were abnormal: Lincoln, emotional in youth to the point of hysteria; Grant, total failure dramatically turned into heroic success—and a drinker; Andrew Johnson, also heroic and also a drinker; Thaddeus Stevens, incarnation of hate, a fury rather than a man; Blaine, popular idol ruined by a genius for making enemies; Greeley, the eccentric; Conkling, with his 'turkey-gobbler strut.' What a stage of Dickensian characters it was! And Hayes the only normal one." [1]

Hayes's life, at nearly every point, touched on his native Ohio. He was born at Delaware, in the central part of Ohio; had a law practice in, and was elected to Congress from, Cincinnati, in the southern part; lived the latter part of his life, and lies buried, at Fremont, in the northern part. He was really a citizen of his state.

When Rutherford Hayes, father of the President, left the Puritanical surroundings of his native Vermont and arrived at Delaware in the Ohio country, together with his wife Sophia Birchard, he was worth $8,000—a considerable sum for those days.

[1] H. J. Eckenrode and Pocahontas W. Wight: *Rutherford B. Hayes: Statesman of Reunion*, p. 40; Dodd, Mead and Company.

Probably most important about not having to worry constantly about money is that one can devote all one's energies to other forms of success. It is not enjoyable, or easy, even for a healthy young man, to devote his best energies to business while following a course of study. Certainly Hayes, who was a frail child, could scarcely have flourished in the face of such a challenge.

Hayes was born—after his father's death—on October 4, 1822, the same year as Grant. One would think that under such circumstances his mother would have been the great influence in his life, but it was a bachelor uncle, Sardis Birchard. This man, who willed him his estate at Fremont, poured out all his unused paternal affection on the boy, paid for his education in public and private schools, and watched his progress avidly.

"Ruddy" was a deserving nephew. He was graduated at the head of his class at Kenyon College, and in 1845 completed his law studies at Harvard. He stayed five years at Fremont, then went to Cincinnati. In 1852 he married Miss Lucy Webb, and their marriage was a happy one, although three of their eight children died in youth.

From the time he was a young man, Hayes was interested in politics. He began as city solicitor in Cincinnati. Then there was an interval while he served in the Civil War. War had a certain fascination for him, and although he had a family, he volunteered as a captain. He was severely wounded at the Battle of South Mountain; was elected to Congress while still serving in the field; and left the war with the rank of brevet major-general. Grant referred to his conduct in battle as "conspicuous gallantry."

Although Hayes was re-elected to Congress, he did not particularly enjoy himself there. But he was a strict party adherent, a "sound money" man, and—what was so important in that era— a war veteran. By running such a man for Governor, the Republicans felt they had a sure thing. The organization named him for the post and he was elected and served three terms, the first Governor of his state to receive that distinction. By this time he had become a national figure and, of course, Presidential timber. It is an interesting commentary on Hayes's popularity to observe, that although he campaigned for an amendment to the state constitution to permit Negro suffrage at the same time that he campaigned for himself, the proposed amendment was defeated while he himself was elected. He was a good and useful Governor.

The year 1876 was the centennial of the birth of the United States and a world's fair was held at Philadelphia to commemorate it. It was celebrated also by the addition of a new state, Colorado, to the Union. But the year was notable also for the occurrence of a very serious crisis in the American Government, the crisis known as the Hayes-Tilden Controversy.

Two able and progressive candidates for the Presidency were put forward by the principal political parties in that year—Rutherford B. Hayes by the Republicans and the bachelor Samuel J. Tilden, successful Governor of New York, by the Democrats. The scandals of the Grant Administrations had caused a reaction making almost certain the election of a Democrat to the White House. In the Congressional elections of two years before, the Democrats had obtained a majority in the House. Now, in the Presidential year, Tilden received 250,000 more popular votes than Hayes and, by the original returns, a larger electoral vote also. But there were some disputed returns, mainly from certain Southern states where Republican or carpetbag governments still were official. Two sets of electors had been sent in from these states, one representing Hayes and one representing Tilden.

Obviously, it was the wish of the majority of the people in these states to vote for the Democratic candidate. But the Republicans would not accept this. An electoral commission was appointed, consisting of members of both houses of Congress and the Supreme Court. Their decision was final; and, since this commission represented a majority of Republicans, they voted along party lines and gave the election to Hayes. It was plainly dishonest. The new President was under a great handicap, from which he never felt entirely free, and was even referred to as "Rutherfraud" B. Hayes. But as his term wore on, the entire nation, including the South, came to respect both President Hayes and his wife.

A deal made in connection with the Democrats' accepting the Hayes decision was that the last Federal troops would be recalled from Louisiana and South Carolina where they had remained since Reconstruction days. Hayes at once withdrew them and that was also the end of the carpetbag governments. It meant in addition that the old-line Southern Democrats would be in control of their state governments and, regardless of the Fifteenth Amendment, would say whether the Negro would vote or not—and, of course, it meant for the most part that he would not. It was thus that the Solid South finally became solid. Strange as it may seem, Hayes still believed in the principle of military intervention in elections and for that reason never consented to repeal the laws with respect to this feature of the old Reconstruction program. Yet he never did actually intervene, and the South did at its elections as it pleased, and voted just as it does to this day.

We cannot write about the period of Hayes without saying something of the rise of Big Business as well as a matter related to it—sound money. In order to finance the Civil War, the national treasury had issued what it called "greenbacks," paper money not backed by gold or any other security, just the good name of the United States. This was called also "cheap money," and the farmers liked it. After the Panic of 1873, money became scarce. Then it was that the Greenback Party was formed whose platform was that enough greenbacks should be "manufactured" by the Government to meet the needs of the times regardless of whether there was gold or silver on hand to back it up or not. The Party entered a candidate for President in 1876, the eighty-five-year-old Peter Cooper, a successful industrialist who had established Cooper Union in New York where Lincoln made his Cooper Union address which brought him national fame.

Hayes vetoed the silver bill and other inflationary measures passed by Congress; although Congress passed them over his veto, the Administration's financial policies were successful in the long run. Confidence was restored, business picked up, farm prices rose, and the agitation for cheap money died down; so much so, that in 1880, with prosperity back, it was easy to elect a Republican as President again, regardless of the fraud of four years before. People forget easily; clearly their enthusiasm for a political administration can depend entirely on their economic condition. The period, lasting from 1879 to 1883, is sometimes called the "Gold Resumption Prosperity."

The dream of Jefferson, that the new American nation would be a democratic society composed principally of agricultural inhabitants, could, of course, not be realized. America was to become an industrial society on which farming was dependent, not the reverse. If there were any doubts about this during the *ante bellum* years, the Civil War settled them. For, after that holocaust, agriculture—and the South—knew that not cotton, not wheat, not packing, but Industrialism was King. And, for all practical purposes, Wall Street and Washington were its servants.

It could not be helped. The transcontinental railroad had been built, making raw materials from one end of the nation readily available to the other. Andrew Carnegie was building his steel empire on the banks of the Monongahela in Pennsylvania where inexhaustible coal fields existed. Oil, which was discovered in the same state, was responsible for another industry, an industry so great that it made America the envy of every other nation on the face of the earth. Great fortunes were being built in steel, coke, oil, transportation—fortunes which made themselves felt in education, art, and the philanthropies. Inventions were coming thick and fast. Westinghouse had brought out his air brake. Alexander Graham Bell, the Scotsman who invented the telephone, showed his discovery to President Hayes who had one installed in the White House. Thomas A. Edison invented the phonograph in 1877; the incandescent light in 1879. That year electric street lights were first put into use. That year Woolworth opened up the first five-and-ten-cent store in Utica, New York, laying the foundations for another fabulous fortune. In northern Minnesota a mighty mountain of iron ore was found, called the Mesabi Range. It is not too much to say that this mountain, owned by United States Steel Corporation, is responsible for transforming the shape of the United States into a nation entirely different from the one the Founding Fathers had in mind.

The population of the nation was growing at an amazing rate, immigrants coming from everywhere—even illiterate ones. This growing, ambitious, multi-talented population, plus big business, plus new technological discoveries, plus the great quantities of natural resources suddenly discovered—all were preparing America for a role in world leadership, whether it was wanted or not. We shall see what all this meant thirty-five years after Hayes left office and where it was leading.

Hayes thought of his job in the Presidency as being the work of "pacification," which meant, of course, the pacification of the

South. It is accurate to say that he succeeded in this job. No state of the South gave its vote to a Republican candidate for the White House until 1920, but the section was pacified just the same, and the important part that the genial Hayes played must be recognized.

A misunderstanding exists about who was responsible for barring intoxicating beverages from White House dinners during this Administration. Because of it and because the Women's Christian Temperance Union honored Mrs. Hayes on occasion, journalists have blamed her, and referred to her as "Lemonade Lucy." This is unfair because she was herself not a prohibitionist: it was her husband who believed in the cause; Lucy was only carrying out the President's wishes. At one of the official dinners, a Cabinet member remarked: "It was a brilliant affair; the water flowed like champagne." [2]

Hayes declared at the beginning that he would not be a candidate for re-election. At the close of his term he retired to his home, Spiegel Grove, the extensive place given him by his uncle, at Fremont. His last years were engaged in prison reform and educational projects; his death came peacefully on January 17, 1893. His funeral was attended by Grover Cleveland who had just been recalled to another term in the White House. Spiegel Grove with its vast collection of letters, books, and memorabilia was donated by the ex-President's son, Webb C. Hayes, to the State of Ohio as a historic shrine. The grave of Hayes is there.

Rutherford B. Hayes was not a great man as historians count greatness. But he was certainly the man of ordinary talents developed to the highest possible peak. He played politics occasionally, but when he did so, it was because of the larger eventual result in view and not because he compromised with his conscience. The entry he made in his diary when he was a young law student he had worthily carried out: "I will strive to become in manners, morals and feelings, a true gentleman."

[2] However, in 1883 Hayes refused to vote for a prohibition amendment to the Ohio constitution.

★★★★★★★★★★★★★★★★★★★★

20

JAMES ABRAM GARFIELD

☆ ☆

		Popular	*Electoral*
VOTE OF 1880:	James A. Garfield, Republican	4,454,000	214
	Winfield S. Hancock, Democrat	4,445,000	155
	James B. Weaver, Greenbacker	309,000	
	Others	10,000	
		9,218,000	369

☆ ☆

AMERICAN PRESIDENTS, OF COURSE, ARE MORE POWERFUL THAN THE kings of today, and more responsible for the fate of their country than contemporary royal rulers are. It can even be said that the history of the United States is read more accurately in the lives of its Presidents than is the history of modern kingdoms in the lives of its monarchs.

The President, who rules for only a specific term, is more powerful than the constitutional monarch, who rules for life, because his position combines the functions of sovereign and prime minister; because in his Executive Department he can initiate legislation; because of the weapon he holds in the veto power over acts of Congress; because of his appointive powers, which include patronage disposal; because of his authority in negotiating treaties; and because he is the titular head of the political party he represents as well as the nation he serves.

We do not hesitate, therefore, to acclaim or condemn men, alive or dead, who have exercised such power, when subsequent evidence and the perspective of time enable us to see beyond contemporary events.

However, as Garfield was President for only six months, two of which were spent on his deathbed, there is little one can say of his short term; but he did have an exceptionally busy life before his elevation to the Presidency. Few men have ever been so busy educating themselves and climbing to the top. His parents were Abram Garfield and Eliza Ballou, the latter of Huguenot origin. The President, the last one to be born in a log cabin, came into the world in the frontier town of Orange, in Cuyahoga County, Ohio, on November 19, 1831. During the whole of his short life he was a resident of this Cleveland vicinity.

His father died when James Abram was only eighteen months old. Helping the widowed mother later with the work on the farm was the main responsibility of the youth, together with his older brother. But he was restless; he soon wanted to leave home, as boys often do. A cousin got him a job with a canal boat, driving mules along the towpath. He was then sixteen. A long illness followed, after which his mother, recognizing the unusual mental capabilities of her boy, urged him to go further in school.

Garfield went first to an academy at Chester, Ohio; then he entered Eclectic Institute, later Hiram College, from which he was graduated in three years with high honors. After spending two years at Williams College in Massachusetts, where he again showed high scholarship, he returned to the Eclectic Institute to become professor of ancient languages and literature in 1856. A year later, at the age of twenty-six, he was made president of the school. One of his pupils was Lucretia Rudolph whom he afterwards married.

Garfield was successful as a college teacher. He also belonged to the sect known as the Disciples of Christ, or Campbellites, and was a lay preacher for them for a time. It was while preaching that he developed his powers of oratory which were such an outstanding part of his personality. But his interest veered toward politics; the classroom presented too narrow a horizon for him. In 1859 he became a candidate for the State Senate and was elected. In 1861 he was admitted to the bar on the strength of what he had taught himself.

The Civil War caught Garfield in its stream as it did most politically ambitious men of the time. He raised a company of soldiers from his district and started off as a lieutenant-colonel. He had had no previous military training, but he was able to get a commission because he held a college diploma. Garfield was outstanding for bravery in the war and showed particular distinction at Chickamauga, as a result of which he was made a major-general of volunteers. He was also chief-of-staff in Rosecrans's army.

Like his predecessor, Hayes, Garfield was elected to Congress while still in the service; unlike Hayes, he resigned his commission and took his seat in the House in 1863. Here he remained seventeen years, eventually becoming the Republican leader. During this period Garfield regrettably joined the Radicals and favored Andrew Johnson's impeachment. He did nothing outstanding in Congress, but he was a tireless worker and an excellent speaker.

Just as in the middle of the twentieth century the Republicans were divided into blocs called "Isolationists" and "Internationalists" and the Democrats into blocs called "Conservatives" and "New Dealers," so in Garfield's time the Republicans were divided into "Stalwarts" and "Half-Breeds." With the latter group, led by James G. Blaine, Senator from Maine and later Presidential candidate, Garfield became affiliated. Opposed to them was the faction led by Roscoe Conkling, Senator from New York and a great political power, the main force behind the idea of a third term for Grant.

When the political conventions of 1880 met, it seemed fairly certain that a Republican would win again in that year's Presidential race. Hayes's policy of pacification and the recovery from the six-year depression which began in 1873 had left the country purring like a cat by the parlor footstool. Conkling saw this as an ideal time to bring the war hero Grant before the people again. And Grant, like Barkis, "was willin'."

Garfield came to the convention as the manager of Senator John Sherman's campaign. However, the contest was strictly between Grant and Blaine and their forces were unyielding. Although Garfield, a Half-Breed, was by no means the best man the Republicans had available in 1880, he was chosen as a compromise. Like Blaine and others whose reputations suffered from the many scandals during the Grant regime, Garfield was tainted; but not enough to do him any permanent harm. To make everybody happy, Arthur, a Stalwart, was made his running-mate. The Republican victory which followed was by no means a walkaway. Garfield and Arthur did not win a majority of the votes cast and had only a 9,000 plurality over the Democratic candidate Hancock, who was a Civil War general and also popular.

Garfield tried hard after his inauguration to reconcile the two belligerent factions of his Party. But the Stalwarts were implacable. It is doubtful whether Garfield with his lack of assertiveness could ever have enjoyed a peaceful Administration. Even Grant complained to him about the appointments he made.

The most noteworthy accomplishment of the Garfield term was the establishment of the American Red Cross, which the founder, Clara Barton, had tried so unsuccessfully to have recognized during previous Administrations. Garfield declined Miss Barton's suggestion that he become the first president of the organization, pointing out that the honor belonged to Clara Barton herself.

It was on July 2, 1881 that the President was shot down in a railroad station in Washington by a fanatic of the Stalwart group who shouted that Arthur was now President. For two and a half months the nation watched and prayed fervently for the recovery of their gentle leader. Garfield himself gave several hints, as dying men so often do, that he would not recover; and at Elberon, New Jersey, whither he had been taken to escape the heat of the capital city, he died on September 19, 1881. He was not yet fifty years old.

Garfield, even if he had lived, would not have been a great man. Nevertheless, it could have been said of him as an adult what was said of him as a youth by one of his classmates: "He was modest and self-possessed and . . . absolutely free from any affectation whatever." He was a man of massive frame, six feet in height, with a large head. One of his contemporaries writes that although he had this impressive appearance, he had what was called a "gander eye," and that one became disquieted as a result of it; it prevented intimacy with him.

Seven children were born to the Garfields, and two of the sons had prominent positions in the Administrations of later Presidents —one under Theodore Roosevelt and one under Woodrow Wilson. As in the families of Grant and Hayes, there were enough boys in the family to keep the name alive for a long time. Garfield's last home was at Mentor, Ohio, and there, on the main road to Cleveland, one may see it today. His body, which lay in state immediately after his death, was later placed in an imposing tomb in Lake View Cemetery, Cleveland. The mausoleum is built of the sandstone of his native state and was erected with funds raised by popular subscription.

★★★★★★★★★★★★★★★★★★★★★★

21

CHESTER ALAN ARTHUR

☆ ☆

VOTE OF 1880: *See* under Garfield

☆ ☆

IN THE CENSUS OF 1880, THE YEAR ARTHUR AND GARFIELD WERE elected, the population of the United States was 50,000,000—an increase of 300% in forty years. In seventy years it was to increase another 300%.

The nation had grown tremendously, surviving a long and bloody civil war in the process, receiving immigrants from every quarter of Europe in unheard-of numbers, finding herself suddenly the beneficiary of every manner of new invention, discovering almost overnight her vast mineral wealth and her immense water-power potential, finding her riches and opportunities the envy of every other great power on the face of the earth.

Depressions came and went. And, we must add, were promptly forgotten. Not only are bad experiences forgotten, but their causes also.

It was during Arthur's time that John D. Rockefeller organized his colossal Standard Oil trust. Carnegie had already made his money and was beginning his benefactions of libraries and church organs. The Vanderbilts and their railroad empire were operating full blast. The banker J. Pierpont Morgan was beginning to be conscious of his power, a power which was to be exerted over the national well-being well into the next century. . . . It was not a time requiring greatness in a leader.

When Arthur was nominated for Vice-President, he was considered a nonentity, while Garfield was considered the man of statesman caliber. We cannot know what would have happened had Garfield lived; but as we study the two men in retrospect, we must conclude that the reverse was true. Garfield demonstrated none of the elements of greatness; Arthur did.

On October 5, 1830, at Fairfield, Vermont, where his father happened to hold a Baptist pastorate, Chester A. Arthur was born. His parents' names were William Arthur and Malvina Stone. Like most minor Protestant clergymen of those years, the father moved from charge to charge until, in 1844, we find him in Schenectady, New York, whence the fifteen-year-old Chester entered Union College. He was graduated in three years.

In 1853 Arthur went to New York City in search of his fortune. He had taught school for a while; but now he was to practice law, also just for a while, because politics beckoned. He became a trusted aide of Conkling, New York's great political boss and Senator. But before this, during the Civil War, he was a quartermaster-general, stationed in New York, in charge of equipping and transporting the State's regiments to the theater of war. He did a praiseworthy job; and then went back to the practice of law.

In 1871 President Grant appointed Arthur to the position of Collector of the Port of New York, a very important place indeed. In this position the new occupant conducted himself in the typical politician's manner, dispensing patronage and requiring support for his causes commensurate with such favors. Although his office, it seems, was somewhat overstaffed, as President Hayes's investigators contended, and some of his subordinates were not above taking bribes, Arthur himself was spotlessly above reproach. Six feet two inches in height, immaculately dressed at all times, and always dignified, he seems to us out of place in the company of these seamy payrollers. Hayes, in his zeal for reform in the civil service, nevertheless asked for Arthur's resignation. When he did not get it, he discharged him from office.

We have stated in Garfield's biography why Arthur was nominated for Vice-President. However, Roscoe Conkling, his mentor, whom the nomination was meant to please, was by no means pleased. It is all right to sponsor somebody, as Conkling had sponsored Arthur, so long as the sponsored one stays in a subordinate position. But if more than that happens, somebody's ego is liable to suffer, and there will be a storm. Conkling's ego was suffering now. He eventually broke with Arthur altogether. The latter humbly stated that the Vice-Presidency was a greater honor than he had ever expected to achieve in this life, and that if it was going to be offered to him, he was not going to decline it. He was imploring Mr. Conkling not to become angry. But Mr. Arthur went on to the Presidency and then Mr. Conkling really became angry.

Arthur's Administration surprised everybody. First of all, the entire Cabinet was overhauled, Robert Todd Lincoln alone being held over from the old regime. Arthur was not going to repeat the mistake of John Adams, who retained his predecessor's Cabinet for the sake of national efficiency only to learn that these men were showing their gratitude by conspiring against their Chief. Although a product of the spoils system in the fullest sense of that term, the President came all-out for civil service reform and signed the act by which the nation at last realized a bipartisan Civil Service Commission, the basic law of the land in that field to this day.

Besides civil service reform legislation, the Arthur Administration is best remembered for its advocacy of an up-to-date navy, the one then serving as such being outmoded and wholly inadequate; and the President's refusal to squander the surplus revenues then pouring into the national treasury. A conservative man through and through, the President insisted on applying the money to the reduction of the national debt, and urged the lowering of taxes.

This was surely not the conduct of a spoilsman. Arthur's prestige with the country grew, but not with the politicians. Mark Twain said of him: "I am but one of 55,000,000; still, in the opinion of one-fifty-five-millionth of the country's population, it would be hard to better President Arthur's Administration."

Although Arthur was a good President, he nevertheless made several mistakes while in office. He interfered in the gubernatorial contest in New York, hoping to get the Republican candidate elected there. This was the old politician coming out in him; and the result was that the Democrat Grover Cleveland, his successor in the White House, won the Governorship. Another mistake was his efforts in behalf of an isthmian canal through Nicaragua. The error here was not in desiring a sea-to-sea waterway in this area, a thing which all the great powers knew for a long time would some day have to be accomplished, but in its violation of a treaty America had with Great Britain respecting the matter. Papers actually were signed by Nicaragua and the United States; but Congress did not ratify and the incoming Administration withdrew the treaty as being a breach of good faith with a friendly power. The entire project, so far as Nicaragua was concerned, was abandoned.

Regardless of how sincerely Arthur attempted to carry out his oath as President of all the people, his political troubles mounted and his renomination could not be realized. He did not openly ask for a second term—he was too dignified for that—but he was known to be receptive to it as a vindication of his policies, just as any other man in his situation would have liked this reassurance. But he had alienated the Stalwarts headed by the "Turkey Gobbler" Conkling to whom he had even offered a post on the Supreme Court. Conkling had declined. The other faction, the Half-Breeds led by Blaine, were his enemies from the beginning. Grant, a perennial moaner and poor loser, also opposed his renomination. One would think that a man as near death as Grant would have other uses for his precious energy than to spend it assailing the policies of his successors in office. The House of Representatives went Democratic in the 1882 elections. There was no harbor in which Arthur could drop anchor. And so he was passed up in 1884 for that controversial man from Maine, James G. Blaine. Before he left office he dedicated the completed Washington Monument, work on which was begun back in 1848.

Arthur was a "high liver." He ate and drank too much, and it caused his premature death on November 18, 1886. He enjoyed being surrounded by nice things and congenial people. His wife had died shortly before he went to Washington, and his sister, as gracious a hostess as he was a host, presided over the social functions during his term. At one time the great singer Adelina Patti gave a concert at the White House for the Arthurs and their guests. That was the sort of thing the President liked. The big house on Pennsylvania Avenue had been comparatively gloomy since the Civil War. Arthur did not at once move into it after becoming President. He did not think the building a proper habitation for any President and promptly had renovations made and innovations installed, living at the Washington home of a friend until they were completed.

There were certain events during Arthur's term of office which, while not bearing on his abilities, are nevertheless milestones in American national life, properly identifiable with the Arthur years. One was an anti-polygamy act passed by Congress and aimed, of course, directly at the Mormons in Utah. Obedience to the law forbidding plural marriages was an absolute prerequisite to Utah's being admitted into the Union. It was 1890 before the Mormon church yielded on this point, and six years more before Utah became a state. Standard Time, by which the entire nation now abides, was adopted in 1884. The American Federation of Labor was organized at Pittsburgh in 1881. The first steel sky-scraper—ten stories high!—was erected in Chicago during this time. And Brooklyn Bridge, that first great suspension bridge in the world, fourteen years in construction and a saga in itself, was completed in 1883; Arthur participated in the dedicatory cere-monies.

Arthur's wife was Ellen Herndon, a Southerner; this partly explains why he got along so well with Southern members of Congress. They had three children. When Arthur died, only a son and a daughter survived. In Albany, New York, where his father eventually had lived, Chester A. Arthur was buried beside his kin in Rural Cemetery. His real home was on Lexington Avenue, New York; it was there that he died at the age of fifty-six.

★★★★★★★★★★★★★★★★★★★★★★★

22

GROVER CLEVELAND

☆ ☆

		Popular	Electoral
VOTE OF 1884:	Grover Cleveland, Democrat	4,875,000	219
	James G. Blaine, Republican	4,852,000	182
	Benjamin F. Butler, Greenbacker	175,000	
	Scattered	162,000	
		10,064,000	401
VOTE OF 1888:	*See* under Harrison		
VOTE OF 1892:	Grover Cleveland, Democrat	5,557,000	277
	Benjamin Harrison, Republican	5,176,000	145
	James B. Weaver, Populist	1,041,000	22
	Scattered	283,000	
		12,057,000	444

☆ ☆

IF THE TWO TERMS OF GROVER CLEVELAND IN THE PRESIDENCY
teach us anything, it is that people simply do not care about a
steady, plodding, unspectacular performance of right conduct;
it is, for the most part, the dramatic and glittering action, which
pleases and gains support. As a study of Cleveland's acts during
that imperialistic era makes us understand that he was almost always correct in his judgments, so it also makes us conscious once
more of the fact that it is the good things of life that are likely
to be undramatic.

There were several precedents realized in connection with
Cleveland's accession to the Presidency. He was the first Democrat
to be sent to the White House since the election of 1856, a long
interval indeed, one that not every political party could survive.
And Cleveland was the first (and only) twice-elected President
whose terms were not consecutive.

We might point out also the incredible fact that three years
before his election he was absolutely unknown to the country!

In 1881, when he was forty-four years old, he was elected mayor of Buffalo on a reform ticket; in 1882 he was elected Governor of New York on the basis of his performance in the mayoralty job; and in 1884 he was nominated for President on the record of his Governorship.

Although he was a reform executive, he was a conservative to his fingertips, as much so as his Republican predecessor Arthur. He was not of the progressive school of Theodore Roosevelt or Woodrow Wilson. Consequently, he was not spectacular, not an opportunist, not an innovator, and may well have been the last conservative Democrat the American nation will ever see in such an important position. His forte definitely was in conserving and guarding that which America possessed.

This President was born at Caldwell, New Jersey, on March 18, 1837. His father, a Presbyterian minister, had his charge in this place, and was named Richard Falley Cleveland; his mother was Anne Neal; there were eight other children besides the child originally called Stephen Grover. When he was four years old, Grover (who was to discard his christened name of Stephen) lived in Fayetteville, New York, where his father's pastorate had been moved; he remained there ten years. What childhood memories he had are of this place. Next, his parents made a short move to Clinton, New York; and finally to Holland Patent, in Oneida County of that state, where his father died. Grover was then sixteen years old.

The death of his father meant that the son's chances for a college education had vanished. The Cleveland boys were no angels, as ministers' sons seldom are; but Grover was a studious and ambitious youth. The tradition of learning had been strong in the family for generations. And it means more to the preparation of a young man for a useful life to have a tradition like that in his strain than it does to possess genius or influence or money without such a tradition. Grover Cleveland could never have become President had he not descended from a long line of educated and clerical forebears. The times were conducive to making the man, as the times always are. The times were still raw when Cleveland was young, and one did not need an elaborate education in order to become a lawyer. After all, there was only twenty-eight years' difference between Lincoln's and Cleveland's ages, so that the latter would hardly have had a harder time being admitted to the bar in New York than the former had in Illinois.

After working for a while with his brother as a teacher in a school for the blind in New York City, Cleveland determined to head West, his destination Cleveland in Ohio, a city founded by a distant relative. At Buffalo he stopped off to visit with an uncle and aunt who convinced him that his chances were just as good in Buffalo. The uncle was a man of means, employed the nephew himself and got him into a law office, which was what Cleveland wanted. In 1859 he was admitted to the bar. Four years later he was appointed assistant district attorney for Erie County; then he became sheriff of the County. It was then only a step into the mayoralty of Buffalo, the home also of Millard Fillmore, where the old ex-President still held forth in legal and educational circles.

Since we are discussing here a man who became a constructive and useful public servant, it is interesting to consider his beginnings and the background of his experience. Why would a man of so conservative a temperament, a dyed-in-the-wool Presbyterian, become a Democrat? His clergyman father's anti-abolitionist views had a lot to do with it, just as Arthur's clergyman father's abolitionist views influenced that President's association with the Republican Party. Although Cleveland lived in the home of his cultured uncle and aunt, he did not follow them politically or socially. Frankly, his companions were of the barroom variety. Like Harry S. Truman two generations and more later, he entered politics at the precinct level. But when he assumed a higher responsibility he was able to forget the precinct and grapple with the issues on a higher level. As his opportunities rose, his horizon widened and his perceptions increased correspondingly. That is what we call growth, and it is this which makes Cleveland the man he remains in our memories.

When he ran for President, his opponents did not hesitate to refer to his ward politics beginnings, his saloon days and questionable company, even trotting out unsavory facts regarding his fathering of an illegitimate child. With courage, an admirable courage but rarely found, he advised his followers about how to meet these charges. "Tell the truth," he insisted.

It is a tribute to the American people that even in those smug

Victorian days unfavorable revelations about a man's moral life were not enough to bar him from public office, especially when he admitted his error and submitted evidence to show he was meeting the responsibilities posed by that error.

When conscription was adopted during the Civil War, a draftee could avoid service by either hiring a substitute or paying the Government $300. Cleveland hired a substitute and this also was a campaign talking-point for his political enemies. But Cleveland, who was a bachelor for so long, had been giving financial support to his mother and sisters at Holland Patent. This, and the fact that his brothers were doing their share in the cause of the Union, he probably felt, did not put a large obligation on him to serve.

Cleveland was not Governor long, but it was long enough to bring him before the people as a reformer at a time when the hue and cry was "Throw the rascals out!" He had governed irrespective of who would be hurt and he had thus alienated Tammany Hall, that great New York City political institution, without whose help no Democrat of the time would have thought of risking a campaign.

In 1884, the people practically demanded Cleveland's nomination as President. His opponent was the popular idol James G. Blaine. Writers like to declare that Blaine lost the election because of an over-zealous clergyman supporter who referred to the Democrats as the party of "Rum, Romanism, and Rebellion," thus making hostile the heavy Irish Catholic vote of New York City, so necessary to the winning of New York State's precious electoral vote. It is more likely, however, that Blaine lost his case before the people because his own past had been tainted and because his personal cause had simply become stale. He had been a contender too long. The people were in no mood for staleness: they wanted a fresh start with a new face, and they turned to a more or less charmless man to give it to them. This unglamorous personality won with a plurality over his opponent of only 23,000 votes. Four years later Cleveland had a plurality of 100,000, but lost in the Electoral College; and four years after that, at his second victory, he had a plurality of 380,000. In the 1884 election, a shift of only 524 votes in New York would have won Blaine the Presidency.

Cleveland at once became a famous veto President. As in his

predecessor's time—and in our own time, for that matter—the treasury was being raided by Congressmen to supply local needs and thus secure their hold on their constituents. In Cleveland's first term these raids took the form of Civil War pensions. Pensions were being voted to everybody and anybody, and President Cleveland simply would not sign these bills without going into the merits of each case.

Whereas in the ninety-six years of American national life before Cleveland's accession, only 132 veto messages had been sent in by 21 Presidents, Cleveland in his first term alone issued 413 vetoes. Not only these vetoes but his attitude toward the civil service made enemies for him. Practically 85,000 positions were added to the classified list and taken out of the patronage machinations while he was President.

In his second term, however, Cleveland did not have so easy a time of it. He had a depression on his hands at once in the Panic of 1893, the year in which the world's Columbian Exposition was held at Chicago. The people blamed the President for the depression just as they were to blame Herbert Hoover thirty-six years later. But, unlike Hoover, Cleveland did not try to relieve the distressed or provide employment or help business. He felt that natural laws would take care of that in their own time. Hundreds of banks failed in this panic; great railroads like the Reading and the Erie went bankrupt. The truth is that the latter part of Cleveland's first term and all of Harrison's term had been a period of prosperity—"railroad prosperity" they called it—and it was now time for a cycle of bad years.

The Pullman strike happened about this time and Cleveland's handling of it would be considered a great blunder today. It was this strike that brought to the national attention Eugene V. Debs, later a frequent Socialist candidate for President, who headed the union of Pullman workers. Although the Governor of Illinois contended that his state's militia was sufficient to deal with the situation, Cleveland, against the Governor's wishes, sent 2,000 Federal troops to Chicago and broke the strike. The President's argument was that he had to see that the flow of mail would be assured. "If it takes the entire army and navy of the United States to deliver a postal card in Chicago, that card will be delivered," was his characteristic assertion. With all the pro-labor legislation on

America's books now, such a step as Cleveland took would be considered politically suicidal today. Debs was sent to jail, but it was not the last the nation was to hear of him nor the last time he would be sent to jail.

Before judging Cleveland for being more concerned with the uninterrupted delivery of the mails than with the fate of the workers in the Pullman community, who had a real grievance, we must recognize that in his time the nation, as well as the Supreme Court, had not yet taken the view that whatever might be covered by the General Welfare provision of the American Constitution was a fit matter for Federal intervention. On the contrary, the feeling always had been that what authority was not specifically delegated to the central Government was still strictly a province of the states, and, by this interpretation, Cleveland was correct. But an act passed in his Administration, the Interstate Commerce Act, later gave the Federal interventionists all the power they needed to settle labor-management disputes in industries whose operations were reflected in interstate trade.

In those days, whenever the times became bad the silver issue came up. A wider coinage of this metal was to be the subject of agitation in and out of Congress for a long time, not just by the Western mining interests but also by the farmers. During Hayes's term a silver purchase act was pushed through and in Harrison's term another. After trying to meet the heavy drain of gold away from the country in several other ways first, Cleveland at last decided that there was only one way to save the money structure of the nation and that was to repeal the silver acts. In this he was successful; but from then on his real enemies were those of his own party, so that he was unable to endorse the Party's nominee for President in the next election.

Periodically in the United States, a new political party has appeared on the national scene, made up of perennial malcontents pointing only to the workingman's plight. They are sometimes led by an eloquent but meagerly informed leader whose real grievance is rooted as much in his own frustrated ambitions as in the condition of the laboring classes. The Populists of Cleveland's time, the Progressives led by LaFollette in 1924, and the Progressives of Henry A. Wallace in 1948 are examples of such third-party movements in recent times.

In the Presidential election of 1892 the Populists carried Kansas, Colorado, Iowa, and Nevada. They advocated the free and unlimited coinage of silver at the ratio of 16 to 1, a graduated income tax, the election of U.S. Senators by popular vote, postal savings banks, Government ownership of public utilities, and a national paper currency by Government issue only.

The Populists and the silver Democrats made common cause and named the same man as their candidate for President in 1896— William Jennings Bryan, a young man of great presence and oratorical gifts. There was another economic depression at the time of this election. The people blamed it on silver, and Bryan, lacking the support of the conservative section of his party, lost the contest.

What really happened in Cleveland's last term was that the defeat of silver showed the complete victory of manufacturing over agriculture in the national economy. In case the Northern victory over the South in the Civil War did not clarify this sociological transformation in the American nation, the silver battles won by the conservatives of Cleveland's stripe clarified it finally for all who had eyes to see.

The foreign policy of Grover Cleveland is a truly noteworthy one. We have remarked about his withdrawal of Arthur's treaty with Nicaragua. He now withdrew Harrison's annexationist treaty with Hawaii. To Cleveland this was imperialism pure and simple. He could not conscientiously take his country down the imperialist path; notwithstanding the educators, journalists, and Congressmen who beat their breasts for the old-fashioned expansionism. It may be that, as his opponents declared, Cleveland was blind to the compulsions of Manifest Destiny; but destiny to him had to be more than manifest: it had to be spotlessly above suspicion. American imperialists—"apostles of democracy to alien peoples," they preferred to be called—saw nothing inconsistent in castigating England for her colonialism while they themselves advocated annexations.

In the Venezuela dispute between that country and Great Britain, Cleveland reaffirmed the Monroe Doctrine, tested it in a truly provocative manner, and compelled Britain to arbitrate the boundary claims, a thing she had been unwilling to do previously.

Cleveland's firm stand strengthened America's world position, naturally, and did a lot for Cleveland's prestige also.

Cleveland was still a bachelor when he entered the White House, but soon thereafter he married his ward, Francis Folsom, daughter of his Buffalo law partner; they had two sons and three daughters. With this family he retired to Princeton, New Jersey, a Presbyterian stronghold in which he felt at home, and where he became a trustee of the University and a friend of its president Woodrow Wilson. He was not to live long enough to see Wilson succeed him as the next Democrat in the White House, for he died June 24, 1908, and was buried in Princeton Cemetery. His grave is not far from that of the tragic Aaron Burr.

The outstanding facet in Cleveland's character was his courage. His vetoes, his defiance of Tammany, his silver and civil service policies, his refusal to endorse Bryan, his refusal to subjugate lesser peoples: we cannot ignore his good Presidency. When he was the county sheriff, one of his duties was to spring the trap at public hangings. This troubled him so that the first time the requirement came up he visited his mother to ask her advice. Since the law permitted it, she suggested that he pay somebody to do this ugly duty; but he declined, saying he would not ask another to do what he would not do himself.

Cleveland's character was little understood while he lived. To us, looking at it from this distance, it is difficult to see why. Unemotional, undramatic, hating publicity, indifferent to money, lover of children, hater of sham, possessor of moral courage to an extraordinary degree: What else can we say of such a man—not a genius, not a mystic, not a philosopher—but a constant, faithful performer of his duty.

Grover Cleveland was not a literary man but he was indeed a phrasemaker, and he is being quoted even to this very day. "It is a condition which confronts us, not a theory," is possibly his best known saying. Another is, "I can bear all I have to bear." These sayings are timeless, but none is so timeless as his last words: "I have tried so hard to do right."

★★★★★★★★★★★★★★★★★★★★★★★

23

BENJAMIN HARRISON

☆ ☆

		Popular	*Electoral*
VOTE OF 1888:	Benjamin Harrison, Republican	5,440,000	233
	Grover Cleveland, Democrat	5,540,000	168
	Scattered	400,000	
		11,380,000	401

VOTE OF 1892: *See* under Cleveland

☆ ☆

THE AMERICAN PEOPLE FOUND BENJAMIN HARRISON'S FOUR YEARS in the Presidential office frustrating. There were at least four reasons for this: he was himself not an imaginative person; the people didn't really want him from the first—they gave him 100,000 fewer votes than they gave his opponent; his term was sandwiched between the two terms of a really forthright executive; and the heroic family name he bore did not confer upon him the expected magic.

President Harrison's boyhood was spent on a farm at North Bend, Ohio, near Cincinnati, which was also the home of his famous Indian fighter grandfather. Here he was born on August 20, 1833, the son of John Scott Harrison and Elizabeth Irwin. His rise, like everything else in his life, was inconspicuous. He was graduated from Miami University in 1852, read law in Cincinnati, married Caroline Scott, and moved to Indianapolis to practice his profession.

He started his career as city attorney; his famous name, naturally, was a big help to him. During the War between the States he took part in Sherman's Atlanta campaign, as well as in other engagements, and came out with a brigadier-general's rank. He ran for Governor of Indiana in 1876 but lost by a slim margin. Hayes named him in 1879 to the Mississippi River Commission.

After taking part in the Garfield campaign, he declined a place in that President's Cabinet in favor of a seat in the United States Senate. After a single term in the Senate, he failed to be re-elected.

In 1888 Harrison was exactly the innocuous type of Presidential candidate the Republicans needed—he had no outstanding talents to which one could point, but also no "dead cats" in his life to which his opponents could point. He "defeated" Cleveland in that anomalous election. The perversity of the American Electoral College system, whereby the winner of the majority of a state's popular vote wins the vote of the entire state, enabled Harrison to become President while receiving only 47.8% of the vote cast by the people of the nation. It is for this reason that an amendment to the Constitution outlawing the electoral system has been so earnestly sought in the Congresses of recent years.

Much of what Cleveland had built up in his pension vetoes Harrison tore down by favoring pensions, and thus America's budget for that sort of expenditure was increased 50%. The Government was still experiencing an excess of revenues over expenditures, even without an income tax, and it is clear that politicians wanted to use that excess as vote bait by spending it where it would gain them the biggest support for the longest time.

Of course, if you are hunting for places to spend your money, people will gladly make the task easy for you; and the disparity between the length of time it takes for a surplus to appear and the time it takes for it to disappear is something men and nations can soon find out. Naturally, the surplus soon disappeared. And the Panic of 1893 was around the corner.

Three pieces of legislation in the Harrison Administration deserve comment: the McKinley Tariff, the Sherman silver purchase legislation, and the Sherman Anti-Trust Act. The silver purchase law had to be repealed, as we have seen, when Cleveland came back to the White House, in order to save the gold basis of the nation's fiscal system. The Republicans weren't enthusiastic about silver purchase in the first place, even though a Senator of their own party had sponsored the legislation; but they passed it to keep the agrarian interests quiet for a while. Fathered by a future President, the new tariff, which raised duties generally, was the Republican Party's declaration to the world that thenceforth Protection was practically to constitute its oath of allegiance to their party; protection, that is, for domestic manufacturers by imposition of prohibitive duties on imports of foreign competitors. There was a reciprocal feature to the law, however, whereby certain nations who granted the United States concessions for its goods received concessions in return. But to high tariffs the farmers and the South were still hostile—their historic position.

As a sop to the people for this tariff bill, the Congress passed the Sherman Anti-Trust Act of 1890. The word "trust" is not, strictly speaking, used properly in this connection. What is really meant is monopoly. The new law was intended to break up big combines or monopolies which often pyramided up to some oddly-named holding company representing a powerful family or group which might be accused of operating in "restraint of trade," thus preventing healthy competition in a free market and depriving the people of potential cuts in prices. There were no teeth in the Sherman law, as it was intended to be more or less harmless; not a single indictment under it was made during the McKinley Administration. It was only in 1914 that an enforcing supplement to the law was realized through the creation of the Federal Trade Commission and the enactment of the Clayton Anti-Trust law. But there were many trusts—and are still—and we hear more about them during the stormy Theodore Roosevelt's term of office, and about prosecutions of them in the term of William Howard Taft.

It was in 1889 that Oklahoma was opened to the public for settlement under the Homestead Act. Originally the section had been set aside by Congress as Indian Territory, for possession by five southern tribes. At noon of the day that Harrison proclaimed the area opened, 20,000 people were poised at the border. All the lands—2,000,000 acres in all—were claimed in less than twenty-four hours, and the scramble gave the future state its nickname of Sooner State; some of the homesteaders entered the area "sooner" than they legally had the right to enter.

In addition to opening up this section, which marked the end of the frontier for Americans, six states were added to the Union during Harrison's Administration—Washington, Idaho, Montana, Wyoming, North Dakota, and South Dakota.

In the 1840's and 1850's, when America really became conscious of her growing pains, the advocates of the territorial extension of the United States were, of course, called Expansionists. In those days the North and East were interested in expansion only if the acquisition in prospect meant territory free from slavery. After America's internal war settled that issue, Northern entrepreneurs favored expansion again—anywhere this time. But now it was to be called Imperialism, in allusion to the imperialist conquests and ambitions of the other world powers.

Pierce, Seward, Grant, Blaine and others were of the imperialist school. When Cleveland came to Washington the second time, the Harrison government presented him with what it thought was a *fait accompli*, the Hawaii annexation. In 1884 the United States had obtained rights to use Pearl Harbor as a naval base. It also had a trade treaty with the Islands. The situation in Hawaii was remarkably similar to that in Texas when Mexican rule was overthrown. First, there was the heavy infiltration of Americans into the Islands; then American capital entered into the picture and tied in with the native production; then there was a conspiracy to overthrow the native government of Queen Liliuokalani; then American marines landed, ostensibly to protect American life and property, but actually to help get the Queen out; then a "republic" was established with an American as its first president; then came the request of the new republic for absorption into the domain of the United States. It was the old formula. In the closing days of his term, Harrison sent the Hawaiian treaty to the Senate for ratification. Because of Cleveland's resistance to this perfect example of imperialism, annexation was held up until 1898.

Since Blaine, Harrison's Secretary of State, was an expansionist, it is interesting to see what he did about Pan-Americanism. Blaine was concerned, and we think rightly so, because Latin America was enjoying the favorable balance of trade in her commerce with the United States. The coffee, rubber, and sugar of the South American republics found an eager market in the United States, but the wares of the United States did not find a similar market in South America. That continent's purchases were made in the part of the globe where she had her strongest cultural ties— Europe and the Mediterranean basin. Blaine called a conference in 1889–90 which formed the basis of the later Pan-American Union. Pan-Americanism and the Monroe Doctrine were intertwined; but the policies of the United States towards South America in Blaine's

time did not have the disinterestedness they had in later times, so
that its motives were always suspect in South America. In fact,
Germany, not a Latin country, was more successful then in her
commercial dealings with South America than was the United
States. Thus, when Hoover and Franklin D. Roosevelt came to
power, the United States had to have a new approach; it was called
the Good Neighbor Policy.

The first Mrs. Harrison died in the White House. After he left
office, Harrison married his deceased wife's niece, Mary Erskine
Dimmick. He had a son and daughter by his first marriage and a
daughter by his second. On March 13, 1901, the 23rd President
died; he lies buried in Crown Hill Cemetery, Indianapolis.

Certainly nobody else in the country had as illustrious an ancestry as Benjamin Harrison.[1] Benjamin Harrison the Signer, who
was also a Governor of Virginia, was the great-grandfather of
Benjamin Harrison the President. General William Henry Harrison, the ninth President, was his grandfather. John Scott Harrison,
a member of Congress, was his father. Nevertheless, the Benjamin
Harrison of 1889–93 failed to rise to excellence of statesmanship.
This is not to say that Harrison was a failure in the Presidential
office: he was simply a disappointment. And the fault for that disappointment may lie as much with the public for having unwar-
rantedly expected great things of a name alone.

[1] There have been Benjamin Harrisons and William Henry Harrisons galore
in the United States. One of the latter, a grandson of the subject of this
biography, was a Congressman from Wyoming in the 1950's.

24

★★★★★★★★★★★★★★★★★★★★★★★★★

WILLIAM McKINLEY

☆ ☆

		Popular	Electoral
VOTE OF 1896:	William McKinley, Republican	7,107,000	271
	William Jennings Bryan, Democrat and Populist	6,533,000	176
	Scattered	312,000	
		13,952,000	447
VOTE OF 1900:	William McKinley, Republican	7,218,000	292
	William Jennings Bryan, Democrat	6,357,000	155
	Eugene V. Debs, Social Democrat	93,000	
	Scattered	300,000	
		13,968,000	447

☆ ☆

DEATH HAS SUCH A PROFOUND EFFECT ON US THAT IN MOURNING WE often do not see the shortcomings of the life cut short. The shortcomings of McKinley's life are now so obvious that it is astonishing to us today that McKinley's contemporaries passed over them.

Today we no longer deprecate McKinley's martyrdom. We deprecate only the uselessness of the war he waged. Theodore Roosevelt, his successor, could clamor for war and nothing particularly inappropriate was noted, for people knew that he was simply acting in character. But when McKinley, a naturally pacific and sober man, took the mighty American people to war against a second-rate power who did not want to fight—then a violation of Nature took place. Considering it, we are surprised and affronted.

Cleveland, in whose last term of office the problem in Cuba arose which led to the Spanish-American War, was handling the situation in a statesmanlike manner—which is to say, he was not trying to show off America's superiority, was seeking honorable solutions, protecting the Monroe Doctrine, and resisting with all his might the imperialists at home. When he left office, he warned McKinley of the explosion which could be touched off if the situation were mishandled; he was satisfied that McKinley believed as he did, and McKinley did—at first.

Cuba, which Spain had ruled for four centuries, had rebelled before 1895, when the revolution began that confronted Cleveland. America had always been sympathetic to the desire for freedom on the part of a dependency, no doubt becauses it was once a dependency itself.

In this latest fight for independence some American investments suffered—the interest of U.S. expansionists in Cuba also was nothing new. Spain made reprisals on the revolutionaries and herded the captives into concentration camps.

Agitation for American intervention in Cuba and for war with Spain had been going on in several American newspapers, notably those of William Randolph Hearst and Joseph Pulitzer; these two men are answerable to as great a degree as McKinley for influencing the decision in favor of needless war. Congressmen, pressed from various quarters to do *something*, were trying to force Cleveland's hand while he was still in the White House. Cleveland was considering buying the island as a final solution. He maintained that buying Cuba would be cheaper than paying for it in a war. But that was not what incendiaries at home wanted. It had been thirty years since the United States had had a war. And savage instincts were stirring.

Theodore Roosevelt, then the immature Assistant Secretary of the Navy, wrote to Henry Cabot Lodge, the Senator from Massachusetts: "The clamor of the peace faction has convinced me that this country needs a war. . . . I rather hope the fight will come soon." He also referred to the President as a "white-livered cur" and said he had "no more backbone than a chocolate eclair."

To some extent, Roosevelt was correct. Had McKinley stood up to the situation, appealed to his countrymen, been faithful to his original feelings, his countrymen would have supported him. But they saw in him no leadership, no assertiveness, so that when the imperialists showed assertiveness, the people allowed them to lead, and let the war come.

When we read of the things prominent men among the imperialists had to say in those days, we are shocked. Listen to the scholarly Albert J. Beveridge, Senator from Indiana and author of a noted biography of Lincoln. He actually stated that God "has made us the master-organizers of the world to establish system where chaos reigns. . . . He has marked the American people as his chosen nation to finally lead in the regeneration of the world. This is the divine mission of America . . ." And the famous editor and friend of Presidents, William Allen White, said: "It is the Anglo-Saxon's manifest destiny to go forth as a world conqueror." Today, it is clear that this babble was uttered to hurry America into a war with a weak Spain.

McKinley's home was in Canton, not far from Cleveland, where his remains lie. His original home was Niles, Ohio, where he was born January 29, 1843. His parents were William McKinley and Nancy Allison, and the father was a foundryman with a large family.

During the Civil War, young McKinley volunteered; he came out of the service a brevet major. He studied law in Mahoning County, Ohio, was admitted to the bar, and settled in Canton where he became active in the local Republican organization. In 1876 he first went to Congress and was re-elected a number of times. His name is attached to the McKinley Tariff Act of 1890, a measure in which the rates were moved sharply upward. The Panic of 1893 was attributed by many people to this tariff. Whether this was so or not, there was general dissatisfaction in the nation with this Act, and Cleveland, upon returning to the White House, was committed to altering it.

Apart from his role in this overwhelmingly protectionist legislation, which pleased business leaders, McKinley's public life was not noteworthy before becoming President. His administration as Governor of Ohio for two terms, 1891–95, was colorless. He had married Miss Ida Saxton, their two young daughters had died. His wife became permanently invalided, and his constant consideration for her received much publicity. America was coming into the age when gentleness toward "our noble womanhood" was as potent a vote-getter as a feeling for "the underdog."

The person responsible more than anybody else for making McKinley President was Marcus A. Hanna, a traction magnate and Senator from Ohio—the very symbol of big business, the *status*

quo, and protective tariffs. With a huge campaign fund, he succeeded in getting his protégé nominated and elected. He had the
campaign stress the gold basis of the American monetary system,
with the assertion that prosperity was the natural corollary of
gold. McKinley had been a bi-metallist earlier in his career, but
his switch now to the anti-silverites was not explained. He did
not need to explain it; it was all too clear. He stayed at home and
conducted a "front porch" campaign, while his opponent Bryan
traveled thousands of miles over the country preaching the
cause of silver.

McKinley was a typical trading politician. One of his friends,
to whom he had promised an attorneyship after he became President, lamented: "If it was necessary to sacrifice a weak friend to
propitiate a powerful enemy he would not hesitate for one moment
to do so." He said further, and at a time when McKinley's popularity was still high, that in no sense did the man have the outstanding qualities of character the people believed.[1] But because
in his dying breath he mentioned the Deity, millions of religious
people concluded that here was not only a man of God, but a great
humanitarian. He was in no sense of the word either thing.

Bryan was a young man when he ran for President—only
thirty-six—inexperienced in too many aspects of life to be telling
Americans what was best for them. The sensation which thoughtful people experienced on hearing him was not unlike what seasoned churchgoers feel when a raw theology student stands in
the pulpit and attempts to expound to them the eternal verities.
The doom of Bryan's silver program, favored by the mining states
and by farmers generally, could already be seen by 1896. The
country was in another one of its cyclical depressions and Hanna
was able to convince the voters that gold alone would save it.
The contest, to state it by oversimplification, was like one between
the powerful forces of capital, and labor.

Bryan lost for another reason, one that men in public life rarely
seem to understand: he tried too hard to win. He was not philo-
sophical and had meager intellectual equipment; it was not the last
time that he was to be on the losing side of a cause. Bryan can be

[1] John S. Wise: *Recollections of Thirteen Presidents*, p. 228; Doubleday &
Company.

described as sincere and personally dramatic, as most men of eloquence are.

In 1900 America had these two candidates before it again. When he lost the contest in 1896, Bryan had moaned: "I have borne the sins of Grover Cleveland"—a rationalization which may have given him temporary comfort. But in 1900 Bryan had a real cause. He ran as an anti-imperialist, fighting against the same thing Grover Cleveland fought against. But it was too late. America had been victorious in battle, had vanquished an ancient colonial power, had acquired distant colonies of her own and—above all— was enjoying prosperity, the kind that war always brings, but which the 76,000,000 Americans of that time did not yet understand was spurious. The Republicans of the time had as their slogan, "The full dinner pail."

The second defeat of Bryan was interpreted as an acquiescence by the people in imperialism, the high tariff, and the gold standard. On March 14, 1900, the nation had officially adopted the gold standard to which the leading European nations had adhered, and by which the American dollar was thenceforth to be comprised of 25.8 grains of gold nine-tenths fine. This step was to hold steady the fiscal structure of the country for thirty-three years.

Meanwhile, the war against Spain, for which imperialists had worked so zealously, had been precipitated. When modern nations go to war, it is ostensibly over what is called an "incident." In reality, they have already made up their minds to have hostilities, but are waiting for that incident which will give them an ostensible reason to start things going. In the Spanish-American War the incident was the sinking of the battleship *Maine* in Havana harbor with the loss of 260 lives. Ostensibly, the battleship was there "protecting American interests," and, ironically, it *was* there for that purpose. Nobody will ever know how this ship was blown up. It lay at the bottom of the harbor and in 1912 was raised, examined, towed out to sea, and sunk again. No board of inquiry has ever been able to establish anything. The incendiaries in America were convinced this was a plot on the part of Spain, and, as a final effort to plunge the country into war, pointed to the incident as a stain on American honor. The more reflective people were not so sure, since the real facts were not known. The facts were not known; but what the country did not know also was that Roosevelt, Hearst, Lodge, *et al* could raise a tumult more powerful than McKinley's weak hand, more powerful than Mark Hanna and the business leaders who definitely did not want war with its inseparable companion—inflation.

There was another "incident" which accelerated the war fever, known as the de Lôme affair. De Lôme was the Spanish Ambassador to the United States who, in writing to a friend in Cuba, referred to President McKinley as "a caterer to the rabble" and disparaged him generally. When this letter was intercepted and its contents made public, de Lôme immediately resigned; but the American people were led to believe that the letter represented Spain's real policy and that in negotiation with respect to Cuba she had all along been insincere.

The Spanish government now made the greatest effort to avert war. Early in April 1898, the month in which the United States declared war, the American Minister to Madrid cabled McKinley: "If you can still give me time . . . I will get you the peace you want so much." And the very day before the President read his message to Congress asking for a declaration of war, the Minister again cabled that Spain was ready to accede to every one of America's requirements respecting Cuba, even to the point of ceding the island to the United States. McKinley deliberately ignored this last message and had war declared April 19, 1898. The clamor for war by certain powerful newspapers; the anti-Spanish feeling among many clergymen who felt they were doing true missionary work by pointing to the plight of the down-trodden Cubans; the criticism of the President by the younger members of his Party for temporizing; the impassioned cry of "Remember the *Maine*" among the people; the disillusionment over the de Lôme letter; the ever-recurring arguments about Manifest Destiny—these were forces McKinley could not stand up against.

The war was a walkaway. The new American navy, begun in Chester A. Arthur's time, operated wonderfully: it destroyed the enemy's fleet in Santiago harbor, while Admiral Dewey destroyed another enemy fleet in Manila harbor. Theodore Roosevelt and his so-called Rough Riders made their much-publicized charge up San Juan Hill by Santiago, as the result of which he was named Governor of New York and, in 1900, Vice-President of the

United States. The military was actually quite inefficient in these campaigns, operating generally in a way that was outmoded. Sanitary conditions were horrifying. There were over 5,400 American deaths in the conflict, almost all of them from disease.

The peace negotiations revealed the full truth: that the United States was interested in something more than the liberties of its weak neighbor Cuba. America wanted Guam, Puerto Rico, and, so as to keep up with everybody else in the empire business, a Far Eastern possession—the Philippines, to be specific. Spain did not understand this last demand, for those distant islands had never been mentioned in any of their correspondence with the United States before.

America agreed at length to pay Spain $20,000,000 for the Philippines, and the rationalization by the President of this act is breathtaking beyond belief. He had met with a group of Methodist churchmen and, of his own volition, brought up the Philippine question, for it was evidently bothering him. He told the churchmen that he had asked God to show him what to do with the Islands and that it had divinely come to him, in a flash, that it was America's duty to take the whole archipelago and its population, "and uplift and civilize and Christianize them," since they were "our fellow-men for whom Christ also died." McKinley said that he then called in the official map-maker of the Government, and instructed him to mark the Philippines as United States property on all future maps.

It is surely by no means difficult to understand why Grover Cleveland, in retirement, expressed feelings of shame and humiliation.

The Philippines were to be a headache for years to come. An insurrection against American rule took place, and was not quelled until 1902. It cost the United States more to subjugate the Filipinos in revolution than it did to fight the war to acquire their country. 4,300 additional American lives and 600,000 Filipino lives were added to the terrible price. American businessmen did not like the idea of annexing territory so far away; the sugar interests were especially fearful of the competition the Islands might give. There were 8,000,000 of these "little brown brothers" at the time of the American conquest of the Islands. By 1946 they were given full independence; and, by their being placed outside the tariff and immigration walls of the United States like any other foreign nation, the fear of their competition in sugar, tobacco, hemp, and cheap labor was removed. In 1947 Puerto Rico was given home rule.

McKinley apologized for himself by saying that if he had been let alone he could have settled the Cuban problem without war. His conscience, apparently, was continuing to bother him; nobody in this world is ever let alone. Pressures are brought to bear on every person living, and certainly nobody must live through more pressures than the President of the United States. Clearly, the President is elected to stand up to the inevitable, often unpredictable pressures—but William McKinley had no such stamina. Just as in his domestic policies he would sacrifice a friend to placate a political boss, in his foreign policies he would sacrifice honorable conduct to silence censure of himself by the most obviously unprincipled jingoes.

On September 6, 1901, while attending the Pan-American Exposition at Buffalo, the Spanish War President was shot down by a demoniacal assassin and September 14th he died. At his death, fund-raisings were undertaken for monuments, and, in typical American fashion, the erection of them from seaboard to seaboard was realized in a very short time. We cannot help but compare this frenzied enthusiasm to memorialize with the more sober efforts made in behalf of a really courageous man and true lover of mankind, Thomas Jefferson, for whom, not until two hundred years after his birth had passed, was a memorial on the beautiful tidal basin in the capital city at last dedicated.

When this author visited the McKinley tomb some years ago, he was horrified to find vendors of mementoes and souvenirs holding forth in the mausoleum only a few feet from the sarcophagi. But, upon reflection, it may not be so inappropriate after all, that this compromise with good taste should have taken place in proximity to the bones of one who during his public life could compromise regularly with principles.

★★★★★★★★★★★★★★★★★★★★★★★★★

25

THEODORE ROOSEVELT

☆ ☆

VOTE OF 1900: *See* under McKinley

		Popular	Electoral
VOTE OF 1904:	Theodore Roosevelt, Republican	7,625,000	336
	Alton B. Parker, Democrat	5,083,000	140
	Eugene V. Debs, Socialist	402,000	
	Scattered	414,000	
		13,524,000	476

VOTE OF 1912: *See* under Woodrow Wilson

☆ ☆

THE LIFE OF THEODORE ROOSEVELT IS INTERESTING TO US BECAUSE IT was exciting. It is also interesting today because of what we have learned about psychology.

Theodore Roosevelt would have been a much more useful public servant if he had not had an inferiority complex which deeply influenced his life. Although he enjoyed an almost unbelievable popularity during his seven and a half years in the Presidency, won world acclaim, and never wanted for a single material thing, Roosevelt was a discontented and thoroughly restless spirit.

Some of Roosevelt's feeling of inferiority was no doubt the result of an embarrassment about his physical qualities, one of which was small stature. Not only was Roosevelt short; he also had poor eyesight from his boyhood on, and in middle life had the use of only one eye, although this was kept from public knowledge during his White House days.

He had the deeper limitation of not being an original thinker; and people who wish to remain most enduringly in the memories of their countrymen must, to some degree at least, have been able to give birth to original thoughts. The performance of original acts is not enough.

Of course, in a mediocre statesman we do not begin to look for anything like intellectual achievement. But Theodore Roosevelt was not mediocre; he was an extraordinarily useful executive. For that reason we feel particularly disappointed by his delight in vociferousness for its own sake.

The first American ancestor of Theodore Roosevelt was a Netherlands immigrant who came to New Amsterdam in the 1640's. While both Theodore Roosevelt and his relative, Franklin D. Roosevelt, bore this Dutch name, we must not think of them as being entirely of Dutch ancestry. The admixture of English and old American stocks was so great that little of the original nationality remained.

From the beginning the Roosevelts were successful merchants; and while they were never philanthropists, various members of the clan were usually available for public service. Theodore Roosevelt was the name also of the President's father. The mother, a Georgia woman, was Martha Bulloch. Besides Theodore, there was another boy, Elliott, whom it is interesting to take note of because he became the father of Eleanor Roosevelt, that controversial lady whose adventures and interests formed such an unparalleled addendum to the terms of the Roosevelt of the 1930's and 1940's.

Sickly, afflicted with asthma and poor sight, Theodore Roosevelt was educated by private tutors in his New York City home, where he was born on October 27, 1858. He knew also the luxury of family trips to resorts, which included trips to Europe and a later trip to Egypt. Simply to have had such experiences, without any later wealth at all, would have been enough to transform many a shy person into a confident person, many an inferior-feeling child into a comparatively assured and serene adult.

The episodes of Roosevelt's life up to the Presidency are in the political tradition. He entered Harvard at the age of eighteen, was graduated in 1880; married Miss Alice Lee of Boston the same year; began practice of law in 1881, only to enter the state legislature, to which he was elected three times successively.

Tragedy came into his life in 1884: his wife died after giving birth to a daughter, the "Princess Alice" of White House days, and his mother died the same day. After these deaths, Roosevelt went to Dakota Territory, where he owned two ranches, and where, except for winters, he was to live the life of a rancher for about five years. Here in the outdoors, which he loved his life long, he strove to build up his health, a task to which he had assiduously set his efforts since he had been in his teens. He never discontinued the "strenuous life," as he called it. It seems somewhat childish to us today, even considering an early sickliness, that any intelligent adult would exaggerate physical activity to the degree Roosevelt did. His life may actually have been shortened by his strenuous living.

In 1886 Roosevelt ran for mayor of New York and was beaten in a three-cornered contest. The same year he married Edith Carow, whom he had known since childhood. She became the mother of five of his six children.

In 1889 President Harrison appointed Roosevelt a Civil Service Commissioner at Washington, and there he remained six years; he was instrumental in the transferring of some 14,000 jobs from the spoils to the merit system. For having done this job so well, the Democratic Cleveland retained him in office. After he became President, Roosevelt's Administration was to increase the number of jobs in the classified service from 110,000 to 206,000.

In 1895 Roosevelt was made president of New York's Board of Police Commissioners. In 1896 he spoke on behalf of the national Republican ticket; and, in appealing for the poor man's vote, declared that the free coinage of silver, which the Bryan Democrats advocated, would never hurt the rich because of their habit of paying bills by check, whereas the poor would suffer because they nearly always used cash; thus it behooved the poor man to vote Republican and for the gold standard. Party leaders of both sides were upset by such explanations of the money system.

In 1897 Roosevelt was appointed Assistant Secretary of the Navy; and then resigned to form the curious regiment of cowboys and adventurers who comprised Roosevelt's Rough Riders in the Spanish War. He received the rank of lieutenant-colonel. In 1898 he was nominated for Governor of New York, elected, and at once showed the assertiveness for which his Presidential years were noted. When the obstreperous young man was named for the Vice-Presidency, it was largely because the party chieftains wanted him out of the way; in those years the Vice-Presidential post did not carry the importance or prestige it had in later years. But Mark Hanna was uneasy and said there was "only one life between that madman and the White House."

When, after McKinley's death, Roosevelt became the President, he stated that he would carry out McKinley's policies. Before long the country realized that the only policies he was interested in were the Roosevelt policies. Not yet forty-three years old, a born crusader, with unbounded enthusiasm, with a young wife and growing children—Roosevelt symbolized the energy of a young country at the acme of its powers. His contemporaries fondly referred to him as the typical American; but this was hardly so. He was a new force, unlike anything the nation had seen before; he was obviously "on the side of the right," and—most important of all—he believed in castigating the rich. This program suited the American people of the first decade of the new century so well that Roosevelt's re-election in 1904 was a foregone conclusion. His plurality, 2,500,000, was then an unheard-of margin. By his victory he also became the first Vice-President who, having succeeded to the Presidency through death, was elected President in his own right. He did what Tyler, Fillmore, Andrew Johnson, and Arthur had been unable to do.

Theodore Roosevelt believed in a powerful centralized government. In this he differed from most Republican leaders before and after him. As he believed in a strong federal government in Washington, so he believed in the President as the focal point of federal rule.

It was strictly in accordance with his concept of the American system that he acted in the anthracite coal strike of 1902. After waiting a reasonable time for the operators and the miners to come to a settlement, he invited the representatives of both to the White House. He urged arbitration. When the operators refused to arbitrate and took an arrogant position toward both miners and the President, Roosevelt took matters into his own hands. He threatened that if the industry would not arbitrate, the U. S. Army would be ordered by him to take over the mines and operate them in the public interest. With winter almost upon them, the industry complied.

Action like this had never been taken before by an American President. The public admired it. So did ex-President Grover

Cleveland who had offered Roosevelt his services in the controversy. The average yearly pay of a miner before the strike, which must of course be evaluated in terms of the value of money during that period, was $560. Roosevelt's interference in this strike is noteworthy indeed, because it signaled the beginning of the end of the attitude of imperious high-handedness which Management had displayed toward workers in the United States. By the time another generation ended, America was to see equally intolerable arrogance of Labor toward industry, and the contempt of high labor leaders for problems of national defense and safety.

The construction of the Panama Canal, which began in 1904, will always be associated with Roosevelt; it is probably the achievement by which he will be best remembered. In beginning this project the President showed the same executive assertiveness that he had shown in the coal strike. In June 1902 Congress had authorized construction of an isthmian canal after years of considering the Nicaraguan route. The French, who had begun operations at the isthmus years previously, were to be paid $40,000,000 for their rights and equipment; Colombia, of whose domain Panama was a part, was to receive $10,000,000; and an annual rental of $250,000 was to be paid Colombia in addition for American use of a narrow strip of 300 square miles to be known as the Canal Zone. The Colombian representative in Washington agreed to this, but when it came to ratification, the then shaky government in Colombia refused to sign, whereupon Roosevelt naturally became furious. The canal had to be built, that was certain; the entire world wanted it. And no nation but the United States could build it without the risk of endangering the Monroe Doctrine. Further, a new treaty with England, superseding the old one which envisioned a canal as a joint venture, now stipulated that America alone should build the canal. A way to build it had to be found.

It has been charged to Roosevelt that he fomented the revolution in Panama which led to America's signing with a new independent republic there, thus enabling digging to begin. There is no proof of this; certainly there were enough unsatisfied French and Panamanians there to incite rebellion. What we do know is that when Colombia wanted to land troops in her province to quell the revolt, American warships were there to prevent such landings. A new Central American nation was born, and recognized by the United States immediately; Panama was paid the $10,000,000 and the $250,000 annual rental, instead of Colombia.[1]

Roosevelt later said: "I took Panama." Years later, during Woodrow Wilson's Administration, an indemnity of $25,000,000 and an apology to Colombia was advocated; but the Senate did not ratify, and it was only in Harding's time that the money was paid—without the apology. The Canal was opened to ships in 1914, although it was not officially declared completed until 1921. The whole story of the Canal and the war against disease in that area is a history in itself.

Many chroniclers hold that Theodore Roosevelt's conservation program was an achievement as great as that of the Canal. The dissipation of American natural resources in the name of the industrial expansion America had experienced was not of real concern to the national Government until Roosevelt came into power, and it would be sheer blindness not to recognize the immeasurable worth of the steps he undertook in this field. The United States Forest Service was established under him, the acreage of the national forests increasing from 43,000,000 to 194,-000,000. Five national parks were added to the system, and thirteen national monuments. The first Federal bird reservation was set aside during this time also; several species of American birds had become extinct, such as the passenger pigeon, the great auk, the Carolina paraquet, and the Labrador duck. Fifty more bird sanctuaries were set aside before Roosevelt left office. In addition, four big game refuges were established.

That Roosevelt was sincere in his love of nature seems clear. He started collecting specimens on his trip to Egypt when a boy. When he left office, he went to Africa not simply to shoot animals for sport, but to collect specimens for the Smithsonian Institution. After his political defeat in 1912, he sailed for Brazil to do collecting for the American Museum of Natural History and to locate the course of a mysterious river in the western wilds of that jungle country. The stream was located and charted, although he was stricken with fever while there and almost perished. The discovery was named for him Rio Téodoro. Certainly, there-

[1] Annual rental to Panama increased to $1,930,000 in 1955.

fore, scientific research was one of the fields open to him after he left the White House.

Another field to which this energetic man had devoted much attention was spelling reform. He was completely sympathetic to this great need in English-speaking countries; in 1906 he had instructed the public printer to issue all Government publications with the reformed spelling he advocated for three hundred specific words. He did not anticipate the hostility aroused among journalists and legislators by this thoroughly progressive matter, and certainly he did not expect that the House of Representatives would actually rebuke him by vote. Roosevelt withdrew his order and admitted he was beaten, a most unusual admission for him; yet he wrote the reformers that his personal interest would not abate, and that he would use the simplified spellings which they had suggested in his own correspondence.

Something that took place all through the two terms of Theodore Roosevelt, which is too little dwelt on today in the teaching of history, was the tremendous immigration—both as to quantity and to quality. As great as the Panama Canal, as great as the conservation program, as great as the incipient dethronement of industrial barons, was this sociological transformation that was taking place in America. Its real effect was not to be felt until almost a generation later, when the children of these immigrants, the new first-generation Americans, began to cast their ballots.

In the twenty-year period from 1870 to 1890, immigration from Northern lands (including Canada and the whole of Ireland) was roughly 6,300,000; that from lands of the Mediterranean basin and from Slavic peoples (including Russia and Greece) was 1,-200,000. In the next twenty-year period, 1890 to 1910, immigration from the North was 3,330,000; and from Southern and Eastern Europe 8,200,000!

In 1907 immigration reached its peak—1,285,000 persons were admitted from foreign countries in a single year. In 1910, when the population of the nation was 92,000,000, almost 15% were foreign-born.

The years in which Roosevelt was President were as striking as any incumbent of that high office could wish. Almost everything was changing. There was high prosperity, broken only by a minor panic in 1907 which was soon dispelled. The inventions of

Edison and others were coming into full fruition. Henry Ford put his Model T on the market for $850.50. The Wright Brothers made their first successful plane flight. The first New York subway was opened. Skyscrapers were being erected. Motion pictures, an indisputable influence on American life and thought, were serving as an antidote to ennui and drudgery for many people. Electricity was becoming more and more a permanent adjunct of living for everybody. Although the internal-combustion engine and wireless telegraphy were conceived by Europeans, many other inventions were having their origins in the ingenuity of American minds. The standard of living was rising steadily. The President enjoyed a personal following not seen since the Era of Good Feeling—since Monroe's time.

In 1905 Roosevelt was the peacemaker in the Russo-Japanese War, as a result of which the combatants signed a treaty of peace at Portsmouth, New Hampshire. For this he was awarded the Nobel Peace Prize, the entire $40,000 of which he donated to a foundation for the promotion of industrial peace.

After the Japanese victory over Russia, Roosevelt did another unheard-of thing. He sent the American fleet of sixteen warships on a sixteen-month journey around the world. He did not counsel with his Cabinet before taking this precedent-shattering step because he felt it was his duty, as he says in his *Autobiography*, "to lead and not to take refuge behind the generally timid wisdom of a multitude of councillors." High naval authorities in Europe were aghast at the proposed voyage. Some years later, when he was in Europe, some of these authorities asked him plainly whether he did not think at the time that his action might have precipitated war. Roosevelt suggests in his autobiography that his prime purpose in the world journey of the ships was to impress the American people by America's sea-power. Probably so; but we suspect that his desire was also to "shake the big stick" at the rest of the world, to give warning that the American fleet would go wherever it wanted—a characteristically Rooseveltian action.

It is of importance to take note of the passage of the Pure Food and Drug Act and the Meat Inspection Act, both signed by Roosevelt in 1906. It is not the acts themselves which are really interesting; more noteworthy is the thinking which led Congress to pass these laws. To legislate with respect to such matters was clearly not granted Congress by the Constitution; but the "embalmed beef" the soldiers had to eat during the Spanish War plus the exposés of the packing houses made by writers of the time forced Federal action. The Interstate Commerce Act and the interstate commerce clause of the Constitution were invoked, by the philosophy of which it was held to be constitutional to regulate respecting products shipped in interstate transit. In a similar way Federal social legislation of a generation later took its cue from the reasoning of 1906, using to validate itself the interstate transit aspect of business operations. The states were slowly, but certainly, losing some of their sovereignty. The right of the ICC to establish transportation rates and fares was also finally determined in these years, and by the same philosophy.

Many people today when thinking of Theodore Roosevelt think of his actions in 1912 and not of what he accomplished before that time. Unmistakably, 1912 was a turning point in American life. There are some individuals who go so far as to say that Theodore Roosevelt was responsible for American participation in the world cataclysms known as World War I and World War II. Had Roosevelt not ignored good counsel in 1912, they say, and had he supported the regularly nominated candidate of his Party, there would have been no Anglophile Woodrow Wilson elected to the Presidency.

It is regrettable for Roosevelt himself that he had to insist on the Presidency again as the proper place for the outlet of his energy; it can only be remarked that powerful men, by reason of both their success and the sycophancy of their adulators, often lose perspective.

There were many places where Roosevelt could have performed admirably. He lacked the vision to see that a far larger role as an elder statesman was ready for him, and—what was transcendently important—the American people were ready for such a statesman in such a role. Herbert Hoover performed notably in the role—and with handicaps that Roosevelt never had. As Roosevelt represented the American people at the funeral of Edward VII, so he might have been the representative of goodwill and the resolver of difficulties for the United States over the entire globe.

With the sacrilegious statement, "We stand at Armageddon,

and we battle for the Lord," Roosevelt accepted the nomination
of a new party, the Progressive Party, when the Republicans
failed to name him again and renominated instead the incumbent
Taft. In his campaign he preached what he called the "New
Nationalism." The Republican vote was split, and the election of
the Democratic candidate was assured. This had happened before
—in 1860: the Democratic vote had been split, insuring the election of the minority Republican candidate. It is hard to believe
that Roosevelt did not see the possibility that all this would recur.
Perhaps one writer's statement that "He had knowledge without
wisdom, enthusiasm without sympathy" applies perfectly here.[2]

At the outbreak of the war in Europe in 1914, Roosevelt immediately said that he distrusted the German emperor; he had always recognized the fraternity of interests between the United
States and the United Kingdom. He advocated openly America's
entering the conflict on the side of the British and their allies, and
after the *Lusitania* sinking was, like many others, wrathful.

But now his life was in eclipse and was to darken until his
death in his sleep on January 6, 1919, at his home in Cove Neck,
Long Island. After America's entry into the war, he wanted to
recruit a division of volunteers just as he had recruited volunteers
in the Spanish-American War, but President Wilson did not
accede to the request. Wilson received a large share of Roosevelt's
abuse during these years.

It is possible that Theodore Roosevelt might have been President again—in 1916. In that year the Republicans probably would
have had a chance with him; but the organization leaders could
not forgive what he did to the Party in 1912 and gave the nomination to Charles Evans Hughes instead. Roosevelt spoke for Hughes
during the campaign, but his bellicosity is believed to have influenced the people to associate entry into the European war with
Hughes's candidacy, and so the victory went to Wilson again.

To add to his many other talents, Roosevelt was a successful
writer—earlier in his life he planned to become one profession-
ally. His four-volume *The Winning of the West*, his *Letters to His*

---

[2] When it was proposed that Roosevelt be made president of Harvard, one of
that school's overseers inquired whether "judgment [is] to be found coupled
with such enormous energy." The post was not offered to Theodore Roosevelt.

Children, and his *Theodore Roosevelt: An Autobiography* are outstanding; he authored many other works. He was a voracious reader and had in his mind an unbelievable collection of facts as a result of it. With his knowledge, his curious mind and crusading spirit, his rich cultural background, his priceless experience, and his rare contemporary prestige there is no end to the number of things he might have done for his country and for the world, had he but possessed that pearl of great price—Magnanimity. It is assuredly because of this lack that many people doubt that he belongs on Mount Rushmore with that high company whose actions and admonishments are still incontestably valid.

Theodore Roosevelt was a product of his times, like most other men. In the first decade of the new century, America was like a great industrial baron who had made the best part of his fortune and was just beginning to pay some attention to philanthropies and causes. Labor unions, Prohibition, woman suffrage, child labor—these were the causes that were beginning to engross men's energies. America had learned how to make money, how to acquire might. It had now to learn understanding of less obvious values.

In Youngs Memorial Cemetery in Oyster Bay, Long Island, the tumultuous twenty-fifth President of the United States has at last found rest.

★★★★★★★★★★★★★★★★★★★★★★★★★

26

WILLIAM HOWARD TAFT

☆ ☆

		Popular	*Electoral*
VOTE OF 1908:	William Howard Taft, Republican	7,678,000	321
	William Jennings Bryan, Democrat	6,408,000	162
	Eugene V. Debs, Socialist	421,000	
	Scattered	379,000	
		14,886,000	483

VOTE OF 1912: *See* under Woodrow Wilson

☆ ☆

ONLY TWO OR THREE TIMES IN AMERICAN HISTORY HAS AN INCUMBENT President been able to pick his successor and get the nation to accept him. Probably it can be said that Jefferson was responsible for Madison's being in the White House. Certainly Jackson named Van Buren as his heir and urged his acceptance. But Theodore Roosevelt practically gave the country an ultimatum to take Taft or take himself for a third time, and the country without a whimper took Taft because "Teddy" told them to. And, as always happens when a glamorous man is followed by an unglamorous one, Taft just could not fill his predecessor's shoes; and this was construed by Theodore Roosevelt's followers, despite the accomplishments of the Taft Administration, as disloyalty to the Roosevelt program. The newspapers, for whom Roosevelt had supplied headlines almost every day of his Presidency, continued to feature the adventures of the dramatic man, so that the people, through their reading, also came to be somewhat disappointed in the Taft regime.

It probably will never be possible to know a public man completely, not even so open and un-complex a man as William Howard Taft. Nevertheless, few other American statesmen have been so clear to us as Taft. No more good-natured man ever occupied the Presidential office. His mind was a judicial one, which Roosevelt's was not, and this difference must be recognized in assessing the attitudes of these two men during that interesting era. Taft could not advertise himself as Roosevelt did, nor did he care to. He always aspired to a judicial career; the Chief Justiceship, rather than the Presidency, was his natural element. Contemporaries and students say that it was his family who had the White House ambitions and that he yielded to them. His father certainly was ambitious for him, as were his wife and brothers. To what degree their interference in his life influenced his decision to run for President in 1908 and to what degree his inner promptings did, we cannot say. Taft inherited Roosevelt's mantle—that we do know—so that nobody else had a chance at the nomination in that year.

All Taft's American ancestors were New Englanders, his father, Alphonso Taft, being the first to migrate westward. He decided to try Cincinnati, where he prospered, lived in a beautiful and spacious house, married Louise Torrey as his second wife and fathered his family, one of whom, William Howard, was born there on September 15, 1857. The influence of the father on the future President and Chief Justice was very great. As the elder man lay on his deathbed, Taft wrote his wife that his father had been his guardian angel "and that as his life ebbs away and ends I shall cease to have the luck which has followed me thus far."

Alphonso Taft had been a member of Grant's Cabinet; also he had been Minister to Russia and Minister to Austria. He was very much concerned about his son's education and lived to see him become Solicitor-General. Like his father, William Howard went to Yale, where he was graduated second in his class. His father strongly urged him to stay out of football and concentrate on his studies, and with this the boy complied. He finished his education with two years at the Cincinnati Law School, where he was graduated first in his class; the same year he was admitted to the bar. Not only was Taft a good student, but he was also popular, as a genial person is likely to be. These two qualities, together with the ambitions of his family for him and the fortuitousness of his association with Roosevelt, made him bound to succeed. It was not long after his graduation that his public life commenced.

His first appointment was that of assistant solicitor for Hamilton County, where Cincinnati is located. Then came other appointments: Collector of Internal Revenue for the district of Cincinnati; judge of the Ohio Superior Court; Solicitor-General of the United States; United States Circuit Court judge; head of the Philippine Commission; civil Governor of the Philippines; Secretary of War. Then followed the Presidency and the Chief Justiceship. Only for the Presidency did he have to make a campaign.

Taft's administration of the affairs of the Filipinos was so successful that the natives called him Santo Taft, or "Saint" Taft. Twice while in the Philippines he rejected offers of Roosevelt to place him on the Supreme Court bench in Washington. He had given very careful thought to the idea of going off to the Islands and, now that he was there, he intended to remain until the work he envisaged for the Filipinos was finished. He made trips into the interior of the 7,000-island archipelago, took part in native fiestas, dances, and christenings, even though his health was seriously imperiled by the climate. Eventually, he had to take a trip back to the States for treatment. Among his achievements were a judicial system, public works and harbors, public health, education of the natives; and always he showed that judicial fairness and conciliatory approach which characterized him his life long. These sorts of things are not dramatic, do not make headlines, but they do contain the germ of enduring accomplishment. So it was only natural that later, as Secretary of War, he should have revisited the Philippines to open their first legislative assembly in Manila.

Taft, in all these tasks, had been getting a steady build-up for his candidacy for the White House after Roosevelt's term. Their friendship had begun when Roosevelt was on the Civil Service Commission and Taft was Solicitor-General. It was a well-founded friendship, natural and warm, and it had the hallmarks of permanence. The Republican convention in 1908, then, had nothing to do but nominate the man Roosevelt wanted, whose election would be a foregone conclusion. In spite of the fact that the Panic of 1907 was not completely over and that there was considerable unemployment in the nation, Taft won easily over Bryan. The Bryan leadership was changing the Democratic Party to a party of social reform, but the nation was not yet ready for this reform: the age still enjoyed its *laissez faire* philosophy. Two weeks after Taft's inauguration, Roosevelt sailed for Africa where he spent a year; traveling thence to Europe where he spent the spring and summer of 1910 luxuriating in its adulation. However else one may care to interpret these journeys at this time, they were in reality only an interlude in an inordinately ambitious life.

Taft, the natural jurist and unnatural politician, had a difficult time in the Presidency from the first. There was no combativeness in his nature to begin with, and large numbers in Congress seized the opportunity of Roosevelt's long-awaited absence to again transfer initiative to the legislative body, where it had been since Johnson's day—with the exception of the Roosevelt interval. Congress was called into special session to deal with the tariff, as Taft had promised in the campaign. Roosevelt very conveniently had ignored this issue and left it in Taft's lap to dispose of as best be could. The tariff law which was the result of this session caused consternation around the country and this consternation was one of the things the fanatical Roosevelt people tried to exploit.

They had started to betray Taft even before their stormy hero returned to the United States from his animal-hunting journeys and the intoxications of popular applause. They reported that Taft had sold out to the "interests," whatever that might mean, and asserted that for the country to be saved Roosevelt should run again in 1912. Among these friends of Roosevelt was Gifford Pinchot, the discharged head of the Forest Service and later Governor of Pennsylvania. The supporters of Roosevelt were almost all of an "agitator" type, like Roosevelt himself; this writer does not recall a single figure among these "insurgents," as they were called, who today enjoys a felicitous reputation. But Taft's name has grown more lustrous with time.

Taft's Administration had just as notable accomplishments to its credit as did Roosevelt's. Human nature being what it is, however, accomplishments must be trumpeted with fanfare if their author is to enjoy the favor of his contemporaries. Although controversial, the Payne-Aldrich tariff bill which Taft supported was a forward step in tariff reduction. Taft also recommended a Federal tax on incomes and the adoption of the Sixteenth Amendment to the Constitution as the means of achieving that long-outlawed method of taxation; the Seventeenth Amendment, providing for the direct election of United States Senators, was adopted during this time. Against the wishes of business interests, the parcel-post and postal-savings bank systems were established. The Department of Labor was set up as a separate Cabinet post. Taft urged the creation of a budget bureau and for the first time in American history submitted a national budget to the country. Arizona and New Mexico were admitted into the Union, bringing into statehood the last territory remaining between the Canadian and Mexican borders. There was also the establishment of a national health bureau; the enlargement of the conservation program, vast additional acreage being withdrawn from the public lands; and the enactment of legislation requiring publicity of campaign expenditures.

Nor were these all the liberal achievements. Taft appointed a Roman Catholic, a former Confederate soldier, to the post of Chief Justice of the United States. The civil service was greatly extended. An eight-hour day was granted all Government employees. Taft had a wide sympathy with human problems and it was during his term that a commission was created to consider additional safety and workmen's compensation legislation. Jurisdiction of the Interstate Commerce Commission was enlarged to include telephones, telegraph lines, cable and wireless systems.

A project dear to Taft's heart, and interesting from the old imperialist angle as well, was his reciprocity treaty with Canada, providing for practically free trade with that neighbor. Congress ratified the treaty, but not before Speaker Champ Clark had uttered some foolish and incendiary language: "I am for it, because I hope to see the day when the American flag will float over every square foot of the British North American possessions clear to the North Pole." Canada was thus told that American imperialism was not dead and that she did not know when she herself would be preyed upon. Her Parliament rejected the reciprocity treaty— and the Democratic chieftains the following year rejected the candidacy of Champ Clark for the Presidential nomination.

For the first time, the Sherman Anti-Trust Act was seriously enforced; there were more prosecutions in Taft's Administration than in any other from the time the law was enacted. There were many monopolies—the beef trust, Standard Oil, the sugar trust, International Harvester, the tobacco trust, and many more. In 1901 J. P. Morgan & Company had formed the greatest manufacturing combine on the face of the earth—the billion dollar United States Steel Corporation. The Government lost its suit to bring about the dissolution of this mammoth.

It is interesting to note that Andrew Carnegie, who sold out to Morgan when the combine was formed, regretted that he had not charged Morgan enough for his Carnegie Steel Company. Once, when the two men were making a voyage on the same ship, Carnegie murmured to Morgan that he should have asked him for $100,000,000 more than he had, to which Morgan with ruthless imperturbability replied, "If you had, I would have paid it"! The incident is symbolic of that age.

The entire first decade of the twentieth century was characterized by onslaughts against the trusts. In Taft's time the Standard Oil Company of New Jersey, American Tobacco Company, du Pont de Nemours, American Sugar Refining Company, and Standard Sanitary were among the monopolies ordered dissolved. America had a progressive government and a progressive administration. In addition, the country was prosperous. . . . Yet, 1912 loomed menacingly—1912, that great American tragedy which need never have occurred.

Some writers say Taft never understood the break between himself and his erstwhile mentor and friend. That is incorrect. He understood it all right, once he saw it clearly, for what it really was. What that conciliatory man could not understand was why it had to be at all. Slowly the two men grew apart until, in February 1912, Roosevelt announced that he would accept the nomination of the Republican Party if it were offered to him. He made some ridiculous statements in advocating his "New Nationalism," among them the astounding proposal to recall judicial decisions by popular vote. This pandering to the people was not appreciated even by the people. The people know instinctively how much they should be deferred to.

When the Republicans failed to give Roosevelt the nomination again, his followers met in convention and formed the Progressive (or Bull Moose) Party and nominated him as their man for President. The election of Woodrow Wilson, the Democratic candidate, was thus assured. Both Wilson and Taft expressed themselves, even before the election, as being relieved that the country would now be spared four more years of Roosevelt. Taft referred to Roosevelt and his followers as "emotionalists and neurotics."

After his defeat in 1912, when only Utah and Vermont swung to him, Taft went back to Yale to teach. He also became president of the American Bar Association. In 1921 the great wish of his life was realized when President Harding appointed him Chief Justice of the United States, at which post he remained for nine years. This was his forte; he was following in the steps of his jurist father and grandfather.

Between the White House and the Supreme Court days came the conflagration known as World War I. Although in his sympathies pro-British, Taft was at heart what in later years would be called an "isolationist"—meaning simply that he was for his own country first and his ancestral land afterwards. Because America in those days actually was second in the affections of many of her prominent citizens, she became a laughingstock among allies and enemies alike and this condition heightened the popular European conception of her as a nation without real culture.

Unlike Roosevelt, Taft was cordial to and friendly with President Wilson. He believed in Wilson's League of Nations and spoke on behalf of it. When he was appointed Chief Justice, the work of the Court was far behind. When he died on March 8, 1930, its business was up-to-date. He was by nature an administrator and a conciliator and, like most jurists, reflective. He had also the habit of thinking aloud, never realizing that so political a person as the President of the United States should not let his left hand know what his right hand is doing. The man was almost naively without guile.

With the exception of his eating, Taft's personal habits were exemplary. He did not smoke and drank liquor sparingly, but his six-foot frame was known to weigh 326 pounds when he was in the Roosevelt Cabinet. His immense weight was always a matter of conjecture while he was President. His marriage was a successful one; his wife, the former Helen Herron of Cincinnati, survived him for some years. It is interesting to note the activity of his two sons in the politics of the nation; the older son, so long the senior Senator from Ohio, Robert A. Taft, one of the co-authors of the Taft-Hartley labor law, had been an active aspirant for the Presidency until his untimely death. Time has yet to reveal the place of Robert A. Taft's political philosophy in the mid-twentieth century; but certainly the aspirations of old Alphonso Taft were echoed "even unto the third and fourth generation."

In Arlington Cemetery in Virginia lie buried the remains of William Howard Taft, a man whose rule for a short time it is indeed pleasant to recall.

★★★★★★★★★★★★★★★★★★★★★★★★★★★★

27

WOODROW WILSON

☆ ✿

		Popular	*Electoral*
VOTE OF 1912:	Woodrow Wilson, Democrat	6,293,000	435
	Theodore Roosevelt, Progressive	4,119,000	88
	William Howard Taft, Republican	3,485,000	8
	Eugene V. Debs, Socialist	902,000	
	Scattered	237,000	
		15,036,000	531
VOTE OF 1916:	Woodrow Wilson, Democrat	9,130,000	277
	Charles Evans Hughes, Republican	8,538,000	254
	Allen J. Benson, Socialist	585,000	
	Scattered	280,000	
		18,533,000	531

☆ ✿

THE FAILURE OF WOODROW WILSON—AND WITH IT THE FAILURE OF the American nation in foreign affairs during the calamitous seven years ending in 1921—is attributable to two things: the fact that the President of the United States was almost exclusively a woman's man; and the parallel fact that he was a schoolmaster.

"America will not bring glory to herself, but disgrace, by following the beaten paths of history," declared this Southern academic in one of his inspired moments. Yet he did lead his country down those very paths, and then rationalized his leadership by instructing America that she was thus serving humanity. The people, though far less cultured than their schoolmaster-President, recognized that serving humanity was not America's prime mission, that the nation ought not to dictate the conduct of other peoples, and that she was doing just what other nations had always done, namely: following a program of enlightened self-interest. The program has not always been enlightened. It has often been characterized by self-interest. See the tragic results of the two world wars.

Woodrow Wilson came of a long line of preachers and teach-ers. His father, the Rev. Joseph R. Wilson, was a remarkable man and a typical Presbyterian. His love for his scholar son was almost inordinate. In fact, Wilson's biographer Ray Stannard Baker de-clares that the letters between father and son were simply love letters. One is reminded of the great love of Alphonso Taft for his brilliant son, and of the all-consuming care of the childless Sardis Birchard for his orphaned nephew Rutherford B. Hayes.

Wilson's mother, Jessie Woodrow, was born in England—a fact most significant to the weal of the American people at the time of World War I. While the father was filling a pastorate at Staunton, Virginia, the son was born in the manse on December 28, 1856, and called Tommy. He dropped the Thomas in later years and made Woodrow Wilson his correct name, an act which psychologists can interpret in a variety of ways. The Rev. Wilson received a call to Augusta, Georgia, when the boy was only two; and it was in that Southern city, all through the Civil War years, that the boyhood of the future President was spent.

Wilson was frail as a boy and obtained his earliest education under his father's instruction and at a private school. When he was thirteen, the family moved again, to Columbia, South Carolina. From there he was sent to Davidson College, in North Carolina, but he was sent home ill before the end of the first year. For a while the family lived in Wilmington, North Carolina. At eighteen Woodrow entered Princeton—the place from which he was to go off to fame. He was not a distinguished scholar, a fact which is bound to surprise many people; but he was an excellent debater. After studying law at the University of Virginia, he opened a law office at Atlanta, Georgia; but he did not care for the law and abandoned it. To earn his doctor's degree, Woodrow Wilson went next to Johns Hopkins in Baltimore. For a while he taught at Bryn Mawr and at Wesleyan in Connecticut.

At last he came to the faculty of Princeton to teach juris-prudence and become its president; and thence onto the world's stage and the provocative eight years in the Presidency of the nation. Unyielding and unforgiving, this self-willed savant entered the lists to win the leadership of the country, and winning it, was catapulted to a tragic death which, disturbing though it was to the world policy of a great power, was nevertheless as natural a denouement as any event in nature.

The rise of Woodrow Wilson was simple. He used his Princeton connection as a pulpit from which to preach his political philosophy to the American people for a number of years. It was in the heydey of Theodore Roosevelt and the progressive movement. Consequently, his liberal utterances were such as to make him talked about for the Presidency even before he entered the political arena. And when at last he got his first public office in the Governorship of New Jersey, which was nothing more than a stopgap till he could win the big prize, he turned his back on the political boss of that state and showed he was serious when he promised a reform administration. His nomination in 1912 for the Presidency naturally followed. Nevertheless, Wilson could never have attained the Presidency had it not been for Roosevelt's defection; he was thus a minority President.

The election of 1916, when the vote for Woodrow Wilson again fell short of a majority of the votes cast, revealed the innately conservative nature of the American people and their reluctance to entrust their fortunes to scholastics and theorists. So close was this election that it was three days before the country knew who was to be the President. Had there been no war in Europe, the Republican candidate Hughes would have been elected; but the people felt that the pacific Wilson would continue to try out peace schemes and thus keep America out of war. In fact, the Democratic campaign slogan was: "He kept us out of war." That alone could have swung the crucial 4,000 California votes in the President's direction and re-elected him in that fateful year—probably the most fateful of all the years since the sundering of the nation in civil strife.

Woodrow Wilson's inaugural address in March 1913 was one of the most lofty in thought ever delivered by an incoming President. There are ideas in it that are phrased with Olympian magnificence. His craftsmanship with words was wonderful, and was fostered by his father who was a great student of style. For the first time in over a century the President appeared before Congress in person to deliver his messages. No one since John Adams had done this, and it came as something of a shock.

The story of Woodrow Wilson's life is indissolubly associated with the prelude and enactment of World War I, and its sequel. Yet there are some real accomplishments in the domestic field during the early days of his first term, which it is necessary to note. Of course the tariff was revised again, really downward this time, Wilson holding it a superstition to say that prosperity depended on a rigid protective system. The greatest achievement was the establishment of the Federal Reserve System. This act was intended to redistribute the money power of the nation, for Wilson had declared that the greatest monopoly in the United States was the money monopoly. In order that it might not have another Bank of the United States as in the early days of the Republic, the nation was divided into twelve Federal Reserve districts with a Federal bank in each. Thus the country has twelve systems instead of one; and although not all the money evils have been removed, the financial structure of the nation generally has been better with these "bankers' banks."

In addition to tariff and currency reform, the Clayton Anti-Trust Act, more specific than the old Sherman law against monopolies, was passed. The bipartisan Federal Trade Commission was created to further supplement the trust acts. To supplement the Federal Reserve Act there were established Federal Land Banks to extend long-term loans to farmers at reasonable rates. The eight-hour day for railroad employees became a reality.

Before the nation became engrossed with the many issues of the war in Europe, it had a situation to handle in Mexico, where there had been a revolution. The American Government was concerned because of investments in that country directly to the south and, naturally, wanted it to be at peace. Wilson took sides in this internal disturbance, but ostensibly pursued a policy he called "watchful waiting." Later he sent General Pershing and a punitive force down to Vera Cruz to compel the new government to salute the American flag. The lives of American marines were lost in this silly exhibition of American power. Wilson mishandled this whole situation because he was temperamentally unable to come to grips with the problem in a magnanimous or masculine way. The war in Europe finally took Wilson's attention away from Mexico and allowed that country to arrive at a settlement of its affairs by itself.

But, in this connection, it is interesting to observe that trait in

Wilson which was to cause the nation so much trouble throughout his terms. To people experienced in Mexican affairs he refused to listen, while he sent down somebody wholly inexperienced as personal envoy to be his listening-post. It was the same when he went to the Peace Conference after the war. Experienced and able men who could do their own thinking he would not take along with him. In fact, with the exception of Secretary Lansing, he ignored everybody in Government connected with foreign affairs, making his associates at the peace table in Versailles as impotent an array as ever dealt with the fortunes of human society.

Why was Wilson unable to tolerate other strong minds? Why did he resort, like a tyrant of feudal times, to "yes men"? The veteran *New York Times* reporter Charles Willis Thompson writes in his book:

> Wilson not only did not desire advice or guidance, but he did not desire information. When, in the course of the World War, Ambassador Walter Hines Page came to the United States to give the President the inside news of what was going on in England—this was before we entered the war and while Wilson still dreamed he could be called upon to make peace—he found it impossible to get the President to listen. Every time he sought to bring the subject up Wilson would side-track it and steer the conversation into other channels. Usually he did this by managing to have others present to whom he could address himself on a different topic. At first Page thought this was accident or coincidence. At last he succeeded in getting Wilson alone, seized the opportunity and started to tell the President what he felt it his patriotic duty to let him know. Wilson looked up with a quick gesture, as if he would dismiss the subject, but Page, who by this time realized that there was nothing accidental about the way Wilson had blanketed him, went right ahead. Seeing that there was no way of stopping Page, the President sprang up, stuck his fingers in his ears, and, still holding them there, ran out of the room.[1]

In the ordinary layman, a trait like this is ludicrous. In the leader of a great people, and at a time of unprecedented crisis, it is benumbing. We see now why Wilson surrounded himself with admiring women who did not understand world problems. These women did not tell him things he did not care to hear.

[1] *Presidents I've Known,* p. 253; The Bobbs-Merrill Company.

The women of Wilson's household also shared this characteristic. The first Mrs. Wilson was Ellen Axson, a Southerner and
an artist, the mother of his three daughters. She was a typically
feminine woman, gracious, deferential to her scholar husband, and
not at all jealous. After she died in the White House, Wilson
married Edith Bolling Galt, a widow and a direct descendant of
Pocahontas. It was she who accompanied him on his European
trips and helped bear his great burden. Wilson never in his life
learned to adjust himself to or work with men, except, as W. E.
Woodward has written, "cat-like men, such as Colonel House."
Mrs. Wilson confides in her memoirs that she protested to her
husband that she did not trust Colonel House because he never
differed with the President and that she did not think that such
"yessing" was good; but Wilson did not share her view. Before
he left Paris, Wilson was to know that his wife's intuition should
have been heeded. And before he died, he had broken with every
one of the male advisers he had left.

In August 1914, the multi-fused powder magazine known as
Europe blew up. On April 6, 1917, the United States officially
became a participant in that conflagration on the side of the
Entente powers. Actually, America had been a participant on that
side from the beginning of hostilities—a participant financially on
the part of huge business interests and emotionally on the part of
many influential classes.

The reason for this partisan action is that the United States had
had an unwritten alliance of understanding with the United Kingdom and its dominions for at least two generations.

During the war the German Kaiser was lampooned in the
Allied world for his reported references to *"Ich und Gott."* Yet
Woodrow Wilson may as well have said "I and God" for the in-
tractable attitude he took as the advocate of righteousness in that
day. In fact, he *did* declare that God led America into the war.
And thousands among the American clergy made rather a sad
spectacle of themselves falling into line with this notion of Wilson's and preaching it from their pulpits instead of the Scriptural
teachings.

The acts of Germany on the seas plus the unwritten alliance
with England forced America into the war. But Wilson would not
let it go at that. He had to idealize America's action into a crusade

for Righteousness. That gave him the status of a new Messiah. There is little doubt that much opposition to him both at home and in Europe stemmed from an aversion on the part of realistic people to bringing any Messianic implications into an old-fashioned war with old-fashioned ambitions and old-fashioned punishments. "The idea of America is to serve humanity." The people had not said it, nor the Bible, nor the Founding Fathers. . . . It was only Woodrow Wilson who said it. And it wasn't going to be enough.

Inasmuch as America's entry into World War I broke an isolationist policy of one hundred years' standing, it is important to enumerate some reasons for the precedent-shattering change other than that of the unwritten alliance. The United States has, of course, a common cultural background with the British. America speaks the same language and lives under the same common law; untold numbers have the same ancestors.[2]

Although it is no longer true that the racial strains in America are preponderantly English, the "ruling classes" in America were primarily of English background. Financiers, captains of industry, college presidents, legislators, were for the most part men who bore Anglican names and often were pillars of the Episcopal Church. America's sympathies with France also, of course, had a historical background; the citizenry never forgot what Lafayette and Rochambeau did for the United States during the Revolution. It was in 1886 that the people of France as a symbol of their friendship for the people of the United States presented the nation with the Statue of Liberty which was erected in New York Harbor.

In 1871 the German states were unified into a powerful, homogeneous whole. At once that nation became England's principal rival in the world, and America, by tying herself up with Britain, automatically found herself opposed to the growth of the rising German imperialism. It was therefore felt that a victory for the Central Powers (Germany, Austria-Hungary, Turkey, and Bulgaria) constituted a threat to America's institutions. Nevertheless, the game that America was playing was power politics.

Power politics, simple and plain, should unquestionably be recognized as power politics, and not confused with God and

[2] Sir Winston Churchill and Franklin D. Roosevelt, for example, are descended from a common Connecticut ancestor of the 17th century.

guilt and the good, as Wilson made the error of doing. God has nothing to do with wars or power politics. It is man's own frailty that leads him toward such courses of catastrophe.

This is but a sketchy presentation of the causes for American sympathy for the Entente nations. Of themselves, these causes might not have been enough to take America to war. But there was also a direct cause—the German submarine menace. Britain controlled the seas and was therefore able to obtain from America all manner of munitions and foodstuffs. Germany could not obtain this contraband-of-war because she was hemmed in by the British blockade. Therefore, as a counter measure, she declared all the waters surrounding the British Isles as being within the area of war and with her submarines undertook to prevent all shipping from arriving at port. This is where German-American relations began to be strained. American as well as belligerent ships were sunk by the subs; and although the United States warned Germany of its rights as neutrals to the safeguarding of its citizens' lives, and Germany made concessions of a sort from time to time, it was the reintroduction of unrestricted submarine warfare in January 1917 which actually cast the die for America's entry into war.

Britain also was guilty of violations of international law on the high seas, and President Wilson was angry with the British on occasion after occasion. In effect, Britain established an unlawful authority over all international trade. Some American ships bound for neutral countries were intercepted and held in British ports for months. When American mails were seized, the Secretary of State, Bryan, was furious, and demanded of Wilson that the Government be truly neutral and impartial. The clash between the view of Bryan and that of Lansing, his successor in the State Department, is well told by the historians Harry J. Carman and Harold C. Syrett:

> Wilson's decision to accept Lansing's rather than Bryan's views of submarine warfare was the turning point in the history of American neutrality. Wilson, basing his stand on principle, insisted that the United States could not stand by while Germany violated the laws of civilization by murdering innocent American citizens. But Bryan, too, relied on principles and stated that Wilson's policy endangered American lives and neutrality. To

Wilson's insistence that Germany was destroying American rights, Bryan replied that England was doing the same. There were, however, certain problems that Bryan refused to face. While it was true that Great Britain interfered with American commerce, it was also true that British policies never resulted in the loss of a single American life. Bryan could argue that Britain was merely in a more fortunate position than Germany in this respect, but the fact remains that the Germans killed Americans and the British did not. . . . Lansing, who convinced Wilson, was himself convinced that an Allied defeat would expose the United States to attack and possible destruction. To Wilson and his principal advisers from the time of Bryan's resignation in June 1915 until the American declaration of war in April 1917, the possibility of a German victory was all important in determining the United States' policy toward war in Europe. To Bryan it was an irrelevancy.[3]

Despite the drift toward war, Wilson desired to achieve peace and hoped that he could be the instrument by which it could be brought about. As late as January 22, 1917, nine days before Germany handed America the note warning that she would again unqualifiedly sink all vessels approaching the British Isles, Wilson appeared before Congress urging "peace without victory." He said further that "victory would mean peace forced upon the loser, a victor's terms imposed upon the vanquished"; that such a peace could not last because it would leave a sting. These were noble as well as realistic utterances; no other head of a great power was talking like that. . . . Yet this was equivalent to talking to oneself in the dark, with an awareness of what was in the dark and of the necessity to face it sooner or later. Publicly, the President called for peace without victory, but privately—as early as 1915—he confided to his intimates that Germany must not be allowed to win the war. The starry thoughts amidst which he lived told him one thing; his sense of reality told him another. Although he told the people that but for the submarine warfare America would not have entered the war, he told a member of the Senate Foreign Relations Committee that whether or not Germany had made any attacks on American shipping, America definitely would have entered the war.

[3] *A History of the American People*, Vol. II, p. 412; Alfred E. Knopf, Inc.

Germany, by her undersea warfare, was fighting for her existence just as desperately as Britain, by her policing of all traffic above the waters, was fighting for hers, but Germany blundered abysmally. Her torpedoing of the British liner *Lusitania* with almost 1,200 deaths, about 120 of which were American, did her no good, despite the fact that the ship carried some munitions and that advertisements had appeared in the newspapers warning Americans not to travel on that ship. What is known as the Zimmerman affair was another blunder. This was an intercepted German note to Mexico urging that country to strike against the United States in the event America became embroiled in the war in Europe, to recover her lost territories of Arizona, New Mexico, and California. There was also the Count Dumba affair, another case of an intercepted note, where Dumba, the Austrian ambassador to America, revealed plans for tying up war production in American plants.

Last, but not least, there was the highly important factor of American investments in the Allied cause. The House of Morgan became the official purchasing agent in the United States for the Allies, and was heavily involved. So were the steel and powder companies. All this was in no sense consonant with America's status as a supposed neutral, and Secretary Bryan wrote J. P. Morgan himself to that effect. Yet, as we have noted, it was the Allies who were able to buy; the Central Powers were unable to buy.

Here, however, we must deal with Woodrow Wilson's life and character, not with the first World War. The history texts tell us well enough what the gigantic undertaking was like, of the preparation and waging of war and the transporting of men across the Atlantic in a mass movement of troops the like of which mankind had never before seen. Although Rudyard Kipling complained that Americans were the eleventh-hour laborers who came in and demanded the same pay as the rest, the country did supply the extra weight that was needed for Allied victory. Without the United States it could never have been accomplished, for the U-boat was winning the war for Germany.

After the Second Battle of the Marne, in which the presence of Americans decided the outcome, and where, according to the German chancellor himself, "the history of the world was played out in three days," it was steady progress up to November 11, 1918, when the war ended. It is not commonly known that quotas of American troops served also in Italy, in northern Russia against the Bolsheviks (who had brought about the revolution in Russia in 1917 and had concluded a separate peace with Germany), and in Siberia to prevent America's ally Japan from taking over on the mainland. From the latter quarter American boys did not finally come home until April 1920.

Although realism compelled Wilson at last to go to war, he never once discontinued his star-gazing about the conflict. Taking the position that America was fighting for the rights of mankind, from time to time he gave utterance to mystical pronouncements articulated in the style of which he was so accomplished an artisan. His most famous proposal was the Fourteen Points, the crowning jewel of which was the idea of a League of Nations to prevent all future wars; and he was foolish enough to believe that the greedy nations of the world would gladly take refuge in such a league after the four years of carnage which took 8,500,000 lives. The allies gave lip service to these aims because, after all, their immediate interest was American military help and, anyway, the Wilsonian precepts had a good moral effect on their peoples.

While the Fourteen Points were for the most part well received in the United States, Wilson's announcement that he would sail for Europe to take part in the peace negotiations was not. It was an unheard-of thing; no President had ever sailed across 3,000 miles of sea to take part in an old diplomatic game fit only for seasoned and tradition-bred fighters. Wilson was completely unable to see that by his two trips to Paris to bargain for idealistic aims with materialists, he was throwing away the dignity of his office. The American people, as well as their statesmen, felt he was going into the lions' den and that both he and the country would somehow be hurt. But such was the willful schoolmaster in him, such his opinion of the blind wickedness of those who wanted to keep their feet on the ground, that he would see no one but himself as the apostle of the New Order.

Wilson was wrong to think that he alone was sincere in wanting a really just peace. He was wrong in believing that overnight he could bring about a new order. He was wrong in having had no bargaining power when he went to Paris: America had naively committed itself fully to the Allied cause without exacting any promises beforehand. Italy acted more intelligently; she came into the war only on the condition that she be awarded specific territories, and after the war she was at the conference table to collect. Wilson was wrong in not taking with him to Europe any prominent Republican or any Senator or Congressman. He was wrong in dropping one after another of his Fourteen Points on the basis of which the new German government had been willing to cease hostilities. He was wrong, to begin with, to have left the United States.

Because, regardless of what Wilson preached, the Allied nations in Europe had divided the spoils of victory long before America came in and this *fait accompli* Wilson had to face at once. Whether or not he knew of these secret deals before he arrived in Europe, one thing is certain: the American people did not know about them; and the disclosure of their existence only made old-fashioned Americans want to pull out of Europe the faster and made them resent the more their President's continued stay in what they felt was only a trap for the uninitiated. But Wilson, with all the disillusion he experienced in Europe, nevertheless felt that if he once succeeded in getting the Covenant of the League incorporated into the peace treaty, future conflicts would be avoided and past wrongs rectified. For the sake of his League, he gave way on many points.

The idea of a league or fraternity of nations was of course not original with Wilson. The Pax Romana, which kept peace by force (it was proposed that the new League also use force), is probably the oldest of such associations we know about. What is known as the Great Design of Henry of Navarre also proposed a league of nations which would keep the peace in Europe—but always, let us observe, *after* certain wicked nations had been subjugated and their rearming made impossible by the good, or victorious, nations. History tells us of many others who had grand schemes for getting nations to live together in peace—William Penn, Rousseau, Immanuel Kant, among them—but all, including Wilson, failed to take account of the invariableness of human nature.

The fight in the Senate of the United States over the ratification of the Versailles Treaty, which had been signed by Wilson and the representatives of the other Allied powers on June 28, 1919, five years to the day that the first shot had been fired in Europe, constitutes one of the most significant struggles in American national life. The controversial Article X of the League Covenant, by which member nations were to come to the aid of a nation who was attacked, was anathema to the Congress which correctly insisted on its Constitutional right as the sole repository of the power to declare war. The implacable Henry Cabot Lodge [4] and other irreconcilable Senators fought Wilson on ratification with savage bitterness. In the end the Treaty was defeated in the Senate. By a simple resolution in 1921, the Congress declared war with Germany terminated. In the Presidential election of 1920, the Democratic candidate, who campaigned on the Wilson policies, was overwhelmingly defeated, corroborating what the statesmen of Europe had known—namely, that the American people themselves did not support Wilson.

The people had shown in the off-year elections of 1918 that they did not approve of the Wilson philosophy by rejecting the President's request that Democratic majorities be returned to Congress that year; instead they had sent back Republican majorities. Nevertheless, Wilson refused to read this verdict correctly, and in late summer of 1919 undertook, against the advice of his physician, a speaking tour of the West to rally support for the League and thus force the Senate's hand. In a few weeks he was felled by a stroke which practically incapacitated him for the remainder of his life. Although an invalid, he was able to ride with his successor Harding on inauguration day and even outlived that robust man by six months. He died in Washington on February 3, 1924, while admirers knelt in prayer on the cold sidewalks outside his home.

Woodrow Wilson's last years were tragic. His being awarded the Nobel Peace Price in 1920 only highlighted the tragedy, for there was no peace. In those last sad years he had said to a journalist friend: "I would like to see Germany clean up France, and I would like to see Jusserand [the French ambassador] and tell him that to his face." It is an incredible statement.

The things Woodrow Wilson wanted were not wrong; they

[4] Not to be confused with Henry Cabot Lodge, Jr., his grandson and America's representative in the UN.

were eminently right—just as the things were right that he fought for at Princeton where his fight with his associates left bitter feeling also because of his arbitrary position. But the things that are right are not attained by pedagogically telling people they must do them. Man's ego will not tolerate this kind of ultimatum.

All peoples want peace. Whether civilization will ever achieve lasting peace no one knows. The United Nations, which today exists as the successor to Wilson's League, may be the expedient necessary to maintain a reasonable peace for these days, under a Pax Americana—in the West at least. But peace is never found in any organization, not even in a religion. Woodrow Wilson never found it for himself. For, like millions of others, he looked without, not within.

If the awesome crypt in Washington Cathedral, where reposes what is yet mortal of the tragic subject of this biography, teaches us anything, it is that no one in this life can hope to accomplish anything of permanence or be himself happy unless he has recognized the Second Commandment as a workable technique of living and the warm human responses which are the basis for apprehending it.

★★★★★★★★★★★★★★★★★★★★★★★★★★★★

28

WARREN GAMALIEL HARDING

☆ ☆

		Popular	Electoral
VOTE OF 1920:	Warren G. Harding, Republican	16,152,000	404
	James M. Cox, Democrat	9,147,000	127
	Eugene V. Debs, Socialist	920,000	
	Others	594,000	
		26,813,000	531

☆ ☆

THERE PROBABLY WAS NEVER A TIME BEFORE IN THE HISTORY OF THE American nation when the choices of the two great political parties for the Presidency made absolutely no difference whatsoever, as in 1920. Because there never was a time before when an incumbent Administration had such indisputable notice from the electorate that its political management would be discharged from office. Any Republican whatever could have won and any Democrat whatever would have lost.

No darker "dark horse" ever ran for President than Harding. With all the big names available in that first post-World War election, it seemed incredible that a country editor, who happened at the time to be a Senator from his state, would be named. When nominating time came, the Republicans were like a child at a toy counter whose father has told him he can have anything he wants, and who in his excited delight and confusion picks the wrong thing after all. To cap the irony: this incorrect choice was elected by the greatest plurality as well as the greatest majority vote ever won by a Presidential candidate up to that time. Even Franklin D. Roosevelt at the peak of his popularity did not receive a greater percentage of the popular vote.

Time and again scholars have pointed out that the American people are essentially a conservative people, but it takes an event like the 1920 election to bring that fact truly home. Even the voters of the Southern states, whom political managers had always counted in the Democratic column, were at heart conservative. It is one of the accidents of American national life that Southerners with their precious 128 electoral votes are in a different camp from the conservatives of the North and West; else the percentage of Harding's majority would have been much greater than 60-plus per cent. Even so, the Democratic state of Tennessee was carried by Harding also.

The reaction against war times and Wilson's internationalism was so great that Harding's campaign slogan of "back to normalcy" accurately designated what the people had in mind. The war seemed an unfortunate adventure. The results left Americans emotionally unsatisfied. There had been no material gains, and even the moral gains Wilson had promised were not in evidence anywhere. The Senate had refused to ratify the Versailles Treaty. The people frankly did not understand what the war had been about and not even the President had clarified the contest for them. No prominent person had told them that Anglo-American hegemony over the Atlantic community was essential to America's way of life. All the people heard was about German submarines, something about the "rape of Belgium," and other comparable issues—but nobody got down to the meat of the matter, and so the people remained confused. Wilson's "making the world safe for democracy" meant nothing to them. They knew only one thing in 1920: they wanted to recapture the old conditions and get back to their old way of life. That was what the election of 1920 meant.

George T. Harding, farmer-turned-physician, and Phoebe Dickerson were the parents of Warren G. Harding, born November 2, 1865, the eldest of eight children. The birthplace was a farmhouse near what is now Blooming Grove, in Morrow County, Ohio. Harding was graduated in due time from Ohio Central College at Iberia, and at seventeen moved with his family to Marion where he was to spend the remainder of his life except for the Washington interlude and a short time in Columbus. Having tried the law and disliked it, the tall handsome youth and a partner bought up a struggling paper, *The Marion Star*. In time he obtained sole control, and although he entered politics in 1898 when he was sent to the state Senate, his real love was the paper and his poker cronies. Prospering, he became active in Baptist, Masonic, and Elk circles and, needless to say, in local civic matters. He fitted in with this kind of life.

Let us pass quickly to this man's Presidency and mention only incidentally that he was Lieutenant-Governor of Ohio for a term and was defeated for the Governorship in 1910. In 1914 he went to the Senate in Washington. When, like the child at the toy counter, the Republicans were undecided about what to pick from the many good things they saw, and there at last emerged from the now famous "smoke-filled room" of a Chicago hotel the choice they finally hit upon, there were all kinds of reactions everywhere. One Republican Senator explained outright that the times did not require first-raters. The most significant reaction came from Harding's own wife: "I can see only one word written over his head if they make him President, and that word is Tragedy." One is reminded of Woodrow Wilson's youngest daughter at inauguration time in Washington, as she lay on the floor of her hotel room weeping hysterically because she said the job her father had taken was going to kill both her parents.[1] And we can say that it did.

Harding made some outstanding Cabinet appointments and also some dismal ones. Among the former were three men of as high a caliber as it has ever been the good fortune of the nation to be served by: Charles Evans Hughes, Secretary of State; Herbert Hoover, Secretary of Commerce; A. W. Mellon, Secretary of the Treasury. Of the latter class there were men who brought disgrace to their office and to the country and literally brought their chief to a premature death; their names are insignificant. On his return from a trip to Alaska, the President began to show signs of worry; it is believed that it was only then that the full impact of the disgraceful acts of his appointees became known to him. Herbert Hoover tells in his *Memoirs* that at one time during the journey the President called him in and asked him what he would do if he were to find that there had been a great scandal in his Administration. Hoover advised: "Publish it, and at least get credit for integrity on your side." As he lay in his hotel room in San Francisco, the President suddenly died on August

[1] Eleanor W. McAdoo: *The Woodrow Wilsons*, p. 202; The Macmillan Company.

2, 1923. Many people feel that the exact cause of death was never fully disclosed.

Harding left the leadership of his Administration largely to his Cabinet and the Congress; and that suited the country perfectly after the nerve-trying eight years of personal assertiveness by Wilson. Upon installation, Harding at once called the Congress into special session. The tariff was raised again, for the "return to normalcy" meant also the return to the old protectionist theories. Harding had declared the League issue "as dead as slavery," but he advocated, as did his Republican successors in office, American adherence to the World Court; Congress refused. Separate treaties of peace were drawn up with Germany and her allies so that America could at last get the European adventure officially behind her.

What is known as the Washington Conference, convened in the fall of 1921, for the purpose of reducing world armaments, is notable. It is notable because here, for the first time, Great Britain yielded to a modification of her complete command of the seas, and that meant only one thing—the beginning of American leadership in the world and the dependence of Britain on America instead of the other way around. A ratio in capital ships was agreed upon among Britain, America, and Japan of 5–5–3, this arrangement to be in force for fifteen years. The Conference involved the drawing up of several other treaties as well, one of which recognized the Open Door policy with respect to China and that country's territorial integrity and sovereignty. It abolished the use of poison gas in international warfare; and although England desired to outlaw the U-boat as well, the other nations did not want to go along with that proposal. The Conference, which unquestionably reduced tension in the Pacific and postponed war for a number of years in that area, was under the management of Secretary of State Hughes, who did a superlative job, as he did of every other job he ever undertook in his life.

The Harding Administration scandals were almost as great as those of the Grant period. The worst of these was called the Teapot Dome fraud, but there were two naval oil reserves involved—Teapot Dome in Wyoming and Elk Hills in California. The Secretary of the Interior persuaded the President to sign a transfer of these reserves from the Navy to his own Department;

and their subsequent leasing to private interests, resulting in Congressional investigations, trials, and personal humiliations, can furnish material for a thesis on many an aspect of the American political system.

But it was not with respect to the nation's oil reserves alone that wrongdoing was uncovered. Before everything was over, the following had to resign: the Secretary of the Navy, the Attorney General, the Director of the Veterans Bureau, the Alien Property Custodian, and the Secretary of the Interior, who was actually sentenced to prison.

During the Presidential campaign of 1952, when Republicans and Democrats were trying to show the people which Party had bred the most corruption, ex-President Hoover said in a radio address:

> There were nine men involved in the Harding episode. The other members of the Administration were aghast. They determined to pursue these men implacably. Before we had finished with them, two of them had committed suicide, one died while awaiting trial, four landed in prison, and one escaped by a twice-hung jury.[2]

Harding had a deep economic depression on his hands shortly after he went into office. Twenty thousand business houses in the country failed; U.S. Steel cut wages three times during the year. But in 1922 there was a revival, wage increases were in evidence once more, and there followed seven years of plenty—the period we now call the Roaring Twenties.

Possibly because Harding was the typical cocktail-drinking, poker-playing, extroverted good fellow, we associate with his name the sociological phenomenon less understandable even than the two World Wars—the Prohibition era. In January of 1920 the Eighteenth Amendment to the Constitution of the United States went into effect. Looking at it from this distance, it seems incredible that such an addition—an emotion—ever got into the Constitution. A recrudescence of Puritanism, beginning at about the time of the Civil War mounted steadily in an immature civilization, championing the underdog and the downtrodden, ex-

[2] *The Constructive Character of the Republican Party*, delivered in New York, October 18, 1952.

tolling Horatio Alger heroes and Pollyanna concepts, providing clergymen zealots an outlet for their dramatic energies, roaring through a heyday with the reform ideas of Theodore Roosevelt. Its fevers found an acme of expression in the crusade against the liquor traffic. It was from here that Prohibition exploded, to leave behind hypocrisy and disillusionment seldom experienced in human society.

It was in 1858 that Maine had gone dry; Kansas was second, in 1880; several other states followed. After 1920, when the entire nation became dry, and widespread lawlessness ensued, it became clear to all that, at the very least, the regulation of liquor had to be returned to the states; in December 1933, another amendment, the Twenty-First, invalidating the Eighteenth Amendment, went into effect. In this expensive, socially disturbing way the nation learned that it could not legislate with respect to private behavior. To a liberty-loving and liberty-nourished people, such as the American people are, the Prohibition experiment represented a monstrous violation of their most sacred prerogatives. It was among the last bits of national excess Americans would be guilty of in the field of moral preaching; any excess they would now be guilty of would be in the field of social enactments. Meanwhile, the Jazz Age, reactionary period to the World War, aided by Prohibition with its graft and excesses and tax evasions and "bootleg" deaths, rolled on during the roaring 1920's, showing perhaps its greatest effect in the so-called liberation of women.

The Harding election was the first in which women voted. The Nineteenth Amendment, also a product of the reform movement in the United States, went into effect in 1920, and provided that sex should not be a qualification for the exercise of the franchise.

Harding's inaugural was the first to be broadcast to the American people by radio—an art and an industry which was to affect American life profoundly. Harding's Secretary of Commerce, Hoover, whose business it was to regulate radio, early recognized the social consequences of broadcasting; and it is through him that the regulation of wave lengths and other phases of the new art were realized and that this new vital force in American life was brought, as Hoover wrote, "out of its swaddling clothes without any infant diseases."

As one studies the lives of the Presidents, observes the unbelievable limitations of the men who serve in that great office which Presidents occupy, realizes the chance the nation takes in selecting any man, one is reminded of how the Earl of Chatham, Benjamin Franklin and others have alluded to the preposterousness of affairs of government caused by mediocre men. In Harding Americans saw this mediocrity and ineptness. Yet Harding was very likable and completely patriotic, the townspeople of his native Marion loved him, and, as one of his employees said, "He never fired anybody." It is true that the office should seek the man, but a corollary should be that the man ought not to accept if in his own heart he knows his inadequacy. Harding himself never really sought to be President.

What has been described as one of the five most ostentatious Presidential memorials in the nation has been erected for Harding in Marion. President Coolidge, wily old Yankee that he was, would not accept the invitation to dedicate the memorial because he felt it would be a political liability to do that. President Hoover, who had more of the milk of human kindness in him, accepted and, while the Great Depression for which he was then being castigated still raged, endeavored in his dedicatory remarks to show how a good man could be betrayed by his friends.

The body of Harding's wife, the former Florence Kling DeWolfe, a widow whom he married in 1891, and who survived him only a short time, lies beside her husband in the memorial. There were no children. Before her death she had destroyed her husband's papers. It is doubtful if these ever would have been of particular value to the historian, since we know approximately all about those ebullient years that we need to know.

★★★★★★★★★★★★★★★★★★★★★★★★★★★★★★

CALVIN COOLIDGE

☆ ☆

VOTE OF 1920: *See* under Harding

		Popular	Electoral
VOTE OF 1924:	Calvin Coolidge, Republican	15,725,000	382
	John W. Davis, Democrat	8,386,000	136
	Robert M. LaFollette, Progressive	4,823,000	13
	Others	157,000	
		29,091,000	531

☆ ☆

"THE ERA OF SMUG SELF-COMPLACENCY." IN SUCH TELLING WORDS did a writer of the times characterize the five and one-half years of the Coolidge Administration. Not only was the era self-complacent, but so, it seemed, was the little red-headed Yankee who happened to find himself in the White House so accidentally at that time.

It was the anomaly of the 1923–29 years that Calvin Coolidge in his private life represented the very opposite of what his age seemed to typify, and the people idolized him for it. Intellectuals were disappointed and even openly expressed shock at the platitudinous sayings of their President. Others, who had learned in childhood that honesty was the best policy, bethought themselves, upon hearing Coolidge tell it to them again; it might really be true that it *was* the best policy!

That Calvin Coolidge was lacking in some desirable traits as a leader did not bother the people at all while he was in Washington. The people were still in revolt from the neurotic Wilson era; and, at the same time, they were happy with the unharnessed materialism of the Roaring Twenties. Calvin Coolidge was the antithesis of both, and the people loved it and wanted their President just to stay nice and quaint as he was and preside over the Prosperity.

The times did not call for profundities, so the President's inability to exhibit profundity was not missed. In his *Autobiography* he says: "I am not gifted with intuition." Truer words never appeared in any autobiography. Yet, because of his taciturnity, a refreshing element in public life, and his thrift and unassumingness, the people were fascinated by him and failed to realize that the country might suffer some day because of their President's lack of "intuition." Had there been an economic depression, he might have been reproached; but since times were booming, the American people, greatly oversimplifying, merely assured themselves that their frugal and honest President would watch over things, continue to believe in his mother's Bible, and by some Yankee alchemy peculiar to him, maintain the formula of good times.

Calvin Coolidge was one of two children born to John C. Coolidge and Victoria Moor at Plymouth, Vermont. The time of the President's birth was July 4, 1872. Between that date and the day of January 5, 1933 when he suddenly dropped dead, his life was of regular habits, unpretentiousness, and rock-ribbed faith in the *status quo*. He came from a rather distinguished old New England line; and, when we look at the pictures of his mother and grandmother, we see beautful, cultured women and not the depressing, hard-lipped kind whose pictures so often appear in biographies as the progenitors of America's great.

Coolidge's was a typical Vermont boyhood with chores on the farm and at the general store which his father conducted. His mother died when he was twelve and his father married again. The boy was given the same name as his father, but since he was always called Calvin, he dropped the John early in life, making his congenital frugality thus evident all down the line.

Coolidge was graduated *cum laude* from Amherst College, which he had entered in 1891. His preparatory schooling was obtained at Black River Academy and St. Johnsbury Academy, both in his home state. He began the study of law in a Northampton, Massachusetts, law office, and after twenty months of work and study, was admitted to the bar. He soon had his own law office. This kind of preparation is a far cry from what law students have to go through today. It is entirely probable that the country might never have heard of Coolidge had it been necessary for him to go for three years to an accredited law school after completing college work. But in 1895 times had not yet become so complicated.

Coolidge was always interested in politics, although he never expected to achieve more in life than moderate success as a small-town lawyer. In 1898 he was elected to the Northampton city council, and after that it was a steady climb to the top; he never once suffered defeat in any contest. He became, in turn, City Solicitor, Clerk of Courts, State House Representative, Mayor of Northampton (two terms), member of the State Senate (two years president of that body), Lieutenant-Governor, Governor, Vice-President, and President.

The utterance of one of his laconisms brought Coolidge to the national eye and his nomination for Vice-President in 1920. In a telegram he sent to the president of the American Federation of Labor at the time of the Boston police strike, he had included a sentence which read: "There is no right to strike against the public safety by anybody, anywhere, anytime." This homely and fortuitous arrangement of words "clicked" in the American mind. It made Coolidge a legend.

Coolidge was apprised of Harding's death by his father, and in the *Autobiography* he says that he knew that the quivering in his father's voice was caused as much "by the thought of the many sacrifices he had made to place me where I was . . . and all the tenderness and care he had lavished upon me in the thirty-eight years since the death of my mother" as it was by the suddenness of the death of the President of the United States.

At two o'clock in the morning, by the light of kerosene lamps, in a farmhouse of an obscure Vermont hamlet, Calvin Coolidge was sworn in as President of the United States by his own father. Was there ever in American life the enactment of greater drama!

The election of Coolidge to a term in his own right in 1924 was easy. Despite the fact that the "progressive" faction of his Party, under LaFollette, entered a separate ticket in the field, he won with a plurality of more than 7,000,000 votes. The prosperity continued, the high duties on imports were retained, and the public debt was reduced. God was in his heaven, the earth revolved in its orbit, and everything was as it should be, despite the saturnalia of speculation on the part of the people and the fact that the chickens from World War I had not yet come home to roost for good. Before the crash was finally to come, $100 par U.S. Steel was to be quoted on the market at 279 and American Tel. & Tel. at 310.

Nor did the economy-minded Coolidge lack support for his policies. His Secretary of the Treasury, A. W. Mellon, the Pittsburgh banker, art patron, and philanthropist, applied his talents toward reducing taxes and lowering the public debt. In ten years the debt was reduced from $24,000,000,000 to $16,000,000,000. The number of millionaires in the country had increased from 4,500 in 1914 to 11,000 in 1926.

It is interesting to note what America did with respect to the $11 billion owed by European countries, 40% of which had been loaned since the close of the war. Herbert Hoover, a member of the Foreign Debt Commission whose job it was to come to a satisfactory disposition of the matter, was in favor of canceling that part of the debt incurred during the war itself and negotiating debt-funding agreements for only the 40%; for he knew what America could in the long run expect from Europe in the way of payments. But the Commission would not hear of this suggestion for they feared Congress, and Congress in turn feared the people. When another proposal was made that all interest charges be waived, the same fears were expressed, and so the debt-funding agreements provided for payment of principal and interest over a period of sixty-two years. One of Britain's Prime Ministers was later to call these agreements "crazy."

It is one of the ironies of the political game that, although Finland alone of the debtor nations regularly met her payments under the agreement, the United States severed diplomatic relations with her during World War II, blacklisted her firms in America, and impounded the funds she had on deposit in American banks—all to please a lukewarm ally, Russia. Again we see how often in the intercourse of nations Justice is adjusted to expediency and opportunism.

Coolidge was not an internationally-minded man. He was a provincial whose horizon was really on the edge of his Vermont hills. Yet, as President, he listened to his Secretary of State, Kellogg, who, with the French Foreign Minister Briand, had en-

visioned a great pacific project for outlawing war as an instrument
of national policy. Called the Pact of Paris, it was adhered to by
sixty-two states and won for Kellogg the Nobel Peace Prize.
The treaty is interesting in a curious sense as the sort of humanitarian venture nations will gladly enter into when all is well, when
prosperity reigns—and when the enemy is securely shackled. It
is interesting in a lamentable sense as the kind of thing nations
will disregard when other plans they develop do not happen to
conform with the requirements of the agreement. Pact-signing in
these postwar years was a mockery. It was conceived in fear and
nurtured in rivalry—a presage of the renewal of war.

Immigration came in for an overhauling again in 1924. The
new Act allowed each country to send to the United States every
year two per cent of the number of persons of that nationality
living in America as of 1890. This did not apply to Western
Hemisphere and Oriental countries. To Coolidge's credit it must
be recorded that he was opposed to the Japanese exclusion provision of the Act as being undemocratic. As if to make up for this
bit of un-Americanism, Congress in the same year declared that
all native Indians were to be counted as citizens of the United
States—a magnanimous pronunciamento that has its own ironic
implications.

Because it was a prelude to the great age of the airplane, both
commercial and military, into which the world was so soon to
move, it is of interest to note that Admiral Richard E. Byrd in
1926 flew over the North Pole, and over the South Pole in 1929.
Peary had reached the former in 1909 and Amundsen the latter
in 1911 through inconceivable hardships. Now the great man-
birds conquered the polar areas easily. Even the shoreline of the
remote, inscrutable continent of Antarctica was further charted
by Byrd on his various trips to that region. Then there was Lind-
bergh's solo flight to Paris in 1927, a sensation for those times,
precursor to the regular transatlantic flights so common today.

Coolidge was fortunate in his wife, the former Grace Goodhue.
Many an embarrassing situation caused by his brusque manner
and uncommunicativeness was saved by his charming and tactful
wife whose extroverted ways were a great relief to her husband's
unsocial disposition. They had two sons. The death of the younger
while the Coolidges were still in the White House was a severe

blow to the President; some say he never really recovered from it and that it contributed to the coronary thrombosis which was the cause of his sudden death.

After he left office, Coolidge became a director of the New York Life Insurance Company, a trustee of Amherst, and an officer in the American Antiquarian Society. For a while he wrote a syndicated column and wails went up again over the platitudinous character of the writings.

In a hillside cemetery in his native Vermont, where six generations of his line are interred, Calvin Coolidge was buried between his father and his son. He had had a foreboding of ill health and therefore chose not to run for President again in 1928, although his popularity was so great that he could have had the nomination on the first ballot by a nod of the head. In 1932 he spoke for Hoover in that President's campaign for re-election.

There has been considerable discussion about the place of Calvin Coolidge among the nation's heroes. His character is uncommon to Americans generally, but it is not difficult to see that he was almost completely an introvert, and, like many introverts, rather self-centered. He could be quite sentimental at times: his devotion to his Vermont hills, for example, was simply nostalgia; the wider love of Nature and her works in the universal sense was an emotion he knew little about. Nor did he care for music, apparently, or art, or even athletics. His looks and personality eloquently bespoke this general impoverishment.

Yet Coolidge filled a need in American life, if only by reminding a complex generation that simple things existed for their benefit provided they met the requirements for receiving them. In a time of stress, which the years of his Administration were not, his pithy admonitions would have been ridiculed. In a time of national well-being, they were given ready approbation. In a certain sense, no other American's life was so dramatic in its stark simplicity. Even his remote burial site, in an old cemetery reached by a narrow dirt road, so secluded in his native state that only few Americans ever have the opportunity of visiting it, communicates an awesomeness to the beholder, insinuating a sense of the evanescence of earthly strivings which few other sights in the United States can evoke.

The American people have always felt good about the Coolidge years, not because they were characterized by provocative leadership, but because they bestir nostalgic memories of a gloriously undisturbed era when the old *laissez faire* was at its zenith. No matter who might have been President, the times would have continued as good; but since they happened to be presided over by one who was a throwback to the farmers of the early, hard-grubbing Colonial era, they are of additional interest.

Nothing could have been more in conformity with Nature's processes than the moment of Calvin Coolidge's death, virtually on the eve of the approach of the New Deal—a situation to which, by his own admission, he could never have become accustomed. The death of Coolidge is a graphic symbol of the death of an era.

It is inevitable and perhaps well that we shall not see this era again.

30

★★★★★★★★★★★★★★★★★★★★★★★★★★★★★★

HERBERT HOOVER

☆ ☆

		Popular	*Electoral*
VOTE OF 1928:	Herbert Hoover, Republican	21,392,000	444
	Alfred E. Smith, Democrat	15,017,000	87
	Norman Thomas, Socialist	267,000	
	Others	97,000	—
		36,773,000	531

VOTE OF 1932: *See* under Franklin D. Roosevelt

☆ ☆

WHEN HERBERT HOOVER LEFT OFFICE IN MARCH 1933, IT SEEMED ludicrous to believe that his name would ever mean anything to his countrymen save as a synonym for outmoded conservatism and economic debacle. That he was unjustly maligned by large sections of Americans is admitted everywhere. And it is seldom that it is given to a maligned public figure to realize in his own lifetime the poet's prediction that "Truth crushed to earth shall rise again." Oftener than not, Error "dies [not] among his worshippers," but continues to sit in the driver's seat and crack the facile whip of half-truth, bigotry, and opportunism.

Nobody like Herbert Hoover had ever been in the American Presidency before. He was a mining engineer, and like most engineers, a man of quiet temperament. He was undramatic as Cleveland, as unpolitical as Taft; and while he faced the issues of his day in a truly patriotic manner, his inability to extrovert himself toward his countrymen in that sore period during which he presided lost him his re-election. His predicament was almost exactly like that of John Quincy Adams whose re-election was impossible because of a like deficiency in temperament, to say nothing of the parallel of the economic depressions which plagued them both.

Son of a blacksmith, Jesse Clark Hoover, and an ordained Quaker minister, Huldah Minthorn, Herbert Hoover was born August 10, 1874, at West Branch, Iowa, the first President to be born West of the Mississippi. The original migrator of his paternal line was a great-great-great-grandfather of Swiss origin. The entire line were Quakers, as were the English ancestors on his mother's side.

Hoover was orphaned at an early age, and this fact doubtless had a lot to do with his feelings for the hungry children of Europe during the two World Wars. Unlike many orphans, Hoover had the good fortune to be brought up by relatives of a high type. It was while serving as office boy in his uncle's real estate office in Salem, Oregon, that he became interested in mining. In 1891 he entered the first class of the newly opened Leland Stanford University in California.

Hoover's mining career began in San Francisco. His performance was such that, when an inquiry came for a young engineer to introduce American methods in the gold fields of Western Australia, Hoover was offered the job. Only twenty-three years of age, his salary was $7,500 per year. After a time in Australia, Hoover's firm gave him another assignment, in China; so, after a visit home during which he married Miss Lou Henry, whom he had met at Stanford and who also was interested in geology, he sailed for China.

For the next dozen or fifteen years Hoover was a world traveler. As a partner in a London firm, he conducted operations in China, Australia, Africa, Central America, South America, Burma, and the Urals. At the outbreak of war in Europe in 1914, we find Hoover in London, and that is where our interest in this singular personality begins. Although he did not know it then, his private life was over.

When war found 150,000 Americans stranded in Europe, unable to get passage home because of the breakdown of international credit facilities, Hoover and some friends took up these responsibilities, which the consular offices could not cope with at all, and personally assisted the Americans, many of whom were school teachers on vacation, to get back home.

When Germany violated the neutrality of Belgium and approximately 10,000,000 Belgians and Northern French found themselves encircled by blockade and armies and threatened with starvation, Hoover again was called upon, and he formed the Commission for the Relief of Belgium. He consulted the governments of both the Allies and the Central Powers, appealed to the Christian instincts of all peoples, and effected the distribution of 5,000,000 tons of food worth $1,000,000,000.

After America's entry into the war, President Wilson appointed Hoover U.S. Food Administrator, in which capacity his organization stimulated production, prevented hoarding, and fostered the conserving of food. He was also chairman of the Interallied Food Council. After the armistice he was adviser to President Wilson in Paris, and head of the Supreme Economic Council. As chairman of the American Relief Administration, he again shipped, with the aid of a Congressional appropriation, five million tons of food in eight months to twenty-three countries. When this relief act expired in 1919, Hoover and some friends continued it privately under the name of the European Children's Fund. During the years 1919–21, an estimated fifteen to twenty million children were nurtured back to health.

In 1921, when he was Harding's Secretary of Commerce, Hoover received an appeal from Maxim Gorky, the Russian author, to come to the help of Russia's suffering, caused by the Ukraine famine of that year. He accepted this undertaking, which lasted into the year 1923; and it brought from Gorky the statement that Hoover had saved three and one-half million children and five and one-half million adults, and from the Russian government a citation for his services. In return for all this, Hoover tells us in his *Memoirs,* the Soviet for years had paid agents in the United States going up and down the land berating his character.

In 1922 Hoover organized the American Child Health Association and became its first president. After the invasion and defeat in 1939 of the honorable Finnish people at the hands of a later ally, Russia, Hoover, who knew the Russians, headed the Finnish Relief in the United States. Finally, after he was inactive during the whole of the Roosevelt years, President Truman called him out of retirement to offer him the job of investigating food conditions in the world, and he headed the National Famine Emergency Committee, going to Europe, Asia, and South America—at his own expense.

Certainly this is a record of epic accomplishment in the relief of human suffering.

In studying Coolidge's life we have seen why those times were called "the era of smug self-complacency." As happens in life when self-satisfaction asserts itself, the smugness was knocked out from under it by disaster. The American people had gone on a debauch of speculation—getting rich by means other than those of production or the rendering of legitimate services. They changed the essential character of the stock exchange which, instead of being a device for the gathering, exchange, or disposal of funds for investment in legitimate enterprise, became at times a mere gambling ring. The inevitable crash came. On October 24, 1929, almost eight months after Hoover assumed the Presidency, the New York stock market collapsed, and 19,000,000 shares changed hands on that day alone. By November 13th following, $30 billion in "capital values" had been swept away.

A calamity like this had never happened before, and the people as well as their Government did not know how to handle it. Their first impulse was to assure themselves that the recession in business would pass just as all others in the country's history had passed. This might have been all right if the depression had had only national origins; but Hoover steadfastly maintained that the storm center of the world catastrophe was in Europe, whose great war of 1914–18, punitive treaties of peace, revolutions, inflation, rearmament programs, and illogical economic policies all contained the very germ of disaster. He stated that a normal recovery was on its way in America in 1931, when the bottom dropped out of everything in Central Europe, followed by Britain's abandoning the gold standard and suspending specie payments both public and private. A score of countries then also went off the gold standard. This was when unemployment in America really began to climb. About this time the figure was 7,000,000. The Depression was deepening. Even municipalities were going bankrupt; school teachers were not being paid. Bread lines were common.

In refusing in 1887 to approve Federal aid for drought sufferers, the forthright President Cleveland had maintained that "though the people support the Government, the Government should not support the people." Neither did Van Buren, Theodore

Roosevelt, Buchanan, Grant, or Hayes feel it to be the duty of the Executive to ameliorate conditions brought on by the depressions of their times. Their theory was to let forces run their course and exhaust themselves.

Because he had a horror of bureaucracy, Hoover opposed a Federal dole to the unemployed. He did, however, believe that his country owed a responsibility to its nationals to try to see that nobody was hungry or ill-clothed during the crisis; but he believed this relief should come from local sources, implemented, when necessary, by the Red Cross or an RFC loan or a Congressional appropriation.

The Hoover Government tried in many ways to combat the Great Depression. Industry was appealed to not to cut wages. The Federal Reserve Bank lowered its rediscount rate in an effort to expand credit. The National Credit Corporation was established to help small banks. The Reconstruction Finance Corporation (RFC) with a capitalization of three and one-half billion dollars was set up to lend money to industry, railroads, promote self-liquidating public projects, and allot money to the states for direct relief. Hoover telegraphed governors and mayors throughout the country to inaugurate public works wherever possible. The bankruptcy laws were reformed. The Administration created the half-billion dollar Federal Farm Board to support farm prices during the Depression. Public works and slum clearance projects were financed. Expansion of the Federal Land Banks to save farm mortgages was secured. The Home Loan Banks to save home owners from foreclosure were created. In spite of all these measures, improvement was rare. The Depression did not leave.

There is no doubt that the banking structure of the nation was faulty and that it contributed to the suffering of that era. The enactment of the Federal Reserve banking system in 1913 was expected to eliminate panics, but only one-third of the 25,000 banks belonged to the Federal Reserve System. The state-chartered banks were a weak link in the financial system; five times as many failed during the Depression as did national banks. In the eight years immediately *preceding* the Depression there were actually 4,000 bank failures in America, while there were none to speak of in Britain or the Commonwealth countries. An additional fifty-one hundred banks failed during the first three years of the Depression itself.[1]

In 1931 Hoover called for a moratorium on all international debt payments, a move which was well received both at home and in circles abroad. But the downward spiral of deflation had yet to run its course, and recovery still did not come.

When Hoover called Congress into extra session early in 1929 to redeem his Party's campaign pledge to do something for the farmer, one of the results was a new tariff, called the Smoot-Hawley Act. Hoover was in reality a moderate protectionist and did not care for all the provisions of the new act; but he signed it because of the protection it gave the farmers from importation of foreign beef, grain, and dairy products. The percentage of imports free of duty in this law was 62%, Mr. Hoover says in his *Memoirs;* the percentage of free items in 1897 was only 45%; so that the accusation that it was the highest tariff in history is not true.

Hoover had scarcely taken over in the Commerce Department when he presented President Harding with a comprehensive program for the reorganization of the Federal Government; the program was defeated by the Congress. While he was President, he asked Congress for authority to consolidate some fifty-eight bureaus and commissions and that body again refused the request. Then in 1947, as if to compensate him for their long-delayed co-operation in these economy measures, Congress created the bipartisan Commission on Organization of the Executive Branch of the Government, and Hoover was offered the chairmanship of it. The recommendations of this commission were designed to save the American taxpayers seven billions of dollars per year; by 1959, 72% of what has become known as the Hoover Report had been adopted.[2] In 1953 Hoover was appointed by President Eisenhower as chairman of a second Government reorganization commission—called the Second Hoover Commission—having a far greater scope of operation than the first commission. Hoover esti-

---

[1] *The Memoirs of Herbert Hoover,* Vol. III, pp. 21–23; The Macmillan Company.
[2] *Reorganization News* for October 1958, published by the Citizens' Committee for Reorganization of the Executive Branch of the Government, New York, N. Y.

mated that the recommendations of the second commission might eventually save the Government three billion dollars a year; by 1959 almost 64% of these recommendations were adopted.[3]

It is not generally known that some of the great water-power projects since completed were begun by the Hoover Administration—Colorado River (Hoover Dam), the Great Valley of California (Shasta Dam), Columbia River Basin (Grand Coulee). Hoover's one fear about all these undertakings was that the Government might go into competition with its citizens in the business of selling power.

Few now know that Hoover was considered a radical by Big Business for his labor views. Alone he fought the United States Steel Corporation for the abolition of the twelve-hour day. First he converted President Harding to this thinking. Then he had Harding convene a White House conference for the purpose of letting the steel men know that the Administration backed an eight-hour day in the industry. Judge Gary, head of U. S. Steel, gave Hoover and the Administration a very difficult time, and his eventual acceptance of the proposal was grudging.

Likewise with social security, Hoover was ahead of his time. While still in Harding's Cabinet he spoke to the heads of the leading insurance companies about a program for unemployment insurance; but the insurance companies weren't interested, the exigencies of the Depression intervened, and the idea was laid aside.

Two sociological studies made by the Government during Hoover's term of office were highly important. One was called *Recent Social Trends* and the other was the report of the Wickersham Commission. The latter is remembered chiefly for its statement that the Eighteenth Amendment was not working in the country. Hoover did not take a forthright stand on Prohibition. He was not a teetotaler himself and it is hard to see what he was to gain by not coming out for repeal of the Amendment, as his opponent Alfred E. Smith had done. It is believed that Elihu Root, the former Secretary of State and a titan in the legal field, advised Hoover that he should uphold the law. The attempts at enforcement of the Prohibition laws were so farcical, that it is

[3] *Ibid.*

not too much to say that, had Hoover come out unequivocally for repeal, some millions of votes he did not get either in 1928 or in 1932 would have come his way. But, unfortunately, politics had a lot to do with Prohibition also, and the Republicans were afraid of the wrath of church groups and others if they forsook the Prohibition cause.

Hoover was the author of several books, all having to do either with the bedrock principle of liberty in which he so strongly believed or the problem of peace. With his wife he also translated Agricola's sixteenth century *De Re Metallica,* a metallurgical treatise theretofore available only in Latin. In 1919 he founded the Hoover Institute and Library at Stanford University, constituting a rich repository of material and memorabilia for scholars on the problems of war and peace, the ever-recurring problems of mankind.

A man, to be a popular president, should know how to make scintillating moves and perform impulsive acts on occasion. This does more to impress the people, who after all are not profoundly informed about their times, than all the iteration of duty being done and alternatives being exhausted. Such iteration the people find tiresome. Herbert Hoover's temperament was too saturnine, too undramatic: he could not electrify. Franklin D. Roosevelt, lover of crowds that he was, knew exactly how to talk to crowds, how to smile at them, how to glamorize what he had in mind for them; for which reasons the people turned to him as the Moses of their day. The trouble with the Hoover policies was not that they were unworkable but that their workability was not communicated to the people: their chief advocate could not communicate them himself.

Hoover's public service was unique in the chronicle of America. No one who would turn down a civil job paying a guaranteed $500,000 a year, such as the Guggenheim interests offered Hoover after World War I, in order to take a $10,000-a-year Cabinet post because such a post afforded him an opportunity of doing something for postwar reconstruction in his country—no one who does such a thing is an ordinary individual. Nor can any right-thinking person be indifferent to such an individual nor indifferent upon learning that in all his Government connections, including the four years in the Presidency, Hoover accepted no salary whatever. For fully half his long life he was of service to the American people without receiving one cent of monetary remuneration.

In his campaign for re-election, Hoover had declared that the contest was between two different philosophies of government. The statement is, of course, correct; but it needs supplementing in order to understand how the people of the time felt. The contest demonstrated the natural impatience of ordinary men with conventional processes which are not giving them bread to eat. It also demonstrated that when human beings suffer, what they want is an unmistakable exhibition of warmth for their plight: nothing short of this will be understood: talk of theories and history certainly cannot be listened to at such a time.

But Herbert Hoover came through this crucible of rejection an unembittered man. He was more highly thought of several decades after his Presidency by his countrymen than ever before in his life. And his friends found additional solace in his example as they saw his lifespan reaching beyond fourscore years—the longest of any President since John Adams, with whose Administration his own had so much in common.

On October 20, 1964 Herbert Hoover died in his New York hotel suite, his residence for 32 years; he was ninety years old. His body was returned to his Iowa birthplace, and in a hilltop grave, while an Army band played *The Battle Hymn of the Republic*, was laid to rest within 600 yards of the tiny cottage in which he was born. No other President had accomplished so much in his retirement.

★★★★★★★★★★★★★★★★★★★★★★★★★★★★★★★

31

FRANKLIN DELANO ROOSEVELT

☆ ☆

		Popular	*Electoral*
VOTE OF 1932:	Franklin D. Roosevelt, Democrat	22,822,000	472
	Herbert Hoover, Republican	15,762,000	59
	Norman Thomas, Socialist	884,000	
	Others	348,000	
		39,816,000	531
VOTE OF 1936:	Franklin D. Roosevelt, Democrat	27,479,000	523
	Alfred M. Landon, Republican	16,679,000	8
	Norman Thomas, Socialist	188,000	
	Others	1,301,000	
		45,647,000	531
VOTE OF 1940:	Franklin D. Roosevelt, Democrat	27,244,000	449
	Wendell L. Willkie, Republican	22,305,000	82
	Norman Thomas, Socialist	100,000	
	Others	171,000	
		49,820,000	531
VOTE OF 1944:	Franklin D. Roosevelt, Democrat	25,603,000	432
	Thomas E. Dewey, Republican	22,006,000	99
	Norman Thomas, Socialist	80,000	
	Others	287,000	
		47,976,000	531

☆ ☆

BIOGRAPHERS AND HISTORIANS HAVE A DISMAYING HABIT OF DECLINING to judge one of their own times by saying that "he is too near to us." They are voluble enough about the happenings of the contemporary scene; but when it involves a major player they tell us we can not pass a cool judgment on one of our own period for perhaps fifty years.

Yet it is the *happenings* we can not judge properly, not the participants in those happenings. It is true that we shall not know for fifty, maybe a hundred years, how near to, or far from, the right answer a public figure's policies may have been. Nevertheless, we still know *him*. And, of course, if *we* do not know him, who lived with him and worked with him, who will know him?

Franklin D. Roosevelt was the most controversial man ever to occupy the Presidential office and he will be a controversial figure for some time to come. His terms contained so many "firsts," the problems he dealt with were so multifarious, his life was so scintillating, the times in which he lived were so revolutionary, the war over which he presided was of such unprecedented magnitude, the loyalties and enmities he evoked were on such an extreme scale, that the chronicler is bewildered by the quantity and variety of the data to be considered, and frustrated in the effort to properly evaluate the era.

America no less than Europe loves its royalty, its Messiahs, its heroes. And at no other time is the desire for a hero so overpowering as when a nation has been through lean years. It is then that the hero-designate must take his people into the fat years and make them happy again. It is that mandate from the people which explains Franklin D. Roosevelt.

FDR was born at the ancestral mansion at Hyde Park, New York, the only child of elderly James Roosevelt and his young second wife Sarah Delano. His education was obtained privately, at Groton, Harvard, Columbia Law School, and abroad. Before he became President, he had held three public offices—State Senator at Albany from his home county, Assistant Secretary of the Navy during the terms of Woodrow Wilson, and Governor of New York. In 1920—that year of the Harding-Coolidge landslide—he had been the unsuccessful Vice-Presidential candidate of the Democratic Party. Shortly after this election, he was stricken with poliomyelitis and spent the next decade fighting to regain his health. He never fully recovered and for the remainder of his sixty-three years walked only with the aid of braces, cane, and a companion's arm.

Roosevelt was a longtime devotee of New York's able Governor, Alfred E. Smith. In 1928, when the latter was running for the Presidency, Roosevelt was prevailed upon by Smith to run for Governor in order to help carry New York for the national ticket. He at once attracted nationwide attention by winning the Governorship at the same time that Smith lost the state. So, when the

Great Depression broke the following year, it was never lost sight of that Roosevelt was Presidential material.

Unmistakably, Roosevelt's greatest asset in 1932 was his name. Millions of Americans of that time remembered with nostalgia the Presidency of his distant cousin Theodore. The Presidency had somehow never been the same since Teddy left. To have another Roosevelt to lead the nation, and in those dreadful days of depression suffering—what portent of boon might that not be! But that was not the whole story of FDR's appeal. As Governor, he was putting through a reform program which included such things as tighter regulation of public utilities, reforestation, and a system of unemployment insurance. This brought about his re-election by the greatest plurality any gubernatorial candidate in New York had ever received.

In the last days of the Hoover Administration, of course, a bank panic had seized the nation. Roosevelt's first act upon coming into the Presidency was to issue an executive order closing all the banks, authority for which he found in an old wartime act of 1917 that had not been repealed. He then called the 73rd Congress into extraordinary session and presented that body with an emergency banking bill, the two Houses passing it almost unanimously. On March 13th following, the panic began to abate and gradually the sound banks were reopened.

In June 1933 the special session of the Congress came to an end. This session is known as the "Hundred Days." Never before in American history had so much important legislation been enacted in so short a time. Bill after bill was sent from the White House to Capitol Hill at regular intervals. Congress, with no policy of its own, was, like the people themselves, only too ready to follow executive leadership. Roosevelt throughout all his Presidential terms unquestionably supplied leadership, regardless of how some people came to criticize that leadership.

When he accepted the nomination of the Democratic Party, FDR had declared for a "new deal" for the American people. Thereafter his Administration was called the New Deal by both its friends and its foes. The legislation of the Hundred Days was the basis of what came to be known as the First New Deal. This legislation, besides the Emergency Banking Law, covered an Economy Act, granting the President wide powers to cut salaries of Government employees and veterans' pensions. It created a Civilian Conservation Corps to give temporary employment to young unmarried men between eighteen and twenty-five, who would probably send the bulk of their earnings home. The Hundred Days provided additional appropriations for the Hoover-born Reconstruction Finance Corporation whose functions were now expanded to include relief. There was created an Emergency Relief Administration, based on the system of outright grants to states and municipalities; a National Industrial Recovery Act with its controversial price-fixing codes; a Public Works Administration; a Farm Mortgage Refinancing Act to enable the Government to assume mortgages of farms about to be foreclosed; a Farm Credit Administration, a loan agency for farmers. Then there was the Agricultural Adjustment Act (AAA), a cutback production program for the farmer by which he was paid for underproduction; a Home Owners Loan Corporation to save private residences other than farm homes. There was created the Securities and Exchange Commission for the Federal regulation of all stock exchanges; and the Federal Deposit Insurance Corporation guaranteeing individual bank deposits up to $5,000.[1]

In addition to all this, Roosevelt took the nation off the gold standard in an effort to regain foreign markets; and, while not coming out for bimetallism as such, he had the Treasury buy great quantities of silver at a price higher than market. In 1934 he pegged gold at 59-plus per cent of its former value.

Probably the most noteworthy act passed during the Hundred Days was the creation of a corporation known as the Tennessee Valley Authority, controlling thirty dams in the Tennessee River basin, created for the purpose of conservation and development of this region, with the right to generate and sell electricity to municipalities and co-operatives. The Socialist candidate for President hailed TVA as one step toward the realization of his Party's aims in the United States. The Supreme Court upheld the unprecedented legislation.

So swift and dazzling were these recovery laws that by the time

[1] It should be recognized that much of the legislation of this time was bipartisan in conception. The late Republican Senator Vandenberg of Michigan, rather than the New Deal, is often credited with being the father of FDIC. Depositors now are insured up to $20,000.

the off-year elections of 1934 came around, there was a further
reduction of Republican ranks in both houses of the Congress
instead of the usual mid-term rebuke to the party in power which
Americans had become accustomed to. And by the time 1936 was
past, the re-election of the President had been accomplished by
an 11,000,000 plurality and the electoral vote of 46 states. No
other Presidential candidate had ever won so sweeping a victory
at the polls. The people evidently were pleased with what they
had seen of the New Deal. After four years in office, Roosevelt's
appeal was no longer merely in his name, but in his glittering
reform program which the common man loved. And whatever
doubts many Americans may have had about the wisdom of the
way in which some of this program was launched were dispelled
the moment they heard the President speak. For Roosevelt had a
voice, the quality and magic of which have never been excelled
by any other American ever to appear in public life.

But Al Smith sulked in his tent. "Alphabet soup," he called
the countless New Deal agencies whose long names could be remembered only by their initials. And the National Association of
Manufacturers sulked. So did the Jeffersonian Democrats who
constituted the life of the Democrary of the South. So did the
banking interests of the nation who were in constant dread lest
Roosevelt tamper further with the currency. So did certain city
bosses and state political moguls who feared the national machine
FDR was building up. So did the ultraconservative Supreme
Court. So did the industrialists of the nation who quaked at the
prospect of the abandonment of *laissez faire* altogether. So did
the majority of the newspapers which, after all, were manned by
editors definitely in the conservative column. So did, of course,
nearly all the Republicans of the country. So did the bulk of the
Protestant Church.

But FDR had his supporters—the widest variety of supporters
any public official in America ever has had. As a Democrat, he
could command without question the 128 electoral votes of the
Solid South. Then there were the great city machines, as in New
York, Chicago, and Jersey City, which were all solidly Democratic. There was Labor, who found in FDR an advocate the like
of which it had never before had. There were the millions of
foreign-born, naturalized and unnaturalized, with their poverty-

conscious outlook on life, who cared little about such abstractions as "liberty" or "private initiative" and to whom the then current slogans of "soak the rich" and "the forgotten man" were the sole indices of how they would cast a ballot. Many thousands of these forgotten men, including many artists, received for a time employment under WPA. Roosevelt had the support of all types of minority groups, racial, religious, economic, and social; and often "leftist" elements who temperamentally had nothing in common with the President's thinking would attach themselves to his cause, embarrassing him by what they did and by evoking the charge of "socialistic" against his Administration. There was, of course, the huge group of Government employees upon whose support the New Deal could always depend. And there were the farmers who, under the Commodity Credit Corporation, AAA, and other legislation, had received Government support such as farmers had never before enjoyed.

Probably the group to come in for the severest criticism were the "intellectuals," of whom great numbers were brought to Washington by department heads. These very often amounted to, in effect, social workers who saw the New Deal as a great laboratory destined to operate for the betterment of mankind; and smart young legal graduates for whom FDR's government was simply *la grande occasion* for erecting on American shores a new Utopia—and cozy niches for themselves whence they could emerge periodically in the role of the prophets of the New Day.

It was inevitable in a traditionally conservative society that the Roosevelt program would sooner or later be brought before the Judicial Department of the Government. So, in 1935, the Supreme Court struck down the National Industrial Recovery Act, the Agricultural Adjustment Act, the Bituminous Coal Stabilization Act, the Railway Pension Act, New York's minimum wage law for women and children. All were unconstitutional, the Court decreed. Roosevelt took these upsets hard and was determined to strike back. There followed bitter acrimony against the Court. "The Nine Old Men," they were called, and their rulings "horse and buggy decisions." The President proposed to Congress legislation enabling him to appoint one new judge for every one on the Supreme bench over seventy who did not resign. This would have given him a majority in the Supreme Court to sustain him in his program.

Many liberals insisted that the Nine Old Men had no right to interfere in social legislation designed for the betterment of individuals. But the Court, ever since Jefferson's time, when it first invalidated an act of Congress in the Marbury *vs.* Madison case, visualized its duty as protecting individual liberties by passing on the constitutionality of legislation, whether Federal or state. In that famous decision, Chief Justice Marshall initiated the principle that "a legislative act contrary to the Constitution is not law . . ." and thus invested in the Court the power of legislative review which it has ever since possessed.

The "court packing" bill of the New Deal failed in committee. But the President continued to fight for his plan for reform of the Court. His opposition now was turned against some of the solons on Capitol Hill, certain Senators in particular; and, against the advice of his political manager, James A. Farley, he attempted a "purge" of such men as had opposed the Court plan. He went into the states where some of the Senators were running for re-election and asked the people in those states not to return those Senators to Washington. In Georgia he spoke from a platform along with the Senator he advocated be unseated, an unusual thing in national politics.

The people were quick to reject Roosevelt's intended purge; they defeated many of the Senatorial candidates who had the Administration's blessing. In 1938 the trend away from the New Deal was apparent from the returns of the mid-term elections.

In the meantime Roosevelt began to realize some of his Court dreams by receiving some resignations from the Supreme bench. With appointees of his own on the Court replacing the retired judges, there began to be handed down various 5–4 decisions which, while not 100% corroborative of the Roosevelt policies, nevertheless were victories for the Administration. In 1937 the Court reversed itself and upheld a minimum wage law for women. The National Labor Relations Act, that important law guaranteeing the worker the right of collective bargaining, also was upheld, and again five votes to four. The oft-quoted observation that "th' Supreme Coort follows th' iliction returns" was receiving fresh meaning. Yet the American people had over a long time come to revere the Court, and Roosevelt did his popularity irreparable harm when he tried to bring it into submission.

Before the New Deal came to an end, there was further progressive legislation enacted; additional quasi-judicial boards were created.

The New Deal came to an end for more reasons than the adverse returns from the 1938 Congressional elections. First, the national economy was beginning to show the strain of the constant experimentation with its functionings. Many people felt that the nation would have been in a better condition had the Depression been allowed to run itself out through natural laws as the old depressions had. After all, they said, the 1837 depression lasted almost ten years and the one of 1893 at least six years. Why should we have been so impatient with the 1929 depression? Why not let this one end itself also? Perhaps America might have had, they said, a sounder domestic condition had it done that.

At any rate, planned economy was not giving the answers. Ten years after the 1929 crash there were reported 11,000,000 still unemployed, a small reduction from the number said to have been idle at Roosevelt's accession.[2] In addition, there were an estimated 19,600,000 on relief. A new depression with some 4,400 strikes had given America a setback in 1937 which was puzzling the Administration as well as the people.

The Supreme Court and the subsequent "purge" campaigns also had a bad psychological effect on the New Deal's fortunes. The people, while not hostile toward Roosevelt, any more than they had been toward Jackson a century earlier, came to distrust Roosevelt's advisers. His Brain Trust, that parallel to Jackson's Kitchen Cabinet, cooled their former zeal. The indications of desertions from the Democratic fold by certain former Roosevelt stalwarts, such as Vice-President Garner, also caused people to have sober second thoughts; and third term talk, too, definitely played a part in the New Deal's loss of strength.

But, most of all, the increasing absorption of the President with the serious world situation and its implications of war compelled him to gear the economy to war production, and thus to

---

[2] The exact number unemployed when Roosevelt took office is disputed. The American Federation of Labor says 13,000,000, but there are claims that the number was as high as 16,000,000.

suspend his liberal program. The dictator nations—Italy, Germany, Russia—were making the familiar land grabs, and sooner or later England would become involved. Automatically that would mean involvement for America just as it had meant that in 1914. Some people thought the President was employing the ancient device of taking the people's minds off the home situation by pointing to bogies abroad. Even the erudite historian Beard was writing in this vein. The criticism still is heard that Roosevelt knew that only through war could prosperity be brought back to the country. But it would be a great presumption to say that because domestic issues were not solved, the President used war as a recourse. At the very least, it must be recognized that as an educated man, he knew too much about history and the very doubtful fate of the reputation of war leaders in history to desire another war.

In May 1939 an unprecedented event took place. The reigning sovereigns of the British Empire paid a visit to the United States. To those who saw with a seeing eye that visit meant only one thing: a reaffirmation of the mutual sympathies of the two great English-speaking peoples in anticipation of war.

In September war came.

As the time for the 1940 elections drew near, it was more and more apparent that the President would seek a third term. James A. Farley and Vice-President Garner indicated to the President that they could not approve a third term. But to one of Roosevelt's temperament, the coming international crisis was something he wanted to handle himself. Also, the resourceful publicity office of the Democratic Party proclaimed to the nation that he, by his experience and intimate knowledge of the diplomatic details, was the man for that hour.

And the third term tradition was broken.

Roosevelt's opponent in the 1940 race, Willkie, gave the impression that he believed in the very things Roosevelt did but that he could somehow do them better. Dewey in 1944 gave the same impression. This was called "Me-too-ism," and it failed to work. If Willkie had declared outright that he would oppose further drafting of young men under the Selective Service Act—a system already in operation by 1940—he could possibly have won the contest. The fear of war on the part of the people, plus an inherent aversion to breaking the third term tradition, might have defeated Roosevelt. But since his opponent had nothing better to offer than a Republican version of Roosevelt himself, the people felt there was no need to make a change in the White House, that it was best for the country to keep an experienced man at the helm.

Whether the United States should or should not have gone into Europe's latest war can not be argued in this biography. But two things are certain about this very trying period in the life of the American people: (1) their overwhelming opposition to war, as evidenced by every public opinion survey made up to the time of the Pearl Harbor attack, the polls showing 85-plus per cent as being opposed; and (2) their continued unshaken faith in Roosevelt as their leader.

Although America's participation in World War II was about as inevitable as it was in World War I, the nation waited for an outright act of hostility against it before entering, because of the unmistakable reluctance of the people to shed the blood of their sons for visionary aims as they had done in 1917. But even so, the Administration never once disguised its sympathy for the Allied cause.[3]

Shortly after the visit of the British monarchs, and before any hostilities in Europe had begun, Roosevelt asked for repeal of the arms embargo in the Neutrality Act. This request was granted on the condition that cash be paid "on the barrel-head" for the supplies bought from America. This redounded to England's advantage, of course, for she was ready with the ships. In the summer of 1940, the national debt limit was raised and Congress adopted tax measures to yield additional revenues needed for the appropriations the President was asking for the expansion of national defense. In September, fifty over-age destroyers were given to England in exchange for the right to build bases in the British possessions of the Western hemisphere. In October registration under the Selective Service Act began, providing for one year of military training for the nation's young men. In Decem-

[3] Secretary of War Stimson wrote in his diary that at a Cabinet meeting in November 1941 the question discussed was how to maneuver Japan into firing the first shot. (See Charles A. Beard: *President Roosevelt and the Coming of the War,* p. 517; Yale University Press.)

ber Roosevelt declared the United States must be "the great arsenal of democracy." Other measures followed fast—the Lend-Lease program, landing troops in Iceland, closing Italian and German consulates, the freezing of Japanese assets in the United States.

In August 1941 the British Prime Minister and President Roosevelt met on board ship off the Newfoundland coast and drew up the set of principles known as the Atlantic Charter, drawing up at the same time what is now known to have been a military alliance. The next month America undertook to convoy Allied ships through the war zones.

Despite all these preparations on the part of the United States, the people hoped war could still be averted. Pearl Harbor alone brought the country face to face with what was in store for it. Unquestionably, the rise of Japan was threatening the other empires in the Orient. In the perspective of history, Pearl Harbor will no doubt emerge as, among other things, one element in the long process of liquidating the white colonial establishments in the Orient.[4]

The American scene during that critical time would be incorrectly depicted if nothing were to be noted of the propaganda efforts made by the proponents and opponents of war prior to Pearl Harbor—efforts by sections of the people, press, and Government. In 1940 there were formed the Committee to Defend America by Aiding the Allies, and the America First Committee. These Committees were highly organized, conducted great mass meetings throughout the nation, and plied the radio networks constantly with the burden of their respective causes. The former group had the title Interventionists; the latter Isolationists. Both terms were inappropriate and unfortunate, and represented perfectly America's outstanding propensity to oversimplify.

On Sunday, December 7, 1941, Pearl Harbor was bombed by the Japanese, who sank or disabled 18 American ships, eight of which were battleships, destroying 177 airplanes, killing 2,403

[4] Other obvious examples of this trend are the German ousting from Kiaochow; the Dutch loss of the East Indies; and the loss by France of Indo-China. Even the granting of self-government to Burma, Malaya, etc. and the complete independence of the Philippines, achieved without violence, can be considered as part of this "manifest destiny" in the Far East.

Americans, and wounding 1,272, most of whom were soldiers, sailors, and marines. On the same day attacks were made on the Philippines, Guam, and Midway as well. The next day the United States declared war against the Japanese Empire. The attack by Japan, we now know, was expected literally for weeks.

Because of the unprecedented global strategy needed in World War II, Roosevelt flew to various parts of the earth for conferences and thus became, in spite of his inability to walk, America's most traveled President. The first of these conferences was at Casablanca, French Morocco, where unconditional surrender of the enemy was agreed upon with Prime Minister Churchill. The next one was at Quebec, again with Churchill. At Cairo, Roosevelt, Churchill, and the Chinese Generalissimo Chiang Kai-shek met to agree on the policy against Japan. At another Cairo conference Turkey was included in the deliberations. Next, at Teheran, the Iranian capital, the Russian Premier Joseph Stalin met for the first time with both the English and the American war leaders. A second Quebec conference with Churchill followed. Finally, when he already was a dying man, Roosevelt met at Yalta, in the Crimea, with Stalin and Churchill, where the secret agreements were entered into which became known only after the war.

Roosevelt had barely returned from Yalta when he died suddenly at his Warm Springs, Georgia, cottage on April 12, 1945. To a nation still at war his death was a stupendous shock, and mourning for him was great and universal. To the grounds of his Hyde Park estate, where he was born January 30, 1882, his remains were taken for burial, and the site at this time of writing is one of the most frequently visited historic places in America.

The Roosevelt era was a time of revolution, and like all revolutions, it had its excesses. Possibly it mattered little who had been President during that stormy time, possibly the emergency would have compelled the changes anyway; we do not know. But it is certain that the reforms of those times were long overdue. American industry had become smug. Old George Pullman's assertion, uttered far back in Cleveland's time—"The workers have nothing to do with the amount of wages they shall receive"—no longer meant anything. Since 1933 Management knew what it was like not to have everything its own way.

What was wrong with the New Deal was not the benefits that

so belatedly had accrued to the working classes of the nation. Those benefits were so sorely needed that Roosevelt's successors were committed to retain—and even enlarge—them. What was wrong was something psychological, namely, where in American life the accent had been placed by these reforms. It has been previously stated in this account that many church people were opposed to the New Deal. A principal reason for this was that religious people so often were dismayed by the stark materialism featured in the Roosevelt revolution. But "reformist" forces, by their very nature, symbolize an extreme materialism. Because of the urgency of their program they cannot become involved with the theory that some of the desired betterment for mankind can best come eventually, and in time: they see only the immediate needs, and think that they are all immediately resolvable. They believe, in other words, in change by revolution rather than by evolution. Naturally, leaders in such movements often become quite unhappy because the improvements they seek never seem to come quickly enough.

If the New Deal's outstanding liability was this disproportionateness just mentioned, then FDR as the No. 1 prophet of the New Deal was also bound to have had some fallacious tenets in his philosophy. "We have nothing to fear but Fear itself," he had proclaimed at his first inaugural. And his widow as late as 1956 was reiterating the dictum to her fellow-Democrats in convention. The statement is a snare. As everyone knows, we have far worse things to fear in life than Fear. The leader of a nation may feel a responsibility to divert the people from Fear; but, if so, he owes it to them also, especially in a time of great social upheaval such as the Roosevelt years were, to warn them of how materialism, envy, cynicism, opportunism, undue reliance on Man—attitudes which invariably control all "have-not" groups—can be more destructive of man's soul than fear.

Roosevelt was not a socialist, as so many of his enemies contended. It is true, as his Secretary of Labor Frances Perkins points out in her book, that he "was not very familiar with economic theory" and that he was an experimenter. Nevertheless, he believed in the capitalistic system: he was himself an outstanding product of that system. He was a scion of an old Hudson River barony, a country squire, genial, presiding over his large family and cognizant of his patrician origins. His wife, who was Anna Eleanor Roosevelt before her marriage, and who became the most influential First Lady since Dolley Madison, had the same type of manorial background. But to Americans generally the Roosevelts appeared as truly democratic people.

It must be recognized that Roosevelt transformed the old Democratic Party into a party of particular—one might even say special—interests. The philosophy by which the Party was born and thrived for more than a century—decentralization—was abandoned. The demands of Labor and of the comparatively new type of American that the immigration of the previous half-century had produced could be met only by centralizing in the Federal authority the important stimuli of American economic life. Such a revolutionary policy was bound to bring disappointment eventually to all earning brackets in the nation. And so we see the Republicans, the traditionally "loose constructionists," today espousing the old Jeffersonian, strict constructionist, states' rights, decentralization type of government—the very opposite of what they originally stood for.

The Roosevelt years were expensive. For example, the national debt increased 240 billion dollars and the taxes to reduce it were burdensome to all classes of people.

The excising of the unhealthier outgrowths of the New Deal is an adjustment that the American people in the second half of the twentieth century have had to accomplish. And they have had to assess the debunking of the Roosevelt myth. FDR had not liquidated the one big problem for the solution of which he had been elected—unemployment, which ceased only when America entered Europe's latest war. And millions of American parents could never forgive him for violating his solemn promise to them that their sons would never be sent to fight in foreign wars again.

Roosevelt was a very capable politician and greatly enjoyed being President. Like his mentor, Woodrow Wilson, he could not deal generously with opponents; but he also could not exhibit Wilson's ability. It is now known how ardently some of his opponents agitated for the reforms for which he received the credit.

The record of the overwrought and passion-ridden 1930's and 1940's has gradually taken shape as a serviceable chronicle for posterity.

★★★★★★★★★★★★★★★★★★★★★★★★★★★★★★★★

32

HARRY S. TRUMAN

☆ ☆

VOTE OF 1944: *See* under Franklin D. Roosevelt

		Popular	Electoral
VOTE OF 1948:	Harry S. Truman, Democrat	24,106,000	303
	Thomas E. Dewey, Republican	21,970,000	189
	J. Strom Thurmond, Dixiecrat	1,169,000	39
	Henry A. Wallace, Progressive	1,157,000	
	Norman Thomas, Socialist	140,000	
	Others	295,000	
		48,837,000	531

☆ ☆

THE DEMOCRATIC PARTY UNDER ROOSEVELT AND TRUMAN TRIED AS hard as it ever was tried in the country to make the United States into a democracy. The Founding Fathers knew too much about the perils of democracy—the will of the majority—to want that form of government for the new nation. They therefore strove for a republic—a government of checks and balances, where the minority's rights were protected with a written guarantee, that guarantee being the Constitution.

This is not to say that Roosevelt and Truman did not value constitutional government; but that, in their Administrations, concerned principally with the rights of the many, the rights of the minority were of secondary consideration. It is possible that after his retirement Mr. Truman did a lot of reflecting as to the difference between a democracy and a republic; but it is certain that while he was President he epitomized the will of the many as graphically as anybody in the nation ever did.

On a farm at Lamar, Missouri, on May 8, 1884, Harry S. Truman was born, the son of John Anderson Truman and Martha Young. His early years were spent in Harrisonville, Grandview, Independence, and Kansas City; but it is Independence, the starting point of the old Santa Fe and Oregon Trails, which is his real home and to which he retired in 1953. His boyhood was a happy and wholesome one; and his people on both sides had a fair amount of means.

One book on the life of Truman [1] points out that in order to understand him we must always take into account the intense influence on Truman of his mother, his books, his music, and his faulty vision. All four are severely personal, and in the ordinary man would be the hallmark of an introverted person. To Truman's credit it must be stated that he was not self-centered enough to develop into such an individual.

Americans generally do not know that the former President for quite a while seriously aspired to a career in music and studied very hard at it. Wearing spectacles at a very early age, he could not partake in boys' games; such a victim is often automatically turned within himself and forced to find his world in books, music, and the home. That was Truman's boyhood. But the youth had another ambition—to go to West Point. At a recruiting station he was told it was hopelessly out of the question with his bad eyes, and he consequently gave up trying for an appointment. There followed ten years of working on his father's farm at Grandview.

Before the public life of Harry S. Truman [2] began, two other things about him are of particular note—his service overseas in World War I, from which he returned as a major in the field artillery; and his unsuccessful venture with a partner in the haberdashery business. Again to Truman's credit, we must recognize that he refused to file for bankruptcy, and as late as his U. S. Senate years he was still paying off his debts.

Truman was a failure—as the world reckons failure—when he entered politics as an initiate of the Pendergast machine of Kansas City. Clean-living and in his middle thirties, Truman appealed to the machine as a promising vehicle for winning victories, and he was appointed overseer of highways for Jackson County. In 1922 he was elected a county judge. Defeated for re-election in 1924, Truman was nevertheless re-elected in 1926. In 1934 came his big chance when Pendergast decided he was the best name

[1] Jonathan Daniels: *The Man of Independence;* J. B. Lippincott Company.
[2] The middle initial S. is only a letter and stands for no name.

they had to run for the United States Senate. In that heyday of
the New Deal his election was assured. It was in his second term
as Senator that he gained national prominence by his vigorous
chairmanship of the committee for investigating war contracts.
By means of this committee, the Government undoubtedly saved
several billions of dollars.

In 1944, when Roosevelt was seeking his fourth term, the
Democrats were looking for a safe running-mate. It was generally
recognized that whoever would be the Vice-Presidential nominee
of the Party would almost certainly become the next President
of the United States; for Roosevelt was failing in health. Truman
did not want to leave the Senate; he was happy there and was well
liked by his colleagues. But politics had its way, Truman was
drafted, and we see for a change the too little experienced condition in America of the office seeking the man.

Truman was a mild and undramatic person when he fell heir
to the grave duties of the White House in April 1945. The country
was enthusiastically behind him and even Republicans affirmed
that they would vote for him at the next election, so favorably
did he impress the nation. But before his first term was over, the
conservative element of the electorate had changed its mind about
him. Truman showed a side of him that people did not think was
there. He was an out-and-out Democrat of the New Deal persua-
sion, and he called his own Administration the "Fair Deal." By
the time the 1948 and 1952 elections were out of the way, he was
to be castigated by his opponents as a strutting, equivocating,
cocksure, rabble-rousing machine politician at the precinct level.

Truman came to power at one of the most crucial times in the
history of the world. World War II was not yet over, although
the end was in sight. Within eighteen days three of the chief
characters in that drama—Roosevelt, Hitler, and Mussolini—were
dead. On May 7, 1945, Truman was able to announce officially
that the war in Europe was over. Following closely on surrender
of the enemy in Europe came the Potsdam Conference in Germany where Churchill, Attlee (Churchill's successor), Stalin,
and Truman met. It was at this conference that the strategy for
Japan and ending the war was decided upon. The matter of defeated Germany's joint occupation by Allied troops also was
settled.

Harry S. Truman tried hard to fill the shoes of FDR, but his chances for success were almost as slim as Andrew Johnson's efforts to follow Lincoln. His own domestic program was therefore not particularly satisfactory. To begin with, the cry of "back to normalcy" resounded in his ears as loudly as in Harding's after World War I. If for no other reason than that, Truman's plans for additional social legislation were not predisposed to easy going. Tired of experimentation, tired of war, and tired of expense, the American people—Labor only excepted—had not the mood to give Truman the support they had so unreservedly given his predecessor. With his plan for more coverage under social security the nation was generally in agreement. But in the South he became so unpopular by his insistence on the continuation of the Fair Employment Practices Committee (FEPC)—a wartime body for outlawing discrimination on account of race or color in any field of endeavor—that his Party became split, entered a separate ticket in the Presidential contest of 1948; and Truman lost four states that year. That discrimination against the Negro is disappearing fast in the United States is evident to all who can see. But in the South this program could not proceed with the speed that was seen for it in the North and East. Truman's beliefs respecting poll taxes, the Negro, and anti-lynching were sound and humanitarian, but he tried to resolve nationally something which, it seemed, each locality would have to do at its own pace.

More labor troubles on a national scale took place while Truman was President than ever before in America's history, and Truman favored the strikers much of the time. In 1946, 4,600,000 workers in different industries struck. Because these strikes threatened the national safety—since they were called at a time when America had a fighting war in Korea on its hands—Truman at different times ordered the Government to seize the railroads, the soft coal mines, and the steel mills. His action in the steel mills was without precedent. It is safe to say that the nation did not support him in this move; for it was Labor, not the mills, which struck against the national defense. Truman came in for special criticism at this time because he did not invoke the provisions of the Taft-Hartley law for dealing with such emergencies. Earlier in his Administration he had vetoed Taft-Hartley and his antipathy to it was impassioned.

The rights of Labor were probably never so violently debated as during the Truman Administration. During the second half of the nineteenth century doughty Wm. H. Vanderbilt had declared, "The public be damned." In the second half of the twentieth century it was Labor who said, "The public be damned." Yet, regardless of how Labor eventually shall fare in the American economy, the words of John Adams, uttered so long ago, echo and re-echo:

> The controversy between the rich and the poor, the laborious and the idle, the learned and the ignorant, distinctions as old as the creation, and as extensive as the globe . . . will continue, and rivalries will spring out of them.

In the conduct of foreign affairs the Truman Administration was truly notable; time alone will reveal the soundness or unsoundness of the many measures and policies adopted. The completion of the war in both Europe and Asia was left on Truman's doorstep, and his was the tremendous decision to drop the atom bomb when Japan refused to surrender. On August 14, 1945 the Japanese accepted the Allied terms and war on a global scale was over for the time being.

In 1947 Truman submitted to a special session of Congress his European Recovery Program, otherwise called the Marshall Plan, providing for economic aid of $17 billion to sixteen countries. The plan, originating with General Marshall, Truman's Secretary of State, proposed to help other countries develop their economics unhampered in a free world—which meant, simply, that the United States would help any nation that refused to become absorbed into the Communist orbit. This program was part of what came to be known as the Truman Doctrine. This doctrine called for "containment," that is, containing Russia and her satellites within their territorial confines by helping all other peoples resist outside pressures, no matter where exerted.

Implementing the Truman Doctrine and the Marshall Plan was the creation in 1949 of the North Atlantic Treaty Organization, signed by fourteen nations. By means of NATO, the fourteen nations declared that an armed attack on one constituted an attack on all. It was the greatest military alliance in all history. The United States included Greece and Turkey under this protection, assuming the responsibilities in that area previously undertaken by Britain.[3] Thus the United States proclaimed to the world that the Mediterranean as well as the entire Atlantic was part of the defensive waters of America. In his 1949 inaugural address Truman announced his so-called Point Four program for giving technological aid to those underdeveloped countries whose policies gave promise of their remaining outside the Russian orbit, and that also became part of the new American foreign policy.

Three more pacts were signed during Truman's time to make American foreign policy what it is today. First, there was the Inter-American Treaty of Reciprocal Assistance signed at Rio de Janeiro with the other republics of the Western hemisphere, lest anyone assume that the Monroe Doctrine was no longer a living thing. Second, there was the Tripartite Security Treaty, or ANZUS Pact, among the United States, Australia, and New Zealand. And a third treaty was signed between the Philippine Republic and America. Of course, by the U.S.-Japanese Peace Treaty America was responsible also for Japan and her islands.

In 1945 Truman by telephone opened the conference in San Francisco establishing the United Nations organization. The following June the charter of the UN was signed by fifty nations. This undertaking was fraught with more omen than that establishing Wilson's old League. In the League of Nations the world's greatest power, the United States, steadfastly had refused to become a member and Soviet Russia had been a member for a short time only.[4] In the UN the United States and the Soviet were the chief members. These two powers with Britain, France, and China comprised the powerful Security Council of the UN.

But as each generation must learn the lessons of life anew, so this generation had to learn that the UN could be as helpless as the old League. This generation saw that the harvest of the dragons' teeth sown in the latest world conflict was but to pit one victor against the other and to create, as some far-seeing Amer-

[3] In 1955 West Germany was added to NATO, bringing the total in that alliance to fifteen.
[4] Soviet Russia was eventually expelled from the League of Nations.

ican leaders had feared, a powerful Soviet Union which would make America regret the day she had ever considered it seriously as an ally. By entering once more a universal and catastrophic war, and then by allying itself to a dictatorship which Roosevelt himself had declared was as vicious as any the world had seen, the United States allowed the Soviet Union to come into control of one-fourth of the world's surface area and the almost 1,000 millions of people who inhabit it.

Eventually, war came again; not between the United States and the Soviet openly, but on an innocent little peninsula called Korea. At the close of World War II, this little country had been liberated from Japan and occupied jointly by the United States and the U. S. S. R., the latter receiving jurisdiction of the Northern part. As the ideological differences between Communism and the free countries became more and more acute, it was evident that Korea could not be united short of a miracle.

In June 1950 North Korean forces—which meant, plainly, Communist forces—struck into the territory of the Republic of Korea, the southern half. The UN then called for withdrawal of the North Korean troops to their own portion and President Truman ordered American naval and air support for the Republic of Korea and a blockade of the Korean coast. General MacArthur was named commander of all UN forces in Korea. Under him was accomplished the virtually complete conquest of the peninsula when, to the surprise of the American people, although not to MacArthur, the Chinese Communists came in and drove the UN forces back to virtually the line of division before hostilities began. MacArthur wanted to bomb China and take other strong measures to end the war, but the Administration opposed this and in the end relieved MacArthur of command.

A truce eventually was signed after three years of fighting, but only after 136,000 American casualties, $15 billion in direct cost, and $65 billion in additional defense outlays had been expended. The war was not won, Korea was not unified, American prestige suffered immeasurably, and the worries of the United States in Indo-China, Formosa, Burma, and other parts of Asia were not over. The whole history of what led up to Korea under the Truman Administration is not yet complete, but it is hardly likely that, given Truman's inheritance from previous Administrations, the President could have acted differently.

Truman must be accorded commendation for his judgment in calling upon the valued talents of Herbert Hoover in two important missions. Hoover was appointed to make a survey of the European food situation in 1947, a job probably nobody else on earth could have done better. He was also appointed as chairman of the First Hoover Commission for outlining a reorganization of the Executive Department of the Government.

In order to reduce quotas from Eastern and Southern Europe, the Immigration Act of 1924, based on national origins as of 1920, was put into law. In 1952 Congress codified immigration laws, retaining the provision of the 1924 law as to national origins. Truman violently opposed this legislation, vetoed it, and complained bitterly when it was passed over his veto. Politics had a lot to do with Truman's feeling about this legislation; for he knew that nearly all immigrants and immigrants' children voted the Democratic ticket.[5]

The adoption of the Twenty-Second Amendment during Truman's time is certainly notable. Forbidding any American to serve more than two terms in the Presidential office, America, by law, fixed something which the Founding Fathers had trusted would be kept fixed without law. Nor, it must be said, did these scholarly men of 1787 anticipate that the ethnic composition of the country would not always remain predominantly Anglican; or that one day it might include nationalities which would be indifferent to precedents which Nordic peoples might consider inviolate.

Truman was fortunate in the selection of his self-effacing and unpretentious wife, the former Bess Wallace, who was a schoolmate. Many Americans had a greater liking for her than for her husband. After the precedent-shattering, global peregrinations of her predecessor, the homespun qualities of Bess Truman were a considerable change in the White House. She was well received by the American people.

The Trumans did not come in for praise over the musical

[5] It is interesting to note also that in the 1952 law the U. S. removed its ban against Asiatics and that they, as well as all Africans, are now permitted to enter the country on the same quota basis as other peoples.

ambitions of their only child. This independent young lady gave concerts and made other appearances during her father's term, but, by all the standards Americans had been used to, this was nothing more nor less than capitalizing on the Presidential office. Truman and his Fair-Dealers saw nothing improper about this, and it was thus only the conservatives who were offended in their souls. In the long run the American people, certainly, did not seem to care much one way or the other.

One way of remembering the years 1932–52 is to consider the period as in a sense the Age of Jackson all over again. More than ever, men in public office stayed in power by appealing to the public's passions. Both Roosevelt and Truman knew how to do this. They also knew the American people's inherent weakness for oversimplification, and gave it to them in large doses.

Truman's language was often careless and inaccurate both during and after his Presidential terms. At one time he said that the Eightieth Congress was the worst in American history. At another time in his Hartford speech in 1952 he declared the Republicans were against the immigration of Catholics and Jews and against minorities of all kinds. During the 1952 and the 1956 campaigns he made statements unbecoming to an elder statesman. Such impetuous utterances made him countless enemies.

Truman's public papers are today housed in a library at Independence, Missouri, where, it is hoped, students may glean the information to enable them some day to make a definitive statement about the usefulness of this Administration. Harry S. Truman died December 26, 1972 at the age of 88, and it was in the courtyard of this library that he was laid to rest.

★★★★★★★★★★★★★★★★★★★★★★★★★★★★★★★★★★★

DWIGHT DAVID EISENHOWER

☆ ☆

		Popular	Electoral
VOTE OF 1952:	Dwight D. Eisenhower, Republican	33,938,000	442
	Adlai E. Stevenson II, Democrat	27,312,000	89
	Others	372,000	
		61,622,000	531
VOTE OF 1956:	Dwight D. Eisenhower, Republican	35,584,000	457
	Adlai E. Stevenson II, Democrat	26,036,000	73
	Others	417,000	1
		62,037,000	531

★ ☆

EVERY TIME A NEW PRESIDENT IS ELECTED, A NEW PRECEDENT IS somehow established. Eisenhower is the first President with a distinctly German name. And he is the first two-term President to hail from a different state at his second election than that at his first.

The aspect of the name is significant. It highlights as nothing else could the changing ethnic composition of the population of the United States. In the more recent national elections this change has been outstandingly reflected in the ballots; in the elected officials of the community and nation we no longer see the preponderance of Anglican names among the winners. We now see more Mayors, Governors, Senators, and even Federal judges bearing surnames bequeathed by Italian, Jewish, Slavic, Scandinavian, and German ancestors.

This sociological revelation about America must not be ignored. More than anything else, it explains why Americans have two conflicting philosophies respecting foreign policy: a populace almost wholly opposed to foreign commitments (isolationist), side by side with an influential class which has been predominantly pro-Anglican (interventionist). Generally speaking, the more recent immigrants and their immediate descendants are for the most part in the former group; while the old colonial stocks are nearly always found in the latter group.

Eisenhower's people on the side of his father, David J. Eisenhower, came from Germany. The people of his mother, who was Ida Elizabeth Stover, came from Switzerland. The families had lived in German-settled Pennsylvania before migrating westward, and belonged, as so many of the "Pennsylvania Dutch" belonged, to one of the small religious sects there. Both the General's parents were deeply religious.

Dwight, born in Denison, Texas, on October 14, 1890, was the third of seven boys, and was brought up in Abilene, Kansas, a typical cow town. The fact that of the last four American Presidents, three were from west of the Mississippi, is significant. Eisenhower's wife, the former Mamie Geneva Doud, came from Colorado. The Far West almost in one generation emerged from a comparatively remote factor into a moving force in American national life.

Although Eisenhower was the first military man since Grant to enter the White House, his caliber was by no means comparable to Grant's. Grant became a politician; and although he became a mighty poor one, it is significant that he was more than willing to become one. Eisenhower, like Generals Washington and Taylor, did not seek the Presidency. And, like those two predecessors, he was by temperament more fitted to be the leader of a nation than the leader of a party. He did not need to become a politician; it was the politicians who needed him. And the fact that he was born in Texas, raised in Kansas, elected the first time from New York, the second time from Pennsylvania, had golfed in Georgia, fished in Colorado, and vacationed in Rhode Island did not detract from his broad political appeal.

When he was approached in 1948 to run for President, Eisenhower was not receptive; he did not like the idea of an army man going into the business of politics. But the Republicans, with whom temperamentally he had the most in common, convinced him that it was only their Party who could save the nation and only he who could save their Party. He was thus drafted for the job of President; his subsequent election ended a twenty-year uninterrupted hold of the Executive Department by the opposition party.

The military preparation of Eisenhower was considerable but it can be described briefly. He was graduated from West Point in 1915 and was by no means brilliant while there. During World War I he served at various training centers in the country, and spent two years in the Canal Zone. In 1926 he was graduated from the officers' school at Fort Leavenworth; in 1929 from the Army War College in Washington; in 1932 from the Army Industrial College. He had a job in the War Department for a time. Then, in 1933, he was made an assistant to Douglas MacArthur and accompanied that general to the Philippines. In 1939 he returned to the United States as a lieutenant-colonel. Early in 1942 he was made chief of the War Plans Division of the Chief of Staff; later in the year he was made Chief of Operations.

In that same year Eisenhower was appointed commander of the U. S. forces in the European Theater of Operations with headquarters in London, and was made a lieutenant-general. In the November following this he was placed in command of the Allied invasion of North Africa; by May 1943 the Germans had been driven out of Africa. In 1943 he was made a four-star general and put in charge of the Italian campaign; by September of that year he had realized the complete conquest of Italy.

At the Cairo Conference in December 1943 Eisenhower was appointed Supreme Allied Commander in the European Theater. Then, on that ominous day in June 1944, followed the invasion of Europe on the beachheads of Normandy accomplished with the previously unheard-of forces of 3,000,000 men, 4,000 ships, and 15,000 planes. The result, with the surrender of Germany less than a year later, is history. He was on the Allied Control Commission for Germany after that. In November 1945 he was made Chief of Staff of the U. S. Army; and the following March he was made a General of the Army (five-star) for life. After that the civic life of Dwight D. Eisenhower began.

Three events are noteworthy before the sweeping Republican victory of 1952 sent him to the White House. First he accepted the presidency of Columbia University in 1947. He wrote a best seller, *Crusade in Europe*. And in 1950 he was appointed Supreme Commander of the armed forces of the NATO countries and left for Europe. America's policy at this time was to strive for a European Defense Community, to be implemented with an army which was to be the bulwark against creeping Communism. Only Eisenhower could give such a project the prestige and force it needed to make an indifferent Europe willing to pool its military resources. Eisenhower came out unequivocally for political unification of the Continent at this time.

While all this was going on, pressure was brought on him to declare himself a Republican. In due course of time he did this. Then came visits to him at his European headquarters from one Party stalwart after another urging him to consent to let his name go forward for the Presidential nomination. In due course he did this also. He then resigned his NATO post and sailed for home to wage the campaign he knew was expected of him and for which he was by nature not fitted. At his election the voting tournout was the greatest in American history—61% of the eligible voting population. Four years before it had been barely 50%. Eisenhower's personal popularity was further accentuated by the fact that at both his elections he received several million more votes than the Republican candidates for Congress received who ran with him. For only the second time since the Civil War a Republican had broken the solid South as Virginia, Tennessee, Texas, Florida, and even Louisiana rode it out with Eisenhower.

One of the reasons for the outstanding Eisenhower verdict by the people is that they believed the General would end the Korean War and bring back their boys. Immediately after his first election he flew to Korea to examine the situation, and the following July a truce was signed.

Eisenhower made it clear before he became President that he would never throw out the social advances made under the New Deal. He came out for enlarged social security legislation, the St. Lawrence Seaway, the franchise for eighteen-year-olds, even for revisions in the Taft-Hartley labor law.

Congress was in no mood to tamper with the basic labor law of the land and refused to amend Taft-Hartley. And although there are two states in the Union which permit eighteen-year-olds to vote, Congress refused to submit to the states a Constitutional amendment legalizing it in the remainder of the nation. The line of reasoning Eisenhower followed, that if a boy was old enough to fight he was old enough to vote, was understandable. Maturing in mind was what was worrying most. Congress was rather unwise in turning down the proposal.

The St. Lawrence Seaway, so long a football of national politics, by which the great inland lake cities would become bustling seaports, was at last authorized in 1954 and the bill for its construction signed by the President.

In Eisenhower's second year the Supreme Court handed down an opinion on the American Negro which rates as the greatest verdict on that question since the Dred Scott decision of 1857. This opinion, which had Eisenhower's unqualified approval, held that segregation of white and Negro children in the public schools was unconstitutional. The Court's ruling is historic. The decision was unanimous, and particularly remarkable because of the fact that three of the justices on the Court came from states which require segregation. The whole problem of civil rights will not be settled in the United States for decades, if then. Meanwhile the Negro's sociological problems, not at all settled by the victory of Northern arms in the Civil War, embarrass candidates for political office even more than they did a hundred years ago.

The fate of American prestige in the world may well hang upon what the Eisenhower Administration has achieved in the field of foreign affairs. Neither Woodrow Wilson nor Franklin D. Roosevelt ever dreamed that the wars over which each presided would loose two opponents against each other—the U. S. A. and the U.S.S.R.—symbolizing the West and the East with their respective cultures, striving to outdo each other in diplomacy, scientific feats, and political cabal so as to make each feel that the accomplishments of the one might conceivably annihilate those of the other.

This threat to the West in the second half of the twentieth century was far more terrifying than those presented by Kaiser William II and Adolph Hitler. At the times of their threats America was energetic, without a huge public debt, and naive. At the time of the Soviet threat America was tired, debt-ridden, and wiser. So were America's allies. All this has made the United States Government very cautious, and the most traveled Secretary of State in American history, John Foster Dulles, tirelessly sought through one program after another to strengthen the position of the country without outrightly provoking war. In 1954 the Southeast Asia Treaty Organization (SEATO) was formed among the United States and seven other countries. Then there was a mutual defense treaty between the United States and Nationalist China (the Formosan government) guaranteeing the defense of Formosa and its offshore islands. In 1957 there was enunciated the Eisenhower Doctrine for the Middle East, by which America served notice that she would undertake to prevent aggression in that quarter if the UN failed to do so.

These moves brought to about 1,000,000,000 the number of people the United States was committed to defend against aggression. America had over 350 military bases established around the world. It was bound in honor to come to the aid of some sixty nations over the face of the earth. The supercession of Pax Britannica by Pax Americana was a *fait accompli*, whether the United States liked it or not.

In addition to these incredible statistics, all of which might conceivably be contravened by the efforts of man, there came an unspeakable potential not easily to be circumscribed by man—the thermonuclear bomb and the inter-continental ballistic missile. The understanding and release of atomic energy has been referred to as "harnassing the basic power of the universe," and we have seen what this energy will do in war. Also during the Eisenhower years came the development of the rocket missile, a weapon not yet tried in war. Both these weapons are possessed by the U. S. A. and the U. S. S. R., but to what degree by each the world did not know. Among other things, the lack of this knowledge made the people of the world apprehensive. The rocket foreshadows a complete change in the method of warfare.

For the first time in the history of mankind the inhabitants of the earth were able to project objects into outer space, and Eisenhower was hard put during his Presidency to reassure the American people after Russia had launched the world's first successful satellite or man-made "moon." In time Eisenhower had a Space Administration created to explore every possible phase of these new discoveries and determine what Americans could do to keep prestige in the world of scientific discovery.

In Eisenhower's second term the design of the American flag was changed for the first time since 1912 as Alaska and Hawaii were admitted into the Union as the 49th and 50th states, respectively. Rich Alaska, three times larger in area than the previously largest state of Texas, looking into Russia's back yard only three miles away, no longer was being called "Seward's Frog Pond." As for ever-beautiful Hawaii, with its many races and nationalities blending so successfully in a common cultural and political unit, it is strangely coincidental that its admission should have been delayed until such time as the mainland was being harassed by its own acute integration problems.

President Eisenhower was severely criticized by both his own Party and the opposition for his spending, the greatest of any peacetime President to that time. His budgets were in excess of $80 billion. But the President insisted that both foreign and domestic tranquillity required that these expensive programs be maintained; that if they were not, America's friends would fall into the waiting arms of the Soviet system. Throughout the States the complaint was made that the welfare state was mushrooming and that in the midst of record prosperity between five and seven million people were still receiving public assistance of some kind or other, exclusive of social security benefits.

It is impossible to say how far we can validly criticize. Probably we should go back to Theodore Roosevelt and Woodrow Wilson and say that, if the doctrines of those men had not been permitted to prevail so that the second half of the Monroe Doctrine had remained as inviolate as the first half, America might have become truly the haven of the oppressed of all the world, and, in addition, been itself spared astronomical costs. On the other hand, had this been so, and had America in her splendid isolation permitted a European hegemony or an Asian hegemony to rise up, as the Russian system has tried to rise, to tell the United States what to do and how to live—would the people of the United States ever have forgiven themselves for having thus forfeited their liberties and their right to leadership? Would this have been fulfilling the dreams of the Founding Fathers earnestly though they sought to disenchant Americans with foreign adventure?

Eisenhower suffered a mild coronary attack in 1955 and underwent abdominal surgery the following year. His recovery from these two setbacks was so rapid that the nation insisted on his standing for re-election, despite the complaints of the oppo-

sition that America had but a "part-time President." After his
second election, he was felled again, this time by a slight cerebral
stroke, and from this also he came back to vigor. Few other
Presidents had so caught the imagination of the people as this
almost "abnormally normal" man; even his handling of his press
conferences was little short of remarkable. He was the first two-
term President forbidden by law to run again; this made his task
somewhat difficult for, regardless of his inability to stand for more
than two terms, the possibility of his remaining in office longer
would have been a check on the purely political conduct of some
members of Congress. Yet, in spite of opposition, Eisenhower had
fewer outright enemies than even George Washington. For a
military man he showed a most acute perceptiveness in the business of government.

Eisenhower visited thirty-one countries during his Presidency
in the effort to strengthen America's position in the world. At
times, as in India, he was welcomed by previously unheard-of
crowds of people. Twice his visits were marked as unwelcome and
were called off.

In 1961 the soldier-hero from Abilene retired to his farm at
Gettysburg, Pa., the oldest man to have served in the Presidency
up to that time. His concern for his country and his Party did not
diminish during his retirement and he did a great deal of writing
about the issues besetting the American people. He lived to see his
protege, Richard Nixon, enter the White House as President, and
died in Washington on March 28, 1969 after a long illness and
further surgery. He was mourned by world leaders and wartime
associates, many of whom came from abroad to attend the days-
long funeral rites. In accordance with his wishes, his body was interred within the chapel in Abilene, Kansas, close to his boyhood
home.

★★★★★★★★★★★★★★★★★★★★★★★★★★★★★★★★★★

34

JOHN FITZGERALD KENNEDY

☆ ☆

		Popular	Electoral
VOTE OF 1960:	Richard Nixon, Republican	34,108,000	219
	John F. Kennedy, Democrat	34,050,000	303
	Harry F. Byrd, Conservative Democrat	293,000	15
	Others	386,000	
		68,837,000 [1]	537

☆ ☆

IN THE DAYS WHEN AMERICA WAS GROWING UP, A CULTURAL ARISTOC-racy had become entrenched in long-settled New England. Never in their most elaborate excursions into fantasy did these "proper Bostonians" ever think that any of their number would be anything other than pure English in stock and the Protestant in tradition.

But the nineteenth-century Irish immigration into this land "Where the Lowells talk to the Cabots and the Cabots talk only to God" changed everything; an entirely new aristocracy was being erected—one that was Hibernian and Catholic.

In the 1960 elections a representative of this new aristocracy was sent to the White House. John F. Kennedy was not the first Irish-blooded man to become President but he was the first Roman Catholic, and at the age of forty-three, the youngest man ever elected President.

As significant as either of these two facts in that election is the circumstance that a Presidential victor had never before worked so hard in the pre-convention months to obtain delegates for himself. It has been the history of American politics that any candidate try-ing so hard would usually wind up in second place on the ticket or eliminated altogether. The United States has never been inclined to hand the Presidency to anyone who worked too hard to get it.

[1] Source: *Statistical Abstract of the United States,* 82nd ed., GPO, 1961.

Kennedy was also the wealthiest man ever elected President,[2] the son of Joseph P. Kennedy, Franklin D. Roosevelt's Security and Exchange Commission chairman and Ambassador to the Court of St. James; and of Rose Fitzgerald, daughter of a former Congressman, one-time mayor of Boston.

President Kennedy was born in Brookline, Mass., on May 29, 1917. His family had always been associated with Massachusetts and their vast clan congregated at a compound at Hyannis Port where the President had a home. He was graduated from Harvard *cum laude;* had degrees also from Notre Dame, Tufts, Boston University, and several other schools. During World War II he served in the Pacific, was invalided home, and awarded the Purple Heart. Before he became President, Kennedy was a Congressman for six years and a member of the U.S. Senate from 1953 to 1960.

The Communist menace with which Presidents Truman and Eisenhower had to grapple had not diminished when Kennedy became the President. In fact, almost immediately upon taking office he was confronted with the specter of Communism right in the Western hemisphere where Cuba's newest revolution had produced in Castro a dictator who openly allied himself with Russia. This alliance was a threat to the security of the United States and all the Latin-American republics.

In the fall of 1962, photographic proof was given to the President and the nation that the Soviet Union had been building missile bases in Cuba only ninety miles from our shores. Then Kennedy acted. At the risk of letting loose a nuclear war, he ordered the island blockaded and all shipping bound thither subject to search. Further, he declared that it would not be enough to halt further shipments of offensive weapons to Cuba but that the bases already erected there would have to be dismantled and shipped back to Russia. The world held its breath. Russia re-routed the arms-bearing ships which were on the seas bound for Cuba. After first attempting a counter offer, which the Administration rejected, Russia yielded.

Although the Soviet Union considered the Monroe Doctrine an anachronism, and no less a personage than Eleanor Roosevelt had declared it was out of date, Kennedy vigorously re-affirmed it; the

[2] Following the example of Herbert Hoover, Kennedy gave all his salaries as a public servant to charity.

Organization of American States voted 20 to 0 to support the United States in its decision to invoke it. This warning by the United States that it would use force, if necessary, to protect the American republics from those powers who would "attempt . . . to extend their system to any portion of this Hemisphere," showed the world that the Monroe Doctrine was anything but dead, and that, together with the Rio Pact of 1947, it was the very keystone of Western hemispheric policy.

Kennedy had many other extremely difficult foreign situations to handle. The fate of the United Nations organization was in doubt as certain prominent men, including ex-President Hoover, charged it was unable to keep the peace. The NATO alliance also was being shaken, and to its very foundations. The Organization of American States (OAS), so important in keeping the Western Hemisphere free, was demanding the President's most assiduous attention. The swift end of colonialism in the world brought many new nations into being, particularly on the African continent; they were not only clamoring for admission into the UN as equal partners but for economic and even military aid in maintaining their newborn, shaky governments. Such spending as the United States did for these new nations was severely criticized in the halls of Congress and in the nation generally; especially so when it was revealed that a million Americans in uniform were standing guard around the world in 41 nations.

Although a Democrat, Kennedy was the son of a somewhat conservative father, and conservative leanings were so frequent in some of his recommendations that Labor expressed its disappointment in him. Many Catholics also were disappointed that one of their number who happened to be the President of the United States did not do anything for the aid of parochial schools.

In the economic field, the rapid development of automation and the resultant unemployment gave the Administration increasing concern. Although the gross national product had risen in the first year of Kennedy's Presidency to the previously unheard-of figure of $540 billion, there were still several million unemployed. The European Common Market was becoming so powerful a force in the lives of Western nations that the Administration was having to re-adjust its thinking altogether on the matter of American tariff policies.

Other problems concerned further explorations into outer space, integration of the Negro, the rapid increase of population and its shift from rural to metropolitan centers, medical care for the fast increasing number of aged. On this last matter Kennedy was definitely committed to Federal underwriting; but many economists, sociologists, and legislators stated that the Administration had not thoroughly thought this problem through, and therefore worked for the defeat of the medical care bill. On the matter of establishing a new Cabinet post for urban affairs, as Kennedy urged, Congress turned down that proposal also.

In the second year of his Administration Kennedy won a signal victory when by the power of his office he influenced the great United States Steel Corporation to rescind its order for an increase in the price of steel. The President's tactics in this instance were sharply criticized by American business and even in Congress; but, objectively viewed, it seemed that the people generally upheld the President, feeling, like him, that Big Steel had misled the country by surprising it with a cost increase the national economy was not yet ready to assimilate.

One of Kennedy's great challenges at home lay in the Republican-Southern Democratic coalition in Congress—a problem which all his Democratic predecessors in the White House during the twentieth century have had—a combination of forces which, by tradition and temperament, had been opposed to the type of liberal legislation begun by FDR, continued by Truman, and espoused by Kennedy himself. But it is only fair to say that, although the people liked these three men enough to vote them into office, the political line-up in Congress, also representing the people's choice, was an index to the nation's fundamental wariness of experimentation with untried social formulae. Political managers often do not understand how the electorate can vote for a highly liberal Executive and a conservative Congressman at the same time; yet ballot-splitting in America is a regular thing, an innate aspect of the checks and balances inherent in the American system.

But the truly great challenge Kennedy faced lay in how to avoid nuclear war and yet keep intact the principles and aims of the free world. The historian Walter Lippmann had declared that the East-West struggle of the twentieth century was more like that which had existed between Islam and Christianity and not the usual type of rivalry heretofore existing between nations. Another historian, Toynbee, had written that after conquering the lion and the tiger, man was safe from extermination; but that now, with the unleashing of atomic energy, man was again threatened with extermination.

Kennedy's youthfulness, at first deplored by some, was later thought by others to be an asset to the United States, because the great issues which an American President must face in the twentieth century could never be handled except by one with resilience and energy. The President's cautiousness and willingness to inquire of others, including his predecessors in the White House, were reassuring to many of his countrymen. Another asset he had was his wife, the former Jacqueline Bouvier, whose background was similar to his, and whose warmth, charm, and linguistic talents contributed to Kennedy's success in his journeys and dealings around the world.

During the early part of his Administration, there was much comment about the number of Kennedy relatives in the Government. The people did not think too much about the President's brother being the Attorney-General nor of his brother-in-law's heading up the Peace Corps. When still another brother, however, became a candidate for the United States Senate from the President's home state and his sister a goodwill emissary to Europe, the opposition complained about a Kennedy "dynasty"—a perfectly understandable complaint. On the other hand, it is also understandable that in so taxing a job as the American Presidency, a man, to carry out his program, is entitled to all the help that those closest to him can give.

The contest in the Kennedy Administration between the element Eisenhower called "the spenders" and that of the conservative tradition to which the President also belonged was absorbing to watch as record-breaking peacetime budgets, exceeding revenues and reviving the charge of "patriarchal government" as well as the fear of further devaluation of the dollar, continued to be advanced. In fact, the accommodation of this duality in Kennedy's political philosophy to the needs of the United States during the agitated times of his Administration was among his greatest challenges of all.

John F. Kennedy was the most scholarly man in the White

House since Woodrow Wilson. His two books, *Why England Slept* and *Profiles in Courage*, reveal him as a historian and an evaluator of human nature. In this age of frustration when, as Mr. Lippmann said, we live "between a war that can not be fought and a peace that can not be achieved," America and the world could take comfort in the thought that in Washington was an executive who had a sense of history; who realized that America in the space age must ever show its disposition toward humanitarianism without allowing the physical might of the free world to diminish or America's role in maintaining that world to be lessened.

The endless caution and resolution required to achieve this magic is something the American people felt was demonstrably present in their 34th President.

On November 22, 1963, America and the world were thrown into stupefying shock as the President of the United States was shot down while riding in his car in Dallas, Texas. The assassination of this handsome young man, his life so full of promise, was an event the American people found hard to accept. Sorrow-torn obsequies were attended by rulers and dignitaries from all over the world and the nation in deepest grief buried its young President in Arlington Cemetery. He was the fourth President to die at the hands of an assassin.

With his work unfinished, Kennedy's death precipitated, as such events so often do, loud encomiums of the dead man's virtues. The Treasury Department at once issued a new savings bond in his honor and struck off a new half-dollar bearing his likeness. Within a short time, biographies, memoirs and tributes by people who had known and worked with him appeared on the market and had a wide sale. The judgments in some of these publications were, naturally, premature.

But the ways of men are such that when tragedy casts its shadow over them, it casts its shadow over their objectivity also. The Kennedy Administration's contribution has been very thoroughly assessed. The British-American author Alistair Cooke, has written of Kennedy that "his public image as a great liberal is a false one" and that if he had not been so charming, young, and handsome, he might not have enjoyed the popularity he did. Cooke states simply: "He was not a great President."

Retrospection and a re-examination of those years may impel thoughtful people to believe this may well be the judgment most likely to stand.

★★★★★★★★★★★★★★★★★★★★★★★★★★★★★★★★★★★

35

LYNDON BAINES JOHNSON

☆ ☆

VOTE OF 1960: *See* under Kennedy

		Popular	Electoral
VOTE OF 1964:	Lyndon B. Johnson, Democrat	43,130,000	486
	Barry M. Goldwater, Republican	27,178,000	52
	Others	337,000	
		70,645,000	538

☆ ☆

THE WISDOM OF THE FOUNDING FATHERS WHEN THEY PROVIDED FOR a constitutional succession to the Presidency in the event of death was never so indisputably corroborated as when Lyndon B. Johnson inherited that office. Without the slightest disruptive act of any kind, the transition was made—as it always has been made—with no agonizing save the grief of a stunned nation and the mourning of the world of nations. A British political writer of the time was impelled to remind the American people that nearly all the political systems in existence in 1789, the year the American system went into effect, had been overthrown, while that of the United States remained stronger than ever.

The induction of Lyndon B. Johnson into the Presidential office was as dramatic as anything that has ever happened on the American shores. The oath administered by a hastily-summoned woman judge, and within the very plane which was carrying the body of a slain President to the capital city and was to carry his successor to the same destination, with the young widowed First Lady and the new First Lady witnessing the grievous observance —this was a sorrow-laden scene of American history the like of which can hardly take place again.

Lyndon B. Johnson was in love with politics from the time he came to Washington as a young secretary to a Congressman from his native Texas. Despite the stories of his rise from poor beginnings, it would nevertheless not have been possible for him to have risen without his quite considerable background. Born August 27, 1908, near Stonewall, Gillespie County, in Texas, he was the son of Samuel Ealy Johnson, Jr. and Rebekah Baines and was of pioneer stock on both sides. Johnson City, in the vicinity, was named for his family, and it was there that his early education was obtained. His wife, known throughout the land as Lady Bird, was Claudia Taylor, also of a substantial Texas family.

Lyndon Johnson was the disciple of Franklin D. Roosevelt who, he admitted, was like a father to him. This relation is the whole index to his performance in office. There was, of course, some conservatism in him, hailing from the section of the nation that he did; and his switch to the far liberal side therefore disappointed his fellow-Southerners deeply. There is no doubt that in the civil rights issue, that domestic matter with which his Administration was to be so deeply involved, Johnson's stand originally was not what it became when he was President. This caused him to be called insincere by his enemies, who pointed out that fourteen times in his House and Senate years he had voted against the repeal of the poll tax. But who is to say whether changes in position taken by a public figure come about through expediency or because of a genuine maturing of the soul?

Johnson had been in the Presidential office only a year before he ran for a term in his own right. He was elected by a tremendous plurality, receiving 61 per cent of the popular vote. There were some precedents broken in that election: Vermont had never before gone Democratic and Georgia never before gone Republican; further, the formerly disenfranchised District of Columbia cast its first Presidential vote under the new 23rd Amendment to the Constitution, ratified in 1961. An estimated 6,000,000 Negro voters were registered—a record.[1]

Since the time when McKinley campaigned on the "full dinner pail," it seems to have been necessary for Presidential candidates to conduct their races on a slogan. Johnson's was "The Great Society." As a devotee of Franklin D. Roosevelt, it was in the very nature of things that he should outline even wider social

[1] The adoption of the 24th Amendment, abolishing the poll tax as a qualification in Federal elections, also had an effect on this vote.

reforms than those his mentor had initiated. He strongly advocated an anti-poverty program—called the Economic Opportunity Act of 1964—and was able to get a $784 million appropriation for its first year of operation. Johnson's opponents called the anti-poverty bill a hoax and mere vote-getting bait. In reality, the Act was mislabeled: it was not a cure for poverty nor were its major programs new. It was a commitment to improve the lot of the nation's 35 million poor who in the midst of unprecedented prosperity were still poor.

But the conservative element in the country could not see why a responsibility that was primarily a local matter should be assumed by the Federal Government—and at a time when the national revenues were still several billion dollars below expenditures every year.

All this emphasized the fear articulated by traditionalists in America since 1932—the eradication of the power of the States. More and more power was being concentrated in Washington. The conservatives felt that the nation could hardly be called a confederation of independent states any more; the states were slowly emerging as mere geographical divisions of a national colossus. Health programs, relief and welfare, highways, education, slum clearance, job training, housing—these were only some of the areas in which the Federal Government in setting its sights for the Great Society kept billions of dollars flowing to the States, counties, and municipalities. In education, parochial and private schools were being given public help for the first time.

In the South this aid was often resented because Federal agencies were authorized to withhold it where racial discrimination could be detected. And the Federal Government was powerful not alone in the field of aid, but also in the ownership of land. In thirteen Western states the Government owned nearly two-thirds of the total land area; in Alaska alone it owned over 90 per cent. Further, the Government was powerful in the field of patronage: one person out of eight was a Federal employee.

Nevertheless, the Johnson domestic campaign forged ahead. The scope of the actions Congress took during this time were without parallel in America's history. Where Kennedy failed in getting medical care for the aged through social security, Johnson succeeded. Where Kennedy failed in getting a new Cabinet office established for urban affairs, Johnson succeeded. Where Kennedy failed in getting tax reduction, Johnson succeeded.

A new immigration law, doing away with the 41-year-old national origins quota system, was enacted, allowing any country outside the Western Hemisphere to send up to 20,000 immigrants to the United States annually. For the first time, a limit was set on immigrants from this hemisphere and on this feature Johnson had to suffer a defeat.

The 1903 treaty with Panama was abrogated; that country was to have absolute sovereignty over the Canal Zone and have a say in the operation of the Canal as well. Johnson also recommended that studies be made for the construction of a new sea-level canal in Central America. The treaty was not ratified.

Johnson also signed a bill creating a National Foundation for the Arts and Humanities, making the Government literally a gigantic patron of the arts. In another esthetic move, he signed a roadside beautification bill.

Two signal defeats handed Johnson were in labor legislation and home rule for the District of Columbia. The Senate by filibuster refused to pare down the Taft-Hartley Act. Compulsory unionism in labor was still anathema to great sections of the American people. As for governing the District, Congress still insisted on retaining control; the charge of politics (in other words, considerations of the Negro vote) was made against both the proponents and opponents of home rule for the heavily Negro capital city.

One day the American people woke up to find themselves engaged in a brutal war in Southeast Asia, in the republic of South Viet Nam. The aggression into this little country was similar in circumstances to that used against South Korea in Truman's time. As the American objective in the Korean War was the independence of democratic South Korea, so the objective in the Vietnamese War was the freedom of democratic South Viet Nam. In both cases Communism was the real aggressor coming from the North; in both cases China was the real power behind the aggression.

It was very hard for the American people to understand why their soldiers had to be in Southeast Asia at all. President Johnson told the people: "We fight because we must fight if we are to live in a world where every country can shape its own destiny. And only in such a world will our own freedom be finally secure." But the people were only puzzled by this statement. They knew that underdeveloped countries like Viet Nam were not only incapable of working out a satisfactory destiny for themselves, but that their peoples did not want to be bothered about it. They wanted peace, safety from bullets, food, and a gradual step-up in their standard of living; and they did not care whether such improvements were accomplished under a democracy, monarchy, Communism, or what.

Nevertheless, the American nation had certain commitments she was bound in honor to fulfill. Principal among them were her obligations under the SEATO Treaty. Johnson contended also that to give in to the aggressor in a little spot like Viet Nam was only to increase the aggressor's appetite for another little spot somewhere else, since the avowed purpose of the Communist system had always been eventual subjection of the entire world to its ideology.

But a new philosophy respecting foreign affairs was emerging in some quarters. In reality, it was the old philosophy of Isolationism. Many people felt that inasmuch as China was the dominant power in Asia, all things pertaining to that continent should be allowed to come within her sphere of influence. The United States took that position when she enunciated her Monroe Doctrine, and she has never allowed the world to forget that, so far as the Western Hemisphere was concerned, she was going to be the ultimate boss.

In Europe, where the NATO alliance was in the most shaky position since its organization, France, in a great show of independence, was striving to dominate her part of the world. Likewise, Egypt felt she should be the determiner of policy in the Middle East; Indonesia felt the same about her role in the Pacific island areas. Even the estimable Walter Lippmann, certainly no appeaser and famous for his pro-liberal views, was advocating in 1965 the sphere-of-influence philosophy instead of that known as "globalism." Everywhere nations were recognizing that no one country would be able to maintain order over the entire world. Certainly the American people, with their very severe social problems and their rising national debt, would not indefinitely agree to the policing of the world.

Yet, the world recognized that it would be folly to assume that America could not win an all-out war in Southeast Asia should she choose to wage that kind of war. And it would also be folly not to recognize that the Vietnamese War was not popular. The policy of Johnson and his aides was calculated to prevent the Pacific from becoming a Chinese lake. In opposition to this theory, men like the historian Toynbee urged immediate withdrawal from Viet Nam to allow that nation to become united even under Communist leadership if necessary. Johnson fervently desired to come to the conference table with the belligerents and arrive at a negotiated settlement, possibly similar to that which ended the Korean War.

But irrespective of the President's ardently expressed desire to end the war, the people associated the escalation with him personally. As a result, his popularity began a descent that was as swift as its ascent had been four years earlier and caused him wisely not to seek re-election. There was in the nation a "credibility gap," a disparity between what was being told the people and the knowledge of things as they really were on the part of Government officials; and Johnson was being blamed for this also. Whether the criticism was valid or not, it became clear that both the President and the people wanted relief from this longest and most unpopular war in America's history which had cost 46,000 lives and $30 billion a year. It became clear also that Johnson, most intensely concerned about his ultimate place in history, was anxious not to bequeath an unfinished war to his successor. He surely knew, as the American people knew, that the country had no business fighting a land war on the Asian continent; his major problem was to find some way to end it honorably.

Pervading the entire sorrowful drama was the temperament of the President. In the cloakrooms of legislative halls, bargaining and maneuvering, he was the expert par excellence. In the White House it was different; there the leadership required would have had to be on such a plane as to transcend the importunities of politicians and populace alike. This kind of greatness Johnson could not deliver. In fact, it can be said that one of the great tragedies of twentieth-century America was that, in the 1930's and 1960's, when the times demanded the most unassailable statesmanship, the Presidency happened to be held by men whose guiding genie could not bring them to the splendid heights.

And so, a few days before the 1968 elections—when Johnson, acceding to the demands the enemy had steadfastly made as a prerequisite to talking peace, ordered a halt in the bombing in the Vietnamese War—he was accused of opportunism aimed at helping the Democratic candidate. The accusation was, of course, unjust; but it showed how large blocs of the people were thinking. It is far more likely that the President was making a last supreme effort to realize peace before he left office. The bombing halt both helped and harmed the Presidential candidates of 1968.

Johnson had one other major foreign problem to handle while in office—the Dominican crisis. American intervention in the Dominican Republic was undertaken suddenly and without prior consultation with the Organization of American States; but the Administration insisted that the crisis was so urgent that any delay in hearing from the OAS or the United Nations would have resulted in a Communist takeover similar to that by Castro in Cuba. America was sharply criticized in both hemispheres for landing troops in Santo Domingo, but when a stable government was installed on the island and public elections were assured, her action was held by many to have been the right one.

Next to the war, the situation worrying Americans most was the crime in the cities. Riots, burnings, lootings, murder in unprecedented degree took place in city after city. In 1967 there were 5,600 deaths from gunshot wounds in the United States, while in England there were fewer than thirty and in France fewer than twenty. Both Negroes and whites took part in the demonstrations which occurred on university campuses as well as in the streets. The outstanding Negro leader and Nobel prizewinner Dr. Martin Luther King was shot down, and soon afterward New York's Senator Robert F. Kennedy, was assassinated. The cry was heard all over the world that America had become a "sick" nation.

But this was the usual oversimplification. Growing in America and in the world generally was an increasingly permissive approach to human behavior, an attitude which marked all facets of life, including the church; and the lawless, present in every society and in every age, took advantage of the opportunity to be less inhibited in their anti-social activities.

As for the public protests, the Negro youths demonstrating for equal rights, the white youths demonstrating against the interruption in their lives by a war 10,000 miles away, were rebelling against a world made by their elders and constituted authority in general. The American people, aghast at this insurgence, sought to find causes and remedies. Some blamed the too easy immigration policies of recent administrations; some blamed the churches for their growing worldliness and the backsliding of the clergy; some blamed arbitrary policies of educational leaders and the pontification of social workers; nearly all blamed the meaninglessness of the Vietnamese War and all foreign involvements. Certainly all these conditions contributed in varying measure to the social unrest of those years. But above all, there was the incontestable fact that inspired leadership was lacking in America. Those who led as well as those who aspired to lead spoke in old clichés, and the people no longer believed them. The Nixon Administration which was to follow would have not only the serious problem of finding a way to end civil disobedience, but the even more serious one of rekindling flickering faith in the traditional precepts of democracy.

A third factor in the distress of sections of the nation was the trend in the decisions being handed down by the Supreme Court, which came to be known as the "Warren Court," in allusion to its libertarian Chief Justice, Earl Warren. By a 3 to 2 ratio,[2] the feelings of the people toward the Court were registered as unfavorable, and the Chief Justice was possibly the most controversial since Roger Brooke Taney.

While Warren conceived of the Court, to use his own words, as the "balance wheel" in the national Government and sincerely sought to execute the duties of his office on that premise, Americans were divided on the Court's ruling that religious devotions could not be required in public schools. Many people, among them the police and others in public life, were shocked at the Court's judgments regarding the Constitutional rights of those charged with crime; others were bewildered by its definition of what

[2] American Institute of Public Opinion Poll, published July 10, 1968.

could rightfully be called obscene; and many politicians were perturbed because it upset the accustomed rural domination of legislative bodies in nation and state. When Chief Justice Warren wanted to resign, President Johnson's replacement appointee, also a member of the Court, was rejected by the Senate, and Johnson was accused of "cronyism"—as Presidents Grant and Truman had been.

A fourth crisis of the Johnson Administration—and one that had world reverberations—was the state of the U. S. dollar as a world currency. There was a run on the dollar in foreign markets; holders of dollars were demanding their redemption in gold. There had been a steady drain on the gold stocks of America from around $24 billion in 1949 to about $11 billion by early 1968 when the crisis took place. The principal reason for the scare was, of course, the Vietnamese War and what it was doing to the public debt; but there were other reasons too. These were the continuing unbalanced budgets and surging Federal deficits; the mounting unfavorable balance-of-payments as the value of imports into the United States rose faster than that of exports out of the United States; and that invisible thief—inflation.

Inasmuch as the American dollar was the reserve currency used by nations of the free world to settle their debts with each other, a loss of faith in it would have compelled the United States to raise the price of gold, which is to devalue the dollar. In the long history of the country the dollar had been devalued only once—in 1934. In conferences with the other Gold Pool countries of the West, certain decisions were made. The price of $35 per ounce remained unchanged in official dealings of governments with each other, regardless of what speculators and hoarders did with the metal. The United States raised income taxes and cut back on domestic programs, at least for the duration of the war in Asia. Interest rates on loans were raised by the Federal Reserve Board. Congress passed legislation removing the gold "cover" as backing for the billions of paper dollars in circulation, thus freeing America's gold stocks for any demands that might be made by holders of dollars abroad. By these moves, confidence in the dollar as the world's leading currency for the time being was maintained.

Meanwhile the economy of the nation boomed giddily with a gross national product exceeding $800 billion; and the controversy between the spenders and the conservatives abated not in the slightest since the Keynes theory of economics was first favored by the Roosevelt Administration in the 1930's. The spenders took the position that when the Government pays out more money than it collects, it creates purchasing power; that when the condition is reversed, it withdraws purchasing power. The conservatives declared that to pile up debt upon debt for our descendants to liquidate was immoral; that the financial debacles of past civilizations testify to this; and that the same catastrophe could happen to America.

Johnson came to the White House with the most extensive Congressional experience of any President in American history— twelve years in the House and twelve in the Senate. He was the most powerful majority leader the Senate had ever known. He wanted very much to be loved, as his mentor FDR had been; to succeed, as FDR had succeeded. This longing, coupled with his interpretation of the 1964 landslide, caused him to pursue an enlargement of the Roosevelt policies with evangelistic fervor. And he got so many of his recommendations through the 89th Congress that he was considered an even more successful manipulator than FDR.

But there was a singular aspect of this reform program which Johnson failed to take into account. Although for the most part the people liked the legislation he had enacted, they were not so devoted to him personally as they were to FDR. The reason for this lies deep in psychology. FDR's was a new voice in the councils of the people. It is true that his program did not arise out of a grand inner philosophy passionately cherished, but rather out of a native shrewdness which prompted him not to resist the social revolution of his time. But that is not what truly made the difference. He was a new voice. And his acts were therefore looked upon as messianic.

But there is only so much of the messianic for which a people can maintain a steady level of enthusiasm. After FDR, Truman and Kennedy, any further laws designed for social welfare would be received in a matter-of-fact way.

It was ironical that in his almost pathological quest for approval, Johnson had to accept the bitter medicine of disapproval. Only the Negro, as a bloc, seemed to be unconditionally for him and his Party. For the black man he had done much. He appointed the first Negro to the Cabinet. He named the first Negro to the Supreme Court. He appointed Negroes as judges and ambassadors, and to other Federal posts. It is another of the ironies in American politics that an adherent of the Southern Democracy, which had always opposed too much liberty for the Negro, should have emerged as the most vociferous advocate of that liberty.

But too many other voter-groups were resistant to Johnson for him to risk running for another term. Large sections of business, of course, had always been in the opposite camp. The South, no longer solid, and demonstrating a two-party system for the first time since Reconstruction days (and in several states a three-party system), was too sensitive to its race problems to be counted on for support at all. Large numbers of church people, adherents of all three faiths, were against him for escalating the war. His relations with the press were not of the best and harsh words were often uttered on both sides. And the 90th Congress had rebuffed him time after time. To make matters worse, the sense of the heaviness of his political personality prevented people from responding to his messages.

Lyndon Johnson had to abandon his plans for the Great Society principally because Congress would not go along and supply him the needed money. This and the unfinished war in Asia were his two great disappointments as he returned to the LBJ Ranch in his native Texas, a retreat visited by so many heroes and visitors from all over the world that it had become as famous as Theodore Roosevelt's Sagamore Hill.

Like most Southerners, Johnson possessed strong sentimental attachments and these softened the dour countenance he so often presented and the driving, sometimes ruthless pace he set for his subordinates during much of his Administration. Perhaps Johnson, the private citizen, writing and working for the Presidential library now located on the University of Texas grounds, will win more approbation than had been given him in the waning years of his Presidency.

But the last days of the Johnson Administration were not without glory. For, on Christmas 1968, three American astronauts broadcast to a spellbound world the news—with simultaneous views—of a voyage to the moon, which they encircled ten times, and then returned to earth with a pre-arranged precision that astonished even the Space Administration. The feat was greater than that performed by Columbus. American prestige in the world, so badly damaged since the close of World War II, was decidedly enhanced as the world beheld what was unquestionably the greatest odyssey in the annals of man up to that time. People began to feel that the universe would at last be conquered, that further explorations into the vastness of outer space were bound to be the inevitable result. Thus, the enthusiastic support of America's space program by Presidents Kennedy and Johnson received illustrious vindication.

The nation was still in official mourning for its 32nd President when it was startlingly informed of the death of its remaining ex-President. Lyndon Johnson had for many years been a victim of heart disease and the fatal seizure occurred on January 22, 1973. His remains were interred in the family burial ground which, like the birthsite and other dependencies, was part of the sprawling 400-acre LBJ Ranch.

★★★★★★★★★★★★★★★★★★★★★★★★★★★★★★★★★★★★★★

36

RICHARD NIXON

☆ ☆

		Popular	Electoral
VOTE OF 1960:	*See* under Kennedy		
VOTE OF 1968:	Richard Nixon, Republican	31,770,000	301
	Hubert H. Humphrey, Democrat	31,268,000	191
	George C. Wallace, Independent	9,897,000	46
	Others	241,000	
		73,176,000	538
VOTE OF 1972:	Richard Nixon, Republican	46,108,000	520
	George S. McGovern, Democrat	28,085,000	17
	Others	1,432,000	1
		75,625,000	538

☆ ☆

IN AN ACTION RARELY TAKEN, THE AMERICAN PEOPLE IN 1968 SENT to the White House a previously defeated candidate for the Presidency. President Johnson and the Party which had been in power were so encumbered with the past, its wars and its miscellaneous nostrums, that change was inevitable.

Although the United States had been experiencing one of the longest periods of prosperity in its history and the workingman's income had never before been so high, the suffering caused by war and the burden imposed by expensive welfare programs had created anxieties and moral disquietude that belittled the material satisfactions of good times. The tax burden, the civil disorders, and the other causes of unrest that we have attempted to analyze in Chapter 35, all created a climate which people felt needed to be transformed. Many living in the 1960's had lived in the 1930's and beheld the vicissitudes and agonies of the years between. Too much blood had been shed in contests not in defense of the homeland. There had been too much disillusionment.

Events revealed that the Republicans recognized these conditions and how the people truly felt about them better than did the Democrats; with a proper candidate the time was ripe for the

return of the former Party to power in national and State councils. The Democrats saw these conditions too; but they had fallen
into the habit of underrating the common man, thinking of him
as principally venal. They campaigned on such slogans as "You
never had it so good," which, together with their promises of still
greater benefits, caused many people to sense that there was going
to be a decided reckoning of some kind somewhere, that the cost
was already evident throughout the country, and in more ways
than money.

For direction to more realistic goals, in 1968 the people turned
to a man who had been a loser in the race for the Presidency. It
was hoped that Richard Nixon with his Quaker upbringing might,
at least, point the way. He had been called an introvert; if so, he
was a tough introvert. He was by nature shy, and his personality
did not come across to the public easily. As a young man, he had
preferred history and music to mathematics and sports.

Nixon was the first President to come from the Pacific Coast.
He was born on January 9, 1913 in a small frame house on a lemon
farm at Yorba Linda in Southern California. His parents, Francis A. Nixon and Hannah Milhous, were ordinary working people.
Richard worked his way through Whittier College, a Quaker institution near his home; then, given a scholarship to Duke University,
he entered the law school there and received his degree. It was at
Duke that he showed a great interest in public affairs. Back in
Whittier, he joined a law firm and met his wife, Thelma "Pat"
Ryan. After the Pearl Harbor disaster, he worked for a while at
a Government desk in Washington and later joined the Navy for
action in the South Pacific, although, as a Quaker, he could have
claimed exemption on conscientious grounds. In the Navy he rose
to become lieutenant commander.

In 1946 Nixon entered politics for the first time, winning the
Republican nomination for Congress; and in 1948 he won both
the Republican and Democratic nominations for that seat. It was
during his second term in Congress that he first received national
notice through his work on the controversial House Un-American
Activities Committee. He constantly called the attention of the
American people to the devious techniques of Communism and
helped draft the famous Taft-Hartley law, voting to pass it over
President Truman's veto. He also supported civil rights legisla-

tion, increased social security benefits, abolition of the poll tax, income tax reduction, home rule for the District of Columbia, and the cautious immigration policies adopted in 1952. His legislative record had thus been a remarkably constructive one. After serving two years in the Senate, Nixon was selected by Eisenhower as his running-mate on the national ticket; in 1956 he won a second election as Vice-President.

Under Nixon the Vice-Presidential office was expanded to its greatest usefulness in American history. It was Eisenhower, of course, who gave Nixon this opportunity. He had great faith in his Vice-President, calling him "my boy." During this time Nixon visited fifty-five countries; these contacts, together with his ten years in the Senate and his experience in presiding over meetings of the Cabinet and the National Security Council during Eisenhower's illnesses, equipped him singularly for the burdensome job he took on in 1969.

However, the task of achieving a sound position on the domestic front as well as in foreign relations could hardly be accomplished in a short time, perhaps not even in one Presidential term. The America of the second half of the twentieth century was far different from the America of the first half. Franklin D. Róosevelt began a new era, one which many students called socialistic. People had become so accustomed to the Federal government's intervention in their daily lives that no candidate for public office could have had victory at the polls without considering the everyday problems of the common man instead of leaving their solutions, as in the past, to local agencies.

For the first time in American history, the Government took a position on the controversial issue of population control. The gigantic relief bequests made by the United States since the close of World War II, both at home and to nations all over the globe, brought the need for family planning urgently into focus. The Department of Health, Education, and Welfare had large sums in its budget for family planning, as did the Agency for International Development. This shift in the American government's policy on a matter formerly considered principally within the realm of religion or, at the least, of private conscience, was most significant; it highlighted one of the greatest problems in the modern world. The American people, although among the most compassionate societies mankind has known, would not consent indefinitely to being taxed to relieve want in countries where the poor were having the largest families. This was the attitude especially with respect to the Western hemisphere; for it was in South America, whose protection from Communism was America's constant preoccupation, that the most widespread poverty was coupled with the largest families—a problem further complicated in that area by the Roman Catholic Church, which historically has opposed artificial limitation of birth.

Related to all this of course was the ever-present welfare system. In a time of unprecedented prosperity for the United States, with unfilled jobs begging for workers, there had been an unbelievable increase of people on relief. In 1973 an estimated 16,000,000 people were on the welfare rolls; for the same year the cost of Federal, state, and local assistance to needy families rose to almost $23 billion. Relief had become a way of life for enormous numbers of people, many of whom had become inured to it. Where offenders could be detected, welfare workers cracked down. But the system was there; it badly needed reform; and reform could not take place quickly because it so often involved politics.

Nixon had been in office only a few weeks when he flew for an information-gathering visit to European capitals. The main purpose of the visit was the strengthening of the NATO alliance. Under Johnson, absorbed with Asia and the Vietnamese war, America's relations with Europe had become badly impaired. The Nixon trip was everywhere considered successful. Europeans, still conscious of what the Marshall Plan had done for them, felt that America was once more concerned with the security and well-being of that part of the world. Especially significant was the rapport the American President seemed to have re-established with the ageing, obdurate French chief of state, Charles de Gaulle, who had expelled NATO headquarters from his country.

Nevertheless, some historians wrote that NATO was showing its age, that its original usefulness was past. There were those who urged that the military pacts of both NATO and its opponent, the Warsaw bloc, be dissolved because of desuetude.

Nixon was soon compelled to make one of the most serious decisions in the realm of national defense that a Chief Executive ever had to make. The anti-ballistic missile system (ABM), had been plaguing American statesmen for some time; the reactions to it had cut across party lines. Nixon's plan differed from that of Johnson's, but it was nonetheless expensive. A workable defense against possible missiles hurled at the United States was a recognized need. But how extensive should this defensive system be, and should the sites for it be centered around populous cities or in open spaces? The answers were far from simple. Those favoring ABM explained that Russia had deployed more land-based missiles than the United States and that the latter had better catch up. They cautioned also that Russia seemed to be returning to the despotism of Stalin and that the free countries should in no wise consider themselves safe from Communist dangers. Those opposing ABM insisted that if America had attained a reasonable security, that was enough; that the nation should be spared the billions of dollars this type of deterrent would cost; that absolute security was an illusion anyway; and that the establishment of anti-missile sites would produce a reaction that would escalate the arms race which could only end in Armageddon.

Nixon said that, besides the protection of land-based retaliatory forces against direct attack, there was the question of defending the American people from the kind of nuclear attack that might come from Communist China in the future. He stressed the threat from that source to both the United States and Russia and the possible community of interest between the two great powers by reason of that danger.

The ratification, early in 1969, by the Senate of the United States of the Nuclear Non-proliferation Treaty, only emphasized the Chinese problem. By this treaty, America, Britain, Russia, France, and China were to pledge themselves not to supply nuclear weapons to any other nation, nor to give help in the manufacture of such weapons, although aid would be given those nations desiring nuclear power for peaceful purposes. China refused to become a signatory to this pact, as did France. Nevertheless, when forty non-nuclear nations join the U. S., Britain, and Russia in ratifying the treaty, it will become effective. Nixon urged ratification as a beginning of arms-control talks with the Soviet Union.

At home the great question of inflation was haunting; something had to be done soon. With a national budget nearing $270 billion, the costly war, and soaring commodity prices, steps had to be taken to put a brake on the overheated economy. The Federal Reserve Board, guardian of the nation's financial structure, raised the discount rate in order to make borrowing more costly; the rate was the highest since 1929. All agencies of the Government, including the Defense Department, were ordered by Nixon to cut spending. Some social programs were singled out for elimination or consolidation with other bureaus. In his first budget, Nixon trimmed $4 billion from original departmental estimates in this effort to halt the inflationary spiral that was seriously affecting the lives of all Americans and rendering the much-publicized "longest peacetime prosperity in history" almost meaningless.

Then, on July 20, 1969, something took place which enveloped the world in awe-stricken wonder. The American astronauts Neil A. Armstrong and Edwin E. Aldrin, Jr., debarked from a space-ship to the surface of the moon while Michael Collins remained in orbit in the Command craft which had brought them into outer space. They had realized an achievement the possibility of which man had lyricized and dreamed about since the beginnings of time. Never before had a human being set foot on another celestial body. With epic-like eloquence, the first words uttered on the moon by Neil Armstrong were: "That's one small step for man, one great leap for mankind." After planting the American flag in the moon's powdery crust, scooping up soil and rocks for scientific study, keeping in touch with the earth constantly, sending back live television pictures of their movements, and answering a call from the President of the United States by radio-telephone, the astronauts left the "magnificent desolation" to return to earth. In the Pacific a recovery ship with President Nixon on board greeted the travelers from another world. Their native world acclaimed these navigators of a new dimension and in ineffable amazement recognized another frontier, the portent of which not even the great technology of the time could predict. Man's concept of the universe could never be the same again.

Only one thing could be construed as mitigating the splendor of this great accomplishment: the reflection that while man's indomitable spirit had at last conquered the heavens, his ego could not conquer the wrongs and injustices on his own planet.

Beclouding everything was the ghastly presence of the war in Asia. To the termination of that human sacrifice the ingenuity of Nixon had to be applied with inexorable perseverance. Because he had resumed the bombing which Lyndon Johnson had ordered stopped, Nixon was severely criticized in and out of Congress. But he regarded the fighting of a war otherwise an absurdity. In the Kennedy Administration the United States had engineered an invasion of Cuba without air support, and the Bay of Pigs undertaking, when Castro completely overwhelmed the invaders, was a humiliating fiasco for the Americans.

After the futile Battle of Hamburger Hill, the people truly wanted disengagement. Their patriotism was tested almost to the breaking point when, after the four years of Nixon's first term, there was still no peace. But the numerous efforts in Paris and elsewhere of Henry A. Kissinger, the German-born Secretary of State, toward peace or at least a cease-fire, has been futile. The President had insisted on "peace with honor," that America would otherwise forfeit her position in the world, her fighting men would be made to feel ashamed, and the world would know that she could not be depended on to stand by her allies.

Peace-at-any-price rallies were held throughout the country; and even professional men, including clergymen, were imprisoned for inciting the youth not to answer the call to arms, thinking thus to force the President's hand to sue for peace. This gave encouragement to North Vietnam. Only after the President's reelection became inevitable could productive negotiations go forward.

The patience of the American Government and people was at last rewarded. In January 1973 a cease-fire was agreed upon, and the 11-year-old war for control of a country not as large as the State of Washington was over for the United States. American casualties had risen to 350,000, military spending to $140 billion, and the number of aircraft lost to 8,600. The terrors of war entered the very livingrooms of the American people who, for the first time, by means of television and satellite, viewed the horrors of combat, the mass burials, the pitiful plight of fleeing refugees, even military executions: it was enough to make pacifists out of hard-core militarists.

In no other war the American people had ever fought was there anything so traumatic for them; they longed for the return of their prisoners-of-war and suffered frustrations over their long-delayed homecoming. All Americans shared this feeling. And when at last the men came home, some from imprisonment for as long as eight years, the joy created was a nationwide emotion experienced by kin and stranger alike.

It may be many years before historians and the people of the world will be able to look upon the American involvement in Indochina with complete detachment. Various explanations are now given, various people blamed. In his memoirs, the French President de Gaulle recounts that he warned President Kennedy to stay out, that Vietnam was a quagmire from which extrication would be well-nigh impossible, and that Kennedy would not listen. Some blamed John Foster Dulles, the Eisenhower State Secretary, for his championing of the SEATO Treaty committing American aid to certain countries in Asia in the fighting of Communism. But the historian Arnold Toynbee explained: "They [the Americans] supposed that they were making war on Communism. They were actually making war on Asian nationalism, which is far more dynamic." This is a reasonable theory; certainly it throws light on the reasons why France could pull out of Indochina without a loss of prestige while America could not do so except "with honor." Communism had ceased being the world's bogeyman. A split between the two great socialist powers —China and the Soviet Union—was already at a stage threatening war. In the New World the Marxist governments in Cuba and Chile were far from stable, while a great country like Indonesia had dramatically rejected entry into the Communist orbit. A "third world" was emerging, with China as the point of polarization.

Nixon saw these changes clearly and adjusted to them, making surprising trips to Peking and Moscow which are now generally considered historic. The case of China was outstanding; the United States had not had diplomatic relations with that vast country for many years; in fact, the West had more or less considered her an outcast in the family of nations. The Chinese had long maintained that America's ties with Taiwan were the biggest obstacle to the normalization of relations between their country and the Americans; but Nixon assured them that eventual withdrawal of all American troops from Chiang Kai-shek's island nation was a certainty. In addressing the Chinese people during his trip, Nixon quoted from the writings of their great leader, Mao Tse-tung, with whom he also had a visit.

The Nixon journey to Russia several months after the Peking trip was most significant. This visit resulted in the signing of several pacts between the two superpowers dealing with health, the environment, and outer space. As the world's largest exporter of farm products, the United States agreed also to meet the critical wheat shortage in the Soviet Union by shipping them almost a billion dollars' worth of grain.

By far the most important agreement reached was the arms pact limiting strategic weapons, the principal feature of which called for limiting to two the anti-ballistic missile systems of each power, one of which, it was agreed, could be aimed at the national capitals of the two countries. America at once ordered construction of another missile site in Montana stopped. So far had the American *détente* with Russia gone.

It was now sanguinely hoped that the Administration would devote its energies to the needs at home. Not the least of these was correcting America's trade deficit—the first since 1888. Exports fell more than six billions below imports in 1972 as compared with a trade surplus in 1964 of seven billion dollars, and the situation was worsening. Within fourteen months the United States twice devalued the dollar, which, although quite important in international transactions, had little effect on consumer prices at home. The American purchaser would feel it only when he bought foreign-manufactured goods or travelled abroad. The steel and auto industries in America welcomed devaluation, for it meant an increase in the purchase of the home product. However, inflation and the high cost of food were still the chief worry of the citizen, although the times were prosperous and the gross national product, for the first time in history, passed the trillion dollar mark.

Despite the label of unbridled materialism with which the world frequently has characterized the United States, there have been few examples in history of a nation's trying so zealously to preserve its primeval natural beauties and protect the environment from the encroachment of the entrepreneur. In President Theodore Roosevelt's time America first became conscious of the need for conserving for posterity the natural wonders of continental

United States and protecting from extinction endangered species
of animals and birds. In Lyndon B. Johnson's term of office it
was no less spectacular. Johnson signed bills creating new national
parks and setting aside millions of acres in wilderness areas, scenic
rivers, and coastal wetlands. Nixon followed by presenting Congress with a program for controlling air and water pollution. The
Environmental Protection Agency was created; and the subsequent vigilance over America's manufacturing centers for violations resulted at times in the imposition of heavy fines on large
corporations. Nixon later reported that the country was "well
on the way to making our peace with nature."

Nixon began his second Administration by stressing decentralization and economy in Government. The two ideas were inter-
related. The aim to reverse the flow of power from Washington
back to the states and municipalities and thus reduce the vast
bureaucracy that had fastened on national affairs since 1932 was
welcomed by all who believed in a true democracy. In this connection Nixon programmed a system of what was called "revenue
sharing" with the states, enabling them to handle such matters as
welfare themselves. At the same time he laid the axe to several
projects begun in previous Administrations. The anti-poverty
program was dismantled[1]; and agencies such as the Peace Corps
were merged with other bodies. Another item severely truncated
was the space program. America had launched altogether seven
moon landing flights, and twelve men had walked on the lunar
surface during the Nixon years. Yet the Administration felt it
had, for the time being, learned what it wanted to know from
these explorations and that further flights did not warrant the
great outlays of money required for them. Nixon wanted also to
reduce the size of his Cabinet, but Congress would not approve
this change.

A change Congress *was* interested in was the reduction of the
American military presence abroad, in particular some 300,000
men in Europe and the money it was costing the taxpayers to
maintain them there. In addition, there were 300,000 men stationed at bases in Asia, Africa, Greenland, in the Mediterranean
and the Caribbean. The concept that all these far-away places

[1] The Bureau of the Census had reported that the number of people in poverty had dropped from 39,850,000 in 1960 to 25,500,000 in 1971.

were necessary in America's defense posture was slowly being eroded. The idea of America as the world's policeman had to be dispelled.

While he was President, Nixon was severely censured by both the press and some members of Congress for his inaccessibility. That he was aloof and possessed a somewhat "heavy" personality is indisputable. However, he was not unlike other Presidents in that he sought to govern without either romanticism or harshness. He did not favor amnesty for Vietnam draft evaders, particularly those who had fled the country; and he urged the re-instatement of capital punishment for certain crimes. The Supreme Court had held that capital punishment as practiced in America was in violation of the Constitution which prohibits "cruel and unusual punishment." But the rise in the crime rate in America, where a murder took place every thirty minutes, a burglary every thirteen seconds, to say nothing of the traffic in drugs and the effect it was having on the youth—all this was threatening the domestic tranquility to such a degree that trenchant and effective measures had to be taken to arrest it. Nixon sharply criticized what he called "permissive judges" and "social theorists" for their leniency with criminals. Crime was unquestionably one of the great worries of the American people in the seventh and eighth decades of the twentieth century.

Perhaps Nixon considered his most important domestic goal changing the composition of the Supreme Court. He was rebuffed twice in this effort, and both times his appointees were U. S. Circuit Court judges from the South. His first choice, Clement F. Haynsworth, Jr., was rejected by the Senate's Judiciary Committee because some of his decisions from the bench were said to have been biased by his corporate holdings. Moreover, he did not have a favorable record in labor or civil rights cases, and the powerful National Association for the Advancement of Colored People came out publicly against him. Nixon next submitted the name of C. Harrold Carswell, like Haynsworth, a Democrat; but Carswell was accused of being a segregationist and also did not have a favorable record in labor cases.

In the meantime another vacancy in the Court had to be filled, and the two men finally confirmed were Lewis H. Powell, Jr., another Southerner and a former president of the American Bar

Association, and William H. Rehnquist, an assistant U. S. Attorney-General. Nixon then appeared before the nation on television to explain these appointments.

Although the President's desire to transform the Court into a basically conservative instrument was understandable, the Senate's meticulous examination of the appointees revealed that a man's conservatism had to be up-dated and consonant with the progressive sentiment of the times in order to win approval. Thus the democratic process was dramatically vindicated and the world knew that the American system of governmental checks-and-balances was real and not just academic verbiage.

As America neared its bicentennial celebration, and realized also with a sort of terrified anticipation that it was on the threshold of the 21st century, foreboding as well as optimism characterized the reflections of thinking people. Four costly wars in a mere half-century had created disillusionment, even if during the 'seventies some sixty percent of Americans could not remember the end of World War II. Nevertheless, since these sixty percent must help by their taxes to pay for World War II, the psychological effect on the young of "getting on" in the American tradition was damaging. Moreover, with the great technological advances made, especially in communication, the people had become too sophisticated to listen to pleas for high-sounding adventures couched in language of dubious idealism. Nothing like Woodrow Wilson's abstract slogans would ever find credence with them. Further, no less than seventy-three percent of the population lived on only two percent of the land area, a statistic which further emphasized the vanishing provincialism in people's outlook. The Presidential election of 1972, when Nixon carried every state but one, indicated that although the Americans' ardent longing for an end to their most unpopular war had not been realized, their maturity was such that oversimplified nostrums for its termination could not win their approval or the approval of the 11,000,000 new young voters who were so suddenly enfranchised by the adoption of the 26th Amendment to the Constitution.

But if the Government thus had to re-assess the wisdom of its past policies, the people, too, had to re-examine the validity of the goals toward which they had been striving. The Roosevelt revolution of the 1930's had unloosed a mighty materialism which furthered rather than assuaged the social unrest. So that even with the war's end the process by which the national malaise in America was to be alleviated would be very complex. Perhaps a revolution of another kind would be required to make the needed corrections.

In the early months of Nixon's second Administration the American people were informed of certain dishonest acts connected with the Executive Department. Most important of these were the scandal which came to be known as "the Watergate" and the bombing in Cambodia. The President had assured the nation in 1970 that, notwithstanding Communist activity in Cambodia, the neutrality of that nation was being scrupulously respected by the United States. Later, by admission of ex-Secretary of Defense Laird, some 3,600 bombings by Americans had been carried out in Cambodia during 1969 and 1970. Further, it was revealed that the kinsfolk of the American dead in these sorties had been notified in falsified reports that their men had died in combat in Vietnam. This deception caused much of the jubilance over the Administration's ceasefire in Vietnam to fade.

The Watergate affair involved the burglarizing during the 1972 Presidential campaign of the Democratic National Committee headquarters in Washington by a Nixon re-election committee; the trial and imprisonment of those apprehended; the firing or resignation of top aides to the President; the resignation of two Attorneys-General; the revelation of illegal campaign contributions; blackmail; wire-tapping of White House conversations without the participants' knowledge; and the sensational televised hearings before a Senate investigating committee examining many Government officials.

The Watergate scandals and convictions were worse than those of Teapot Dome or the Grant era; for they resulted in both the President's and the Vice-President's being driven from office. During the time of the Senate hearings, it was revealed that Vice-President Agnew, both before and during his incumbency, was regularly paid "kickbacks" for State government work in his native Maryland. Further, Agnew had evaded payment of income tax for much of this money. He was forced to resign as Vice-President, fined, put on probation, and disbarred from the legal profession.

As if this were not shame enough for an Administration, it was finally uncovered through White House tapes which the Supreme Court had ordered turned over to the special Watergate prosecutor that, contrary to what Nixon had been assuring the country right along, the President had known from the beginning about the break-in of the Democratic headquarters and had even aided in the cover-up of that burglary.

The Judiciary Committee of the House had already begun hearings on impeachment when the contents of the tapes were revealed together with Nixon's admission of complicity in the cover-up of the burglary. The Committee recommended impeachment of the President on three articles: (I) obstruction of justice, (II) abuses of Presidential power, (III) disobedience of the Judiciary Committee's subpoenas. Other articles were proposed but a majority vote on them could not be obtained.[2] Each article concluded with the words that the President "has acted in a manner contrary to his trust as President and subversive of constitutional government, to the great prejudice of the cause of law and justice and to the manifest injury of the people of the United States . . . [and] by such conduct, warrants impeachment and trial, and removal from office." After the tapes had become public, the Judiciary Committee, Republicans and Democrats alike, stood 100% for impeachment. Later a delegation from the Senate called on the President and told him there was no hope. So on August 9, 1974, Richard Nixon became the first President to resign from office.

The climate of disillusionment with the Presidential office had infiltrated the entire nation. Irregularities had been found in the President's income-tax returns over the years, causing people to feel that he was as guilty as Agnew. The Government then assessed Nixon around a half-million dollars in back taxes and interest, which he promptly promised to pay. Further, it was revealed that he had used about $17 million of Government money to improve his two homes in Florida and California under the guise of national security for the President. It was not proved whether Nixon directly authorized these expenditures or not; but

[2] Eleven articles of impeachment were returned against Andrew Johnson in 1868.

the sycophants with which he had surrounded himself naturally sought to accrue all manner of benefits for their chief.[3]

After a good beginning, the Nixon second term was a disheartening experience for the American people. Democracy itself seemed threatened; imperialism was regnant in the White House certainly. The prospect was a sad one, for the people had liked their President—if for no other reason than that he had at last liberated them from their longest and most hated war.

The President was not the only Watergate casualty. Criminal charges were filed against forty-five members of the Executive Department, the White House staff, and the Nixon Re-election Committee. Worst among these, possibly, were those in the last-named group whom President Ford called "an arrogant, elite guard of political adolescents." Andrew Jackson had his Kitchen Cabinet, Franklin D. Roosevelt his Brain Trust, and Richard Nixon his Elite Guard; all three represented to some degree circumvention of the Executive Departments of the Government. But when such circumvention developed into tyranny and after that into crime, retribution had to come: the Constitution had to be upheld.

The toppling of Nixon and his aides intensified the lesson that there is no substitute in life for integrity and maturity. It was a tragedy for the nation that Nixon should have entrusted such young men with so much power, especially the unbelievable power wielded by the Elite Guard. The temptation to make decisions beyond the law and be so self-important in perpetrating such acts is too great; when fueled by the hunger for reprisal of an insecure chief, only those of the stoutest character would be able to avoid eventual fall into ruin.

Watergate created a crisis without parallel in American history. What caused it was the character of Richard Nixon himself. We stated earlier in this acount that he was a tough introvert. His defects rose to the surface and distorted his entire Presidency— poor judgment of people, suspicion, inability to treat opponents with any degree of magnanimity, dislike of criticism, and so forth. Also, Nixon exercised a greater than normal assumption of

[3] The situation was considered especially intolerable because Nixon had gone into office at a salary of $200,000—double the highest amount paid any previous Chief Executive.

the authoritarianism of his office. This was most unfortunate, for the man had both unusual ability and unusual knowledge of statecraft. His mistakes confirm what this writer has long maintained and what people in past elections have demonstrated, namely, that it is not in the best interests of the country to elevate to the highest office in the land one who has striven too hard to attain that office. It is now generally recognized that it was better that men like Henry Clay, James G. Blaine, and William Jennings Bryan never reached the Presidency; all wanted the job too badly, betraying a longing for fulfillment of ego more than a pure desire to be of service to the nation.

When the fuming Thaddeus Stevens failed in his attempt to expel Andrew Johnson from the White House, he declared from his deathbed that it would never again be possible to remove a President except by assassination. He was, of course, wrong. That peerless Gibraltar of human rights—the American Constitution—again demonstrated to the world its durability and the monumental wisdom of its far-seeing authors; demonstrated that Presidents could be chosen and Presidents be removed by its mechanisms; that all men are truly equal under the law; and that that great boon of all peoples—good government—could prevail in spite of any traumatic experience to which its citizens may be subjected.

Richard Nixon, who had reached the pinnacle of power and fame and been hosted by the great figures of the world, returned home to San Clemente in California, a broken man. He was hospitalized for a time and could not comply with subpoenas issued for his appearance at trials in connection with Watergate. Time, the great healer, will eventually enable the American nation to balance the accomplishments of his administration against the lamentable events with which his name is irretrievably associated.

★★★★★★★★★★★★★★★★★★★★★★★★★★★★★★★★★★★★★

37

GERALD RUDOLPH FORD

☆ ☆

WHEN GERALD R. FORD SUCCEEDED TO THE PRESIDENCY SO SUDDENLY in late summer of 1974, observers declared that he was handicapped by being the first President not elected by the people. They were citing the fact that he had been appointed, not elected, Vice-President as a handicap also.

To say that Ford was the first President not voted into office by the people is not strictly correct. In the first ten Presidential elections—those from Washington to John Quincy Adams—the people had nothing to say about who would be their President; and that was the way the Founding Fathers wanted it. They had inserted into the Contsitution Section 1 of Article II providing for the choosing of the President, not by the people, but by electors. Moreover, these electors were named by the state legislatures. This was anything but democratic.

This method of choosing the President still prevails, except that the people now vote directly for the electors. They do not know who these electors are, and could hardly care less; for they know that when the Electoral College meets in December of a Presidential year, its members will register the will of the people as expressed at the polls the month before. There is nothing in the laws or the Constitution to prevent an elector from voting for any person his caprice or change of conviction may dictate, but this seldom occurs; most electors respect the verdict of the people at the polls.

Under the 25th Amendment to the Constitution, the President appoints a new Vice-President, subject to Congressional confirmation, when that office happens to fall vacant. This contingency arose for the first time when Spiro T. Agnew resigned and Nixon named Ford. When Nixon resigned, Ford automatically succeeded to the office of President, and in turn named Nelson A. Rockefeller, who was then confirmed as the new Vice-President.

Ford's only other political office had been as Representative in the House from his district in Michigan, a position he held from the 81st to the 93rd Congresses; he was the minority leader there from 1965 to 1973.

Born in Omaha, Nebraska, on July 14, 1913, Ford was six months younger than Nixon. His parents were Dorothy Gardner and Gerald R. Ford, Sr., his stepfather who adopted him. His natural father was named Leslie King, which was originally also the name of the future President. His wife was Elizabeth Bloomer, known throughout the nation simply as Betty Ford.

Ford received his bachelor's degree from the University of Michigan, his law degree from Yale; and from 1942 to 1946, he was a lieutenant commander in the Navy. In Congress he had a reputation for being forthright, conciliatory, and hard-working.

Three months after Ford took office, elections were held in which the Democratic majority in Congress was further increased, and few Republicans won anywhere in the nation. There was nothing unusual about such a switch in a mid-term year; what was regarded as unusual was this rebuff to a new President. What triggered it was Ford's pardoning of Richard Nixon. Ford maintained that the country had to get the Watergate nightmare behind it so that it could move forward with its great domestic problems, severest of which was the inflation. So, in order to prevent "prolonged and divisive debate over the propriety of exposing to further punishment and degradation a man who has already paid the unprecedented penalty," Ford, pursuant to the pardoning power conferred upon him in the Constitution, granted the ex-President "a full, free, and absolute pardon . . . for all offenses against the United States . . ."

The pardon was not well received in the country—which came as a surprise to Gerald Ford. Experienced people thought it badly timed. So was Ford's recommendation that Nixon be paid $850,000 in "transition expenses." The public was outraged by this exhibition of munificence to a public official it felt had enriched himself enough at the public trough already, and Congress pared the amount down to $200,000. Later, Ford voluntarily appeared before a Congressional committee to explain the Nixon pardon, and thus became the first incumbent President to submit to questions by Congress over an act of his Administration.

While Nixon was still President, there arose what was called an "energy crisis," meaning, simply, a scarcity of that commodity which keeps the civilized world in operation—oil. It hit the entire Western world suddenly. Nixon named an Energy Czar, rationing of all fuel and other measures were advocated in and out of government, and the price of gasoline to the consumer rose so high that little long-distance traveling could be afforded except by the transportation agencies. When ordinary citizens learned that the oil producers in America were reaping the greatest profits in their history, they felt that they were once more being offered as a sacrifice to the great Moloch—the corporations. This also influenced the voter revolt of 1974.

Oil and politics were intertwined. In the Middle East, where so much of America's crude oil originated, the Arab countries— their profits already bulging with their enormous oil revenues— increased prices yet more, in retaliation for America's having supplied Israel with arms in the Arab-Israeli wars. America's interest in Israel had not strictly been the humanitarian thing she hoped the world would believe: it was a political thing. To the degree that the Soviet Union supplied the Arabs with arms, America aided Israel in the same way; so the Mideast problem, like that of Korea and Indochina, was in reality a manifestation of Russian-United States rivalry.

Yet America retained the initiative in the Mideast and the Arabs recognized this. By the many flying trips there by Secretary of State Kissinger in the quest for peace in that area and the success he achieved in getting the Suez Canal re-opened, to say nothing of the Americans' part in cleaning up that waterway and making it navigable again after seven years, the United States secured a leverage by which it hoped to get lowered oil prices and relieve the burden on its citizens.

Because of Watergate and related scandals, a tough Federal Campaign Reform Act was demanded; for it was revealed that, in addition to the many individuals indicted, more than a dozen corporations had made illegal contributions to the 1972 Presidential candidates and were duly fined. In the new Act, strict limits were put on spending by candidates for both President and Congress; and, for the first time in history, Government financing for Presidential campaigns was offered. Federal aid was to be given on a "matching" basis, that is, if money is available from voluntary income tax check-offs, the Federal Government would match, with certain provisos, private funds collected. Nothing like the $90 million dollars spent by both parties in the 1972 contest would be allowed again. Ford signed this Act and it became law.

Ford fervently urged Congress to limit Government spending as the first requisite in whipping inflation. What he did not say and what no man in public seemed to be willing to say was that the four costly wars fought within a half-century—none of which had been paid for—were at the root of the country's inflation.

Conspicuous in Ford's character were his unaffectedness and his compassion. He rejected the policy of revenge for the 50,000 Vietnam war resisters, whether draft evaders or deserters, and felt he had ample precedent for this in the amnesty proclamations of Lincoln, Andrew Johnson, and Truman. "I want them to come home," he said in an address to a convention of veterans only ten days after he took office; but he said also that he wanted them to "work their way back," that a condition for their return would be their performing some kind of unselfish service for society.

It is always encouraging to discover a charitable nature in a public figure. Unfortunately, human opportunism is such that an exemplary personal life is seldom the deciding factor in the people's determination of a man's worth. Ford had to grow into the Presidency; that would take time, particularly in the economically besieged nation which his Administration had inherited.

BIBLIOGRAPHY

Adams, Charles Francis, Ed., *The Memoirs of John Quincy Adams*, Lippincott, 1874/77.

Adams, Henry, *Letters of Henry Adams*, Houghton, 1938.

Adams, James Truslow, *The Adams Family*, Little, Brown, 1930; *The Epic of America*, Little, Brown, 1931; *Jeffersonian Principles and Hamiltonian Principles*, Little, Brown, 1932.

Agar, Herbert, *The People's Choice*, Houghton, 1933.

Anthony, Katherine, *Dolly Madison: Her Life and Times*, Doubleday, 1949.

Baker, Ray Stannard, *Woodrow Wilson: Life and Letters*, Doubleday, 1927.

Barck, Oscar T., Jr. (with Nelson M. Blake), *Since 1900*, Macmillan, 1947.

Bartlett, J. Gardner, *The Henry Adams Genealogy*, privately printed, 1927.

Barton, William E., *Life of Abraham Lincoln*, Bobbs-Merrill, 1925.

Beard, Charles A., *President Roosevelt and the Coming of the War 1941*, Yale University Press, 1948; *The Presidents in American History*, Messner, 1946; (with Mary R. Beard), *The Rise of American Civilization*, Macmillan, 1927.

Beloff, Max, *Thomas Jefferson and American Democracy*, Macmillan, 1949.

Bemis, Samuel Flagg, *The American Secretaries of State*, Knopf, 1927/64; *John Quincy Adams and the Foundations of American Foreign Policy*, Knopf, 1949.

Bent, Silas (with Silas M. McKinley), *Old Rough and Ready*, Vanguard, 1946.

Beveridge, Albert J., *Abraham Lincoln*, Houghton, 1928.

Binkley, Wilfred E., *American Political Parties*, Knopf, 1943.

Blake, Nelson Manfred (with Oscar T. Barck, Jr.), *Since 1900*, Macmillan, 1947.

Bowen, Catherine Drinker, *John Adams and the American Revolution*, Little, Brown, 1949.

Bowers, Claude G., *The Young Jefferson*, Houghton, 1945; in *Times of Trial*, Knopf, 1958.

Boykin, Edward, *The Wisdom of Thomas Jefferson*, Doubleday, 1941.

Brant, Irving, *James Madison*, Bobbs-Merrill, 1941.

Bruce, David K. E., *Revolution to Reconstruction*, Doubleday, 1939.

Buehrig, Edward H., *Woodrow Wilson and the Balance of Power*, Indiana University Press, 1955.

Bundy, McGeorge (with Henry L. Stimson), *On Active Duty in Peace and War*, Harper, 1948.

Burns, James MacGregor, *John Kennedy: A Political Profile*, Harcourt, 1960.

Carman, Harry J. (with Harold C. Syrett), *A History of the American People*, Knopf, 1952.

Catton, Bruce, *This Hallowed Ground*, Doubleday, 1956; *Stillness at Appomattox*, Doubleday, 1953; in *Times of Trial*, Knopf, 1958.

Cavanah, Frances, *They Lived in the White House*, Macrae-Smith, 1959.

Chamberlain, Ivory, *Biography of Millard Fillmore*, Thomas & Lathrops, 1856.

Charnwood, Lord, *Abraham Lincoln*, Holt, 1916; *Theodore Roosevelt*, Atlantic Monthly, 1923.

Childs, Marquis W., *Eisenhower: Captive Hero*, Harcourt, 1958.

Chitwood, Oliver Perry, *John Tyler: Champion of the Old South*, Appleton-Century, 1939.

Cochran, Thomas C., et al., *An American History*, Harper, 1950.

Colman, Edna M., *White House Gossip from Andrew Johnson to Calvin Coolidge*, Doubleday, 1927.

Commager, Henry Steele (with Richard B. Morris), *Encyclopedia of American History*, Harper, 1953; (with Allan Nevins), *A Short History of the United States*, Random House, 1945.

Coolidge, Calvin, *Autobiography of Calvin Coolidge*, Cosmopolitan, 1929.

Corwin, Edwin S., *The Presidency Today*, New York University, 1956.

Coyle, David Cushman, *Ordeal of the Presidency*, Public Affairs Press, 1960.

Crook, W. H., *Memoirs of the White House*, Little, Brown, 1911.

Cunliffe, Marcus, *George Washington: Man and Monument*, Little, Brown, 1958.

Current, Richard N., *The Lincoln Nobody Knows*, McGraw-Hill, 1958.

Curti, Merle, et al., *An American History*, Harper, 1950.

Curtis, George Ticknor, *Life of James Buchanan*, Harper, 1883.

Daniels, Jonathan, *The Man of Independence*, Lippincott, 1950.

Dewey, Davis Rich, *Financial History of the United States*, Longmans, 1934.

Dewitt, David Miller, *The Impeachment and Trial of Andrew Johnson*, Macmillan, 1903.

Eckenrode, H. J. (with Pocahontas W. Wight), *Rutherford B. Hayes: Statesman of Reunion*, Dodd, Mead, 1930.

Eddy, Sherwood, *The Kingdom of God and the American Dream*, Harper, 1941.

Eisenhower, Dwight D., *Crusade in Europe*, Doubleday, 1948.

Farley, James A., *Jim Farley's Story*, McGraw-Hill, 1948.

Faulkner, Harold U., *From Versailles to the New Deal*, Yale University Press, 1950.

Fiske, John, *Essays Historical and Literary*, Macmillan, 1902.

Fleming, Thomas J., *First in Their Hearts*, Norton, 1967.

Flynn, John T., *Country Squire in the White House*, Doubleday, 1940; *The Roosevelt Myth*, Devin-Adair, 1948.

Ford, Henry Jones, *The Cleveland Era*, Yale University Press, 1919.

Ford, Paul Leicester, *The True George Washington*, Lippincott, 1896.

Freeman, Douglas Southall, *George Washington: A Biography*, Scribner's, 1948/58.

Fuess, Claude M., *Calvin Coolidge: The Man from Vermont*, Little, Brown, 1940.

Furman, Bess, *White House Profile*, Bobbs-Merrill, 1951.

Gallup, George, *The Political Almanac*, Princeton University Press, 1952.

Gay, Sydney Howard, *James Madison*, Houghton, 1884.

Gibson, Hugh (with Herbert Hoover), *The Problems of Lasting Peace*, Doubleday, 1942.

Goebel, Dorothy and Julius, Jr., *Generals in the White House*, Doubleday, 1945.

Goldman, Eric F., *The Crucial Decade*, Knopf, 1956; *Rendezvous with Destiny*, Knopf, 1952.

Grant, U. S., *Personal Memoirs of U. S. Grant*, Webster, 1885.

Griffis, William E., *Millard Fillmore*, Andrus & Church, 1915.

Gunther, John, *Eisenhower: The Man and the Symbol*, Harper, 1951.

Hamilton, Holman, *Zachary Taylor: Soldier of the Republic*, Bobbs-Merrill, 1941; *Zachary Taylor: Soldier in the White House*, Bobbs-Merrill, 1951.

Haraszti, Zoltán, *John Adams and the Prophets of Progress*, Harvard University Press, 1952.

Harrington, Fred Harvey, et al., *An American History*, Harpers, 1950.

Hathaway, Esse V., *The Book of American Presidents*, McGraw-Hill, 1931.

Hay, John (with John G. Nicolay), *Abraham Lincoln: A History*, Century, 1886.

Henry, Reginald B., *Genealogies of the Families of the Presidents*, Tuttle, 1935.

Henshaw, David, *Herbert Hoover: American Quaker*, Farrar, Straus, 1950.

Hertz, Emanuel, *The Hidden Lincoln*, Viking, 1938.

Hesseltine, William B., *Ulysses S. Grant*, Dodd, Mead, 1935.

Hoover, Herbert, *The Memoirs of Herbert Hoover*, Macmillan, 1951/52; (with Hugh Gibson), *The Problems of Lasting Peace*, Doubleday, 1942; *The Ordeal of Woodrow Wilson*, McGraw-Hill, 1958.

Howe, George Frederick, *Chester A. Arthur: A Quarter-Century of Machine Politics*, Dodd, Mead, 1934.

Hull, Cordell, *The Memoirs of Cordell Hull*, Macmillan, 1948.

Hurd, Charles, *The White House: A Biography*, Harper, 1940.

Hutchins, Frank and Cortelle, *Washington and the Lafayettes*, Longmans, 1939.

Hyde, Arthur M. (with Ray Lyman Wilbur), *The Hoover Policies*, Scribner's, 1937.

Ickes, Harold L., *Secret Diary of Harold L. Ickes*, Simon and Schuster, 1953/54.

James, Marquis, *Andrew Jackson: The Border Captain*, Bobbs-Merrill, 1933; *Andrew Jackson: Portrait of a President*, Bobbs-Merrill, 1937.

Jefferson, Thomas, *Autobiography of Thomas Jefferson*, Putnam's, 1959.

Johnson, Allen, *Jefferson and His Colleagues*, Yale University Press, 1921.

Johnson, Alvin Page, *Franklin D. Roosevelt's Colonial Ancestors*, Lothrop, 1933.

Johnson, Gerald White, *American Heroes and Hero-Worship*, Harper, 1943.

Kennedy, John F., *Profiles in Courage*, Harper, 1955.

Keogh, James, *This is Nixon*, Putnam's, 1956.

Kerney, James, *The Political Education of Woodrow Wilson*, Century, 1926.

Koch, Adrienne, *Jefferson and Madison*, Knopf, 1950.

Koenig, Louis W., *The Presidency Today*, New York University Press, 1956.

Krock, Arthur, *Memoirs: Sixty Years on the Firing Line*, Funk & Wagnalls, 1968.

Kull, Irving S. and Nell M., *A Short Chronology of American History*, Rutgers University, 1952.

Lewis, Lloyd, *Captain Sam Grant*, Little, Brown, 1950; *Myths after*

Lincoln, Readers Club, 1941; *Sherman, Fighting Prophet*, Harcourt, 1958.

Lewis, William Draper, *The Life of Theodore Roosevelt*, Winston, 1919.

Lorant, Stefan, *The Presidency*, Macmillan, 1951.

Lynch, Denis Tilden, *An Epoch and a Man*, Liveright, 1929.

Lyons, Eugene, *Our Unknown Ex-President*, Doubleday, 1948.

Marshall, Thomas R., *Recollections: A Hoosier Salad*, Bobbs-Merrill, 1925.

Mayo, Bernard, *Myths and Men*, Harper & Row, 1963.

McCormac, Eugene Irving, *James K. Polk*, University of California Press, 1922.

McCormick, Robert R., *Ulysses S. Grant*, Appleton-Century, 1934.

McElroy, Robert, *Grover Cleveland: The Man and the Statesman*, Harper, 1923.

McKinley, Silas B. (with Silas Bent), *Old Rough and Ready*, Vanguard, 1946.

Mellon, Matthew T., *Early American Views on Negro Slavery*, Meador, 1934.

Moley, Raymond, *After Seven Years*, Harper, 1939.

Moran, Thomas Francis, *American Presidents*, Crowell, 1928.

Morgan, George, *The Life of James Monroe*, Small, Maynard, 1921.

Morris, Joe Alex (with Ira R. T. Smith), *Dear Mr. President*, Messner, 1949.

Morris, Richard B. (with Henry Steele Commager), *Encyclopedia of American History*, Harper, 1953; in *Times of Trial*, Knopf, 1958.

Morse, John T., Jr., *John Quincy Adams*, Houghton, 1882; *Thomas Jefferson*, Houghton, 1883.

Myers, William Starr (with Walter H. Newton), *The Hoover Administration*, Scribner's, 1936.

Nevins, Allan, *Grover Cleveland: A Study in Courage*, Dodd, Mead, 1932; (with Henry Steele Commager), *A Short History of the United States*, Random House, 1945; in *Times of Trial*, Knopf, 1958.

Newton, Walter H. (with William Starr Myers), *The Hoover Administration*, Scribner's, 1936.

Nichols, Ray Franklin, *Franklin Pierce*, University of Pennsylvania Press, 1931.

Nicolay, John G. (with John Hay), *Abraham Lincoln: A History*, Century, 1886.

Olcott, Charles S., *Life of William McKinley*, Houghton, 1916.

Padover, Saul K. (Ed.), *A Jefferson Profile*, John Day, 1956.

Perkins, Frances, *The Roosevelt I Knew*, Viking, 1946.

Polk, James K., *The Diary of a President* (Allan Nevins, Ed.), Longmans, 1929.

Preston, John Hyde, *Revolution: 1776*, Harcourt, 1933.

Pringle, Henry F., *The Life and Times of William Howard Taft*, Farrar & Rinehart, 1939.

Pusey, Merlo J., *Eisenhower, the President*, Macmillan, 1956; in *Times of Trial*, Knopf, 1958.

Randall, J. G., *Lincoln the President*, Dodd, Mead, 1952.

Randall, Ruth Painter, *Mary Lincoln: Biography of a Marriage*, Little, Brown, 1953.

Randolph, Sarah N., *Domestic Life of Thomas Jefferson*, Ungar, 1958.

Rayback, Robert J., *Millard Fillmore*, Buffalo Historical Society, 1959.

Rhodes, James Ford, *History of the Civil War*, Macmillan, 1917.

Roosevelt, Anna Eleanor, *This Is My Story*, Harper, 1937.

Roosevelt, Franklin D., *Public Papers and Addresses of Franklin D. Roosevelt*, Random House, 1933/41.

Roosevelt, Theodore, *Theodore Roosevelt: An Autobiography*, Scribner's, 1913.

Rossiter, Clinton, *The American Presidency Today*, Harcourt, 1956.

Russell, Phillips, *Jefferson: Champion of the Free Mind*, Dodd, Mead, 1956.

Sandburg, Carl, *Abraham Lincoln*, Harcourt, 1939.

Schachner, Nathan, *Thomas Jefferson*, Yoseloff, 1951.

Schlesinger, Arthur M., Jr., *The Age of Jackson*, Little, Brown, 1945; *The Age of Roosevelt*, Houghton, 1957; *The Bitter Heritage*, Houghton, 1966.

Shepard, Edward M., *Martin Van Buren*, Houghton, 1888.

Sherwood, Robert E., *Roosevelt and Hopkins*, Harper, 1950.

Shryock, Richard M., et al., *An American History*, Harper, 1950.

Sidey, Hugh, *A Very Personal Presidency*, Atheneum, 1968.

Sinclair, Andrew, *The Available Man*, Macmillan, 1965.

Smith, Bessie White, *The Boyhoods of the Presidents*, Lothrop, 1929.

Smith, Ira R. T. (with Joe Alex Morris), *Dear Mr. President*, Messner, 1949.

Smith, Theodore Clark, *James Abram Garfield: Life and Letters*, Yale University Press, 1925.

Stanwood, Edward, *A History of the Presidency*, Houghton, 1916.

Stephenson, George W., *American History Since 1865*, Harper, 1939.

Stephenson, Nathaniel W., *Abraham Lincoln and the Union*, Yale University Press, 1918.

Stettinius, Edward R., *Roosevelt and the Russians*, Doubleday, 1949.

Stewart, Randall, *Nathaniel Hawthorne*, Yale University Press, 1948.

Stimpson, George, *A Book About American Politics*, Harper, 1952.

Stimson, Henry L., *On Active Service in Peace and War*, Harper, 1948.

Stoddard, Henry L., *As I Knew Them*, Harper, 1927; *Presidential Sweepstakes*, Putnam's, 1948.

Stoddard, William Osborn, *The Lives of the Presidents*, Stokes, 1887/88.

Stryker, Lloyd Paul, *Andrew Johnson: A Study in Courage*, Macmillan, 1929.

Syrett, Harold C., *Andrew Jackson*, Bobbs-Merrill, 1953; (with Harry J. Carman), *A History of the American People*, Knopf, 1952.

Tebbel, John, *George Washington's America*, Dutton, 1954.

Theobald, Robert A., *The Final Secret of Pearl Harbor*, Devin-Adair, 1954.

Thomas, Benjamin P., *Abraham Lincoln*, Knopf, 1952.

Thompson, Charles Willis, *Presidents I've Known*, Bobbs-Merrill, 1929.

Thompson, Richard W., *Recollections of Sixteen Presidents*, Bowen-Merrill, 1894.

Truman, Harry S., *Memoirs by Harry S. Truman*, Doubleday, 1955/56.

Tugwell, Rexford G., *The Democratic Roosevelt*, Doubleday, 1957.

Tumulty, Joseph P., *Woodrow Wilson as I Know Him*, Doubleday, 1921.

Umbreit, Kenneth B., *Founding Fathers*, Harper, 1941.

Upton, Harriet Taylor, *Our Early Presidents*, Lothrop, 1890.

Van Deusen, Glyndon G., *Thurlow Weed: Wizard of the Lobby*, Little, Brown, 1947.

Wallace, Lewis, *Life of Gen. Ben Harrison*, Hubbard, 1888.

Warren, Louis A., *Lincoln's Youth: Indiana Years*, Appleton, 1959.

Warren, Sydney, *The Battle for the Presidency*, Lippincott, 1968.

White, William S., *Majesty and Mischief: A Mixed Tribute*, McGraw-Hill, 1961.

Wight, Pocahontas W. (with H. J. Eckenrode), *Rutherford B. Hayes: Statesman of Reunion*, Dodd, Mead, 1930.

Wilbur, Ray Lyman (with Arthur M. Hyde), *The Hoover Policies*, Scribner's, 1937.

Williams, Charles Richard, *Life of Rutherford B. Hayes*, Houghton, 1914.

Wilson, Edith Bolling, *My Memoir*, Bobbs-Merrill, 1938.

Wilson, James Grant, et al., *The Presidents of the United States 1789–1894*, Appleton, 1886.

Wilson, Woodrow, *The New Democracy*, Harper, 1926; *War and Peace*, Harper, 1927.

Winston, Robert W., *Andrew Johnson: Plebeian and Patriot*, Holt, 1928.

Wise, John S., *Recollections of Thirteen Presidents*, Doubleday, 1906.

Wister, Owen, *The Seven Ages of Washington*, Macmillan, 1929.

Woodward, W. E., *A New American History*, Garden City, 1938; *George Washington: The Image and The Man*, Liveright, 1926; *Meet General Grant*, Liveright, 1928; *Years of Madness*, Putnam's, 1951.

INDEX

Abolitionists, 164, 167-8
Adams, Abigail, 61, 68, 101
Adams family, 61, 63, 68, 99, 102-3, 107 n, 110
Adams, John, 43, 58, 60 et seq., 69, 75-7, 79, 81-2, 88, 99, 101-3, 107, 109-10, 120, 158, 220, 265, 318
Adams, John Quincy I, 63, 68, 92-3, 95-7, 99 et seq., 111, 120-2, 124, 126, 130, 139, 143-4, 291, 299
Adams, Samuel, 48, 61, 84, 99
Alaska, 104, 144, 162, 194, 279, 328-9
Albany Regency, 126
Alexander I, 104
Alexander the Great, 135
Alien and Sedition Acts, 66
Allen, Ethan, 49
Altgeld, Gov. John P., 227
Amendments to the Constitution (see also Bill of Rights):
  I, 66, 109; XII, 77; XIII, 190, 192, 193; XIV, 192; XV, 192, 193, 211; XVI, 205, 258; XVII, 258; XVIII, 281-2, 297; XIX, 282; XXI, 282; XXII, 55, 321
American Civil War, 53, 82, 103, 153, 157, 162, 172, 178 et seq., 191, 194, 197, 199, 200 et seq., 209, 211, 212, 215, 219, 221, 226, 229, 231, 234, 238, 264, 281, 326-7
American Federation of Labor, 222, 286, 307 n
American Museum of Natural History, 249
American Red Cross, 217, 295
Anglo-American fraternity, 65, 253, 268-9, 278, 308
Anti-Federalists, 64, 86
Anthracite strike of 1902, 247
Anti-Masons, 111 n., 127-8, 158
Appomattox Courthouse, 183, 203
Arnold, Benedict, 52
Arthur, Chester Alan, 216-8 et seq., 224, 229, 241, 247; family, 219, 221-2, 225
Articles of Confederation, 54, 85
Article X of the League Covenant, 275
Astor, John Jacob I, 147
Atlantic Charter, 310
atomic energy and warfare, 318, 328
Attlee, Lord Clement, 316

Baker, Ray Stannard, 264
Barton, Clara, 217
Bastille, Fall of, 75
Battles:
  Antietam, 180, 202; Bennington, 49; Brandywine, 49, 93; Buena Vista, 151, 153, 177; Bull Run, I, II, 180; Bunker Hill, 49, 101; Camden, 52; Chan-

cellorsville, 181, 202; Charleston, 52; Chicamauga, 182, 215; Cold Harbor, 182; Concord Bridge, 49; Corinth, 201; Cowpens, 53; Fallen Timbers, 133; Fort Harrison, 150; Forts Henry and Donelson, 181, 201; Fredericksburg, 180, 202; Germantown, 50, 93; Gettysburg, 181, 202; Guilford Courthouse, 53; Horseshoe Bend, 115; Kings Mountain, 53; Lake Erie, 88; Lexington, 49; Long Island, 49; Lookout Mountain, 182, 202; Manila Bay, 241; Marne II, 272; Missionary Ridge, 182, 202; Mobile Bay, 182; Monmouth, 51, 93; Monongahela, 47; Monterrey, 151; New Orleans, 89, 115; Okeechobee, 150; Palo Alto, 151; Princeton, 49; Resaca de la Palma, 151; San Juan Hill, 242; Santiago Harbor, 241; Saratoga, 49, 50; Savannah, 52; Shiloh Church (Pittsburgh Landing), 181, 201; South Mountain, 209; Spotsylvania, 182; Thames River, 88, 134; Tippecanoe Creek, 134; Trenton, 49, 93; Vicksburg, 53, 181, 201-2; Waterloo, 53, 95; White Plains, 49, 93; Wilderness, 182, 198, 203; Yorktown, 51, 53, 56, 133
Beard, Charles A., 79, 153, 308, 309 n
Bell, Alexander Graham, 212
Bell, John, 171
Benson, Allen J., 263
Benton, Thomas Hart, 114 n., 163
Bessemer process, 164
Beveridge, Albert J., 238
Biddle, Nicholas, 117-9
Bill of Rights, 86
Birchard, Sardis, 209, 213, 264
Birney, James G., 142-3
Black Friday, I, 204, II, 206
Black Hawk War, 116, 150, 176
Blaine, James G., 205, 208, 216, 221, 223, 226, 234
Bolívar, Simón, 135
Booth, John Wilkes, 163 n., 184
Boston Massacre, 61-2
Boston Tea Party, 133
Braddock, Gen. Edward, 47
"Brain Trust," 119, 307
Breckenridge, John C., 168, 171
Briand, Aristide, 287
Brown, John, 163, 168
Bryan, William Jennings, 229-30, 236, 239-40, 255, 257, 270-2
Buchanan, James, 130, 161, 164-5 et seq., 189, 204, 295; family, 165, 169
Buckner, Gen. Simon B., 201

377

INDEX TO CHAPTERS 34-37 (PAGES 331-368) IN REVISED EDITION